DEMOCRATIC PROCESS, FOREIGN POLICY AND HUMAN RIGHTS IN SOUTH ASIA

DEMOCRATIC PROCESS, FOREIGN POLICY AND HUMAN RIGHTS IN SOUTH ASIA

JOSEPH BENJAMIN

GYAN

Democratic Process, Foreign Policy and Human Rights in South Asia

Rs. 750

ISBN: 978-81-212-1044-7

Published in 2010 in India by
Gyan Publishing House
23, Main Ansari Road, Darya Ganj
New Delhi-110002
Phones : 23282060, 23261060
Fax : 011-23285914
E-mail: books@gyanbooks.com
Website: www.gyanbooks.com

Lasser Type Setting by: Rudra Computer Graphics, Delhi
Printed at : Gian Ridhi Offset Printers, Delhi

Contents

Preface

The term South Asia is used for the countries lying South of Himalayas and Hindukush mountains and surrounded by the Indian Ocean from three sides. The countries of this region include India, Pakistan, Bangladesh, Sri Lanka, Nepal and Bhutan. Afghanistan and Maldives are included in this region. South Asia can be considered as a subsystem, which has great geo-strategic significance along with the Indian Ocean, with which it is symbiotically related. Many geopolitical thinkers like Halford Mackinder, Alfred Thayer Mahan, Nicholos J. Spykman and others influenced the thinking of ruling elites of many Western Colonial powers; emphasizing the fact that geography is destiny. Many western countries, therefore, have their eyes on this region. It is true that it was dominated and exploited by western countries for many centuries during the post Vasco-de-Gama age of Asian history. The aftermath of Second World War saw the retreat of Western powers, as decolonization process gathered momentum. India, Pakistan, Myanmar, Sri Lanka became new independent nations from British yoke. Of course, Philippines was granted freedom by USA in 1946. French, Dutch and Portuguese had to march with the time and lost all their colonial possessions. No doubt South Asian region is politically and economically better than African continent. These countries too are rich in natural resources.

The South Asian region should have been economically sound, but due to internal problems, namely terrorism, ethnic clashes, democratic deficit, military coups and monarchical structure, these countries are facing many problems. An effort is to be taken up to have mutual economic co-operation with each other. An organization, SAARC (South Asian Association for Regional Co-operation) on the model of other regional groupings like the European Union (EU) has come up to tackle socio-economic impediments for collective growth and prosperity. Young Indian Prime Minister late Mr Rajiv Gandhi took this initiative in 1985. The association was formed in 1985 with India, Pakistan, Bangladesh, Nepal, Bhutan, Sri Lanka and Maldives. Afghanistan was admitted at 14th SAARC summit held in New Delhi in April 2007. Afghanistan President Hamid Karzai, participated in the SAARC summit for the first time in 2007. Again, in the recent summit held at Colombo on July 19, 2008, Afghan President attended the summit. What has been the outcome of these summits? The discussion moved around only on one issue, i.e., the problem of terrorism in this region. This forum has become the forum of confrontation rather than cooperation. These countries have more child labour, drug trafficking, sex trafficking and poverty is the central issue.

The present book is an attempt to evaluate the Human Rights situation in South Asian region. It is a volume of research papers by eminent scholars engaged in their specialized fields. The scholars have taken great pains to portray a picture of Human Rights violation in South Asia. It is felt that South Asia has become the hub of human right violation. All South Asian countries are signatories of UN Charter on Universal Declaration of Human Rights, yet, Human Rights violations are more in these countries.

In preparing this book, I have been helped by Professor John Alexander. At familial level I have been backed up to the hilt by my wife Smt Pratibha and sons Prashant and Jayant who have shown unusual patience and forbearance when I was too involved in my work. My friends Prof. S. N. Malakar (JNU, New Delhi), Prof. Sanjukta Bhattacharya (Jadavpur University), Prof. Abdulrahim Vijapur (Aligarh Muslim University) and Prof. Sanjay Srivastava (Banaras Hindu University) have helped me in this project and also assisted in selecting experts in the field of Human Rights and South Asia.

I acknowledge my heart-felt thanks to Gyan Publishing House, New Delhi who has so kindly consented to publish this path-breaking book entitled *Democratic Process, Foreign Policy and Human Rights in South Asia.*

Nagpur
Dated; 16/6/2009

Joseph Benjamin

Introduction

Joseph Benjamin

Human right is paramount and pre-eminent to all laws of the globe. No law is superior to this.[1] Human rights are those rights, to which an individual has a claim by virtue of birth. Human Rights imply the rights relating to life, liberty, equality and dignity of individuals. In order to protect the rights of individuals in the whole globe, the UN General Assembly adopted the Universal Declaration of Human Rights on December 10, 1948. But the stirrings of Human Rights go back nearly eight hundred years in Magna Carta, passed during King John in the year 1215 A.D. So, as logical corollary, one witnesses the flowering of the concept in the 1948 document, which has been translated in 334 languages of the world. It "remains the fundamental standard for measuring progress or regression in civil society. It was to serve as the guidepost for setting goals for the future and to which states should aspire".[2] Consequently, all the member countries of the UNO who have put their signature on the document, have to abide by it. Besides the civil and political rights (Article 3-21), the UN Declaration has also outlined economic, social and cultural rights clearly mentioned in Articles 22 to 27. These Articles outlines, (i) right to social security, (ii) right to work the right to equal pay for equal work and the right to form and join trade unions, (iii) the right to rest and leisure, (iv) right to a standard of living adequate for health and well being (v) the right to education and (vi) the right to participate in the cultural life of the community. The UN has convened various meetings on different problems of Human beings. In order to make civil and political rights legal the UN General Assembly adopted two covenants on Human Rights on the December 16 1966. These two covenants are namely, International Covenant on Economic, Social and Cultural Rights and the International Covenant on Civil and Political Rights. In 1963, the UN General Assembly adopted a Declaration of Elimination of All form of Racial Discrimination. The Declaration affirms fundamental equality of all persons and opposes discrimination between human beings on the basis of race, colour or ethnic origin. In 1993 the General Assembly proclaimed the decade (1993-2003) to Combat Racism and Racial Discrimination and called on all states to take measures to combat all forms of racism. The UN took interest in protecting the rights of children and women. Long before, in 1959 the General Assembly had adopted Declaration of the Rights of the Child, which affirms the rights of children to special protection, opportunities and facilities for healthy normal development.

In December 1993, the General Assembly created the office of UN High Commission for Human Rights, which works under the directions and authority of the UN Secretary General. The High Commissioner is responsible for promoting and protecting the enjoyment by all of all civil, cultural, political and social rights through the Centre for Human Rights, based in Geneva. It also provides advisory services, technical and financial assistance in coordination of UNO's education and public information programme on human rights. Over and all this, it helps in the removal of obstacles in the way of full realization of all human rights and preventing the continuation of human rights violations throughout the world, by engaging in dialogue with governments.

South Asia is a region with distinct political, economic, cultural and geographical identity and coherence. It has a common past in terms of its civilization and cultural orientation. Most of the countries namely India, Pakistan, Sri Lanka and Bangladesh were British colonies for more than a century and became sovereign nations in the aftermath of Second World War in 1945. Besides India, Pakistan, Bangladesh and Sri Lanka, Nepal, Bhutan, Afghanistan and Maldives can be included in this region. It is a very strategic area in terms of World politics. All these countries are in geographical contiguity with one another. The region is wracked by problems of underdevelopment, poverty, and population explosion, ethnic and communal conflicts. To top it, they have inter-state boundary conflicts and contentious issue of sharing of river waters. The litany does not end there, as social problems of Child labour, Child and Women trafficking, fill the brim of the cup of woes.

The present book is an attempt to evaluate the Human Rights situation in South Asian region. It is a volume of research papers by eminent scholars engaged in deeper study their specialized fields. They have taken great pains to portray a picture of Human Rights violation in South Asia. It is felt that South Asia has become the hub of human right infringement, despite all being signatories of the UN Charter on Universal Declaration of Human Rights.

I personally developed an interest in Human Rights issue in South Asia and invited well known scholars to contribute for this volume on Human Rights in South Asia. The present book contains twelve papers, which are arranged in alphabetical order. Professor John Alexander in his paper *Communism, Military, Democracy, Civil Society and Human Rights in Afghanistan* has discussed the history of Afghanistan since 1747. He explained how Afghanistan has passed through different stages of political evolution and finally they have a democratically elected government now, however flawed it may be.

Indra Mohan Jha, an expert on South Asia in his paper *Democracy and Human Rights in Bangladesh* has tried to give the detail political history of Bangladesh. He says that after independence of Bangladesh, it followed the path of Pakistan. After about four decades of independence, it resembles another Pakistan. There is no place for democracy and human rights. Mullahs and military have ruled the roost in all these years except for some intervals of weak elected governments, managing anyhow to survive merely to remain in power. In their quest for power, respective governments, right from 1971, have contributed to further weakening the values of liberation struggle. In such a situation, human rights violations of the weak and marginalized is abominable. Perhaps, Bangladesh today has the lowest rating on human rights measurements. Ironically, Bangladesh is a party to International Covenant on Economic, Social and Cultural Rights, Covenant on Civil and Political Rights, Convention on the Rights of the Child, and Convention on Elimination of All forms of Discrimination against Women, though with reservations. He expects that newly elected government (December 2008) would, at least protect the rights of women.

Ms Sreya Maitra, in her paper *Bangladesh: Assessing Democratic consolidation and human rights situation under Civil-Military Regime* has tried to evaluate the process of democracy in Bangladesh. She has divided her paper into five sections. She said that Bangladesh was bound by certain international principles to ensure safeguarding of human rights. Bangladesh has not yet adopted any specific legislation incorporating the provisions of the United Nations Convention against torture or the International Covenant for Civil and Political Rights, despite its ratification of these treaties that constitute customary bedrock of international law.

Bhutan has adopted a democratic system as recently as in March 2008. At the same time monarchical system too exists in Bhutan. Dharam Pal Singh in his paper *Bhutan: - Monarchy and Simulated Democracy in the Amphitheatre of Hills* has proposed to examine and analyze the threat perception of Bhutan, since pre and post Indian Independence era. History is the testimony of the fact that Bhutan had faced threats from its toxic neigbourhood. He has also discussed the problems of Bhutanese refugees living on Indo-Nepal boarder.

Ram Puniyani in his paper on *Attack on Minority and Minority Commission in India* has highlighted the problems of religious minorities in India. He said that there were many commissions, which tried to find out the status of minorities in India. The status of minorities has still not appreciably improved. He suggests that minority commission should have more teeth to implement various recommendations of such commission.

Subhash Gatade has discussed the problems of *Dalits* in India. In his paper *Dalit and Law in India,* he has explained the various constitutional provisions in Indian Constitution, which safeguards their rights. Unfortunately their rights are brazenly violated. The old social malady of untouchability, is still is alive in many pockets of country. Both, Ram Puniyani and Subhash Gatade have tried to evaluate the violation of human rights of different communities of India.

Flavia Agnes in her paper *Women and Violation of Human Rights* has tried to study the violation of women in India. She says that human rights of women in India continue to be in a deplorable condition, despite the international conventions and declarations and domestic statutes and Constitutional protection. She says we have National Women Commission to protect the rights of women. The campaigns initiated by the women's movement and the statutory reforms, which were effected in response, have helped to bring public attention to the issue. But they have not served as a deterrent. The reported cases of rape and dowry death continue to be on the increase. In 2007 the official statistics brought out by the National Crime Record Bureau (NCRB) revealed that every hour two women are raped. Total 20, 737 rape cases have been registered in 2007. This shows 7.2 % increased over the previous period. This ought to be a grave cause of concern for all human rights activists.

Joseph Benjamin in his paper *Civil Society, Polity and Human Rights in Maldives,* has tried to explain how human rights is violated in South Asia's smallest nation. The inherent dignity, equality and inalienable rights of all members of society are the foundation of freedom, justice and peace in society. The principles of justice serve to ensure that any government does not infringe human rights overtly or covertly by unconstitutional methods. The Universal Declaration of Human Rights, December 10, 1948, is not country specific. It is a universal law binding on all human beings across the globe, only because all are human beings. After 30 years of President Maumoon Abdul Gayoom rule, the citizens of the country have elected new President Mohamed Nasheed. There is a great hope from the newly elected President to protect the democratic rights of Maldivians and usher a new era of democratic government in name and deed.

Rajneesh Kumar Gupta in his paper *Recent Development in Nepal and Indian Foreign Policy Dilemma* attempts to explain the peculiar situation that bedevils the bilateral relations between India and Nepal. He takes up Neo-realist approach to study the different contours of fluctuating relationship. Neo-realist perspective in the study of international relations, is an advanced version of classical realism. The basic premise of the approach is that, the national security is a prime objective of any country's foreign policy. India proved to be a good practitioner of this world view.

Arjun Karki and Neeraj Joshi in their joint paper *Civil Society and Struggle for Human Rights in Nepal* argue that civil society in Nepal played a critical role in protecting and promoting human rights, besides influencing the political system by means of advocacy and campaigns, for well functioning of the government, be it democratic or otherwise. This paper first gives a brief description about the emergence of modern civil society in Nepal and its relationship with the State. It then highlights the recent trend of human rights followed by a description on the contribution of CSOs to the Struggle for Human Rights in Nepal and the significance of such a struggle. The paper rounds up by highlighting the challenges facing Nepali CSOs, in time of political transition and end of the monarchy in the only Himalayan Hindu Kingdom of Nepal.

Sangeeta Mahapatra in her paper *Human Rights in Pakistan: A Heuristic of Hope and Despair* tries to review the human rights scenario in Pakistan. She has divided her paper into three parts. The first part briefly touches upon the concept of human rights that is widely accepted and assesses the extent to which Pakistan has legalized and institutionalized these precepts. The second part deals with those groups of the society that continue to suffer human rights abuse in Pakistan and Pakistan occupied Kashmir (PoK), despite unflagging efforts by Pakistan's Human Rights Commission and international organizations to put an end to their privations and sufferings. This paper especially focuses on the different religious minorities and women who have been subjected to draconian laws and have no one to turn to but an indifferent establishment. The concluding parts tries to evaluate the political, institutional, religious and societal dimensions of ensuring human rights in the country.

Rohini Hensman in her paper *Self-Determination, Sovereignty and Democracy: The Reality Behind The Rhetoric in Sri Lanka,* has discussed the various parameters of ethnic conflict between the Sinhalese majority and Tamil minority. In her concluding remarks, she has said that the conflict in Sri Lanka is primarily between fascism and democracy, and second between Sinhala and Tamil ethnic groups. The solution lies, therefore, in the restoration of democracy and human rights of people, ravaged by never ending ethnic conflict, which has caught the benighted people in its cross hairs.

I thank each and every contributor who has helped enormously in the preparation of this volume. All these contributors are experts in their own fields. I would further submit that these research papers are original and of high quality of scholarship. My sincere thanks to Prof. S N Malakar, Prof. Sanjukta Bhattacharya, Prof. Abdulrahim Vijapur and Prof. Sanjay Srivastava, who have helped me in identifying the experts on South Asia.

I would be happy to have comments and feedback on this book entitled, *Democratic Process, Foreign Policy and Human Rights in South Asia*, which is becoming a turbulent and intractable issue in the arena of political discourse, not only in South Asia but in other parts of the world as well.

References

1. Joseph Benjamin (2007), "Human Rights in Indian Situation" Indian Social Institute, New Delhi, p. iv.

2. William Kovey (2001), "NGOs and the Universal Declaration of Human Rights" Palgvave, Basingstoke (UK), p.1.

List of Contributors

Joseph Benjamin has done considerable research on the problems of weaker sections of Indian society. He has published a number of high quality articles in papers and prestigious national journals. Currently, he is Reader and Head, Department of Political Science, St. Francis de Sales' College, Nagpur. He has been teaching in this college since 1987.

Dharam Pal Singh is a senior lecturer in Government P. G. College, Dausa, Rajasthan.

Rohini Hensman is a social Activist and expert in Human Rights in Sri Lanka. She has written extensively on the Human Rights problems in Sri Lanka.

Rajneesh Kumar Gupta is a Doctoral Fellow in the School of International Studies, Jawaharlal Nehru University, New Delhi. He has specialized on Nepal.

Ram Puniyani, is retired professor of IIT, Bombay. Currently he is attached to Centre for Study of Society and Secularism, Bombay. He has published many books on Human Rights and Secularism in India. He has been awarded National Foundation for Communal Harmony Award of 2007 on August 11, 2009.

Ms Sangeeta Mahapatra is the Executive Editor of *Business Economics*. She has done her Masters Degree in International Relations with a specialisation in Central and West Asia from the Department of International Relations, Jadavpur University, Kolkata. She is currently working on her doctoral thesis on Terrorism and Counter-Terrorism Strategies.

Ms Sreya Maitra is doing her Ph. D. from Jadavpur University, Kolkata. She has done her Masters Degree in International Relations. She is Research Fellow of Global India Foundation, Kolkata.

John Alexander is a retired Professor of History. He has published number of research papers in reputed journals.

Arjun Karki is the President of Rural Reconstruction, (RRN), Kathmandu, Nepal.

Neeraj Joshi, is the Research Director at Rural Reconstruction Nepal (RRN), Kathmandu, Nepal.

Subhash Garade is a Human Rights activist based in Delhi. He has been writing on the issue of *Dalit* rights and has many published papers against his name.

Flavia Agnes is women's rights advocate based in Bombay and director of *Majlis* a Bombay based NGO dealing with women's rights initiative and interdisciplinary arts initiative.

Indra Mohan Jha is reader in the Department of Political Science, A. R. S. D. College (University of Delhi), Delhi. He is expert on South Asian Politics. He has published number of research papers in reputed International and National Journals.

1

Communism, Military, Democracy, Civil Society and Human Rights in Afghanistan

John Alexander

Introduction

Afghanistan is partly a colonial creation with boundaries delineated by the British Raj in India; though Ahmad Shah Abdali, a lieutenant of Persian invader Nadir Shah had in 1747 carved out a separate Afghan state with his capital at Kandhar. It is a multiethnic, multicultural and multilingual country, with no strong spirit of national identity. It is a nation of minorities with Pashtun, Hazara, Uzbeg, Tajik, Kirghiz, Kazaks, Baluch, Nuristani etc being innumerable tribes, which composes this failed state. It has become a victim of its geographical location.Pashtus forms the largest ethnic group, followed by Tajiks, Hazara,Uzbegs etc. The ethnic and linguistic composition is mixed and complex.

Six countries – Tajikstan, Turkmenistan, Uzbekistan, Iran, Pakistan and China, surround Afghanistan. It is located east of central Asia and lies astride trade and invasion routes of innumerable foreign conquerors. Silk route to China caravan moving towards Iran had to pass invariably through rugged terrain and mountain passes of Afghanistan. It is a landlocked country. Pushto-Persian is major language but each tribe speaks in its own language and dialect. Thus, there are more than 70 languages.

International Setting

The Great Game was played between Russia and Britain in the nineteenth century to have influence and control over Afghanistan. East India Company during the Governor Generalship of Lord Auckland fought the first Anglo-Afghan War 1839-42 and then during the Governor-Generalship of Lord Lytton fought Second Anglo-Afghan war 1878-1880. The third one was fought in 1919.The aim had been to install a ruler who was friendly to the English and who kept reasonable distance with the Russian power. Russia was feverishly expanding itself on its southern side and the British power in London was not willing to see Afghanistan coming into the orbit of Russian supremacy.

The 1945 post world war II witnessed radical change in configuration of political power in the world. Emergence of two superpowers, was the dominant factor of this paradigmatic shift.

United States of America stepped into the role of Britain as the significant power in Asia. Decolonization process, which started in 1945, created vacuum in certain regions. Though Washington had formed pacts like Baghdad Pact, Southeast Asia Treaty Organisation, Anzus besides NATO in Europe, it did not take much interest in Afghanistan affairs. The internal political dynamics of Afghanistan had perennially remained turbulent. When Cold War was at its height, King Zahir Shah, the ruler of Afghanistan turned to erstwhile USSR for economic assistance and closer ties with it. His political stance was at variance with the previous ruler Emir Amanullah, who had successfully won the third Anglo-Afghan War in 1919 over the British and obtained complete independence. In 1926 is he founded the short lived monarchy. He was quite westernized in his approach. It is to be remembered that he was contemporary of Reza Shah of Iran and Kemal Attaturk of Turkey. Both were modernizers.

King Zahir Shah gave a new orientation to foreign policy of Afghanistan and Soviet influence increased correspondingly. But his cousin Daoud Khan deposed him in 1973. He declared Afghanistan as a Republic. But soon found his nemesis in a coup, which snuffed out his life in 1978.The next person, Noor Taraki set up a Marxist regime but as in game of musical chairs, he was removed and executed in 1979.He was followed by Hafizullah Amin as President of the Republic, but in three months time he was killed and Babrak Karmal took over the reigns of office in December 1979. Najibullah who changed the nomenclature Democratic Republic of Afghanistan to Republic of Afghanistan followed him. Both the Flag and emblem were changed.

President Najibullah tried to win over frontier tribes and many malcontents including the mujahideens, who were fighting to unseat him from power. He tried to rope in even Afghan diaspora on his side. The Marxist party of his, was Peoples Democratic Party of Afghanistan (PDAP). He wanted parleys with his opponents in holy city of Mecca, but opposition to his Marxist regime remained unabated.

The Soviet, for geo-strategic reasons had always desired influence in Afghanistan. They extended military and economic assistance to the regime of Najibullah. The policy makers of Moscow had miscalculated the fact that the traditional society of Afghanistan, which was much controlled by mullahs and Islamic radicals, would not co-exist with the ideology of Communism.

To shore up and support the regime of President Najabullah, the Soviet Union made a policy blunder in occupying it physically by invading the benighted country in 1979. The year also saw the ouster of Shah of Iran and installation of the rule of Ayatollah Khomeini in that country. This cataclysmic event made a seismic change in the whole region seething with volatility and turbulence. Many regional players and the superpower USA got involved in a proxy war and orchestrated it with its surrogates.

The number of actors who took part in violent, unceasing civil war to overthrow the President Najibullah, communist regime was too large; often working at cross-purposes at times. The Communist party itself had split into two factions Khalq and Pavcham. The Jamai-i-Islami, Sufi order Mahaj-e-Milli Islami of Gilani Sufi order under Pir Sayyid Gilani, Jebh-e-Nejat-e-Milli of Sibghatullah Mojaddedi of Peshawar, Hijab-i-Islami of Yusuf Khales, Itehad-i-Islami of Rasool Sayyaf etc added religious dimension to the conflict. Leaders like Burhanuddin Rabbani, Gulbaddin Hekmatyar and Ahmad Shah Masood with their groups, all waged war of attrition against the occupying Soviet forces. From sanctuaries in Pakistan and Iran, pincer movement was launched, and many fighters including Osama bin Laden came to add their mite.

At the back of it, President Jimmy Carter and then President Ronald Reagan put in lot of resources and helped their proxies to oust Soviet Union lock, stock and barrel from Afghanistan. They were determined to turn this a Soviet defeat as Soviet Vietnam in Afghanistan. In the upshot, the last Russian soldier left Afghanistan on 15 December 1989. In the unraveling of Soviet Union in 1992, Afghanistan fiasco was one of the contributory factor.

Afghanistan down the ages has seen invaders pouring down the plains of Punjab through its territory. Different tribes had fought off Persians and others who tried to control its heartland. Afghans though congenitally averse to combine with each other, had always been averse to any outside power turning it into its real estate. It had neither military academy nor a centralized command structure. Much of it has to do with its geography. It is a land of mountains and valleys where, no roads or other infrastructural facilities are there. The weapons by no stretch of imagination were technologically advanced. As communication facilities became better, various tribes of Afghanistan bought weapons from outside. It is no surprise they were defeated by outside invaders and conquerors.

Russia, Britain, USA in that order have controlled Afghanistan, though it is symbiotically connected for trade with Iran and China. Britain fought wars with Afghanistan in 19th century and in the second decade of the twentieth century. But it never physically occupied it. Soviet Union had a bitter experience between 1979-89 and now it is USA and NATO led coalition which has occupied it after ejecting out the Taliban as a consequence of 9/11 attack on World Trade Centre in 2001, masterminded by Al-Qaeda headed by Osama bin Laden.

Afghans has hopped for weapons and other military hardware first from its neighbors and as time rolled on, the spatial reach has also widened. The fighters have also looted the national armories or obtained it clandestinely through smuggling. Today even one may see a bearded Afghan soldier going on his deadly pursuit of his enemy, holding an American Stinger missile on his shoulder and other weapons captured or obtained illicitly.

Military

Due to continuous wars and struggle, military has played a larger role in Afghan society and culture. Peace is a luxury in this war ravaged country. If it is not fighting an outside power, then it is fighting within the country between different contestants for power and authority. Internecine conflict between different tribes is one constant of Afghanistan's chequered history. In an insightful editorial, it is mentioned "in Afghanistan and in Somalia, the world calls them warlords, a word that first came into general usage 75 years ago in connection with the then anarchy in China. They are tribal and clan chiefs who take advantage of a political vacuum at the centre to maintain or extend their traditional power base, through the use of force and then prevent central authority being reasserted".[1] That paraphrases or in nutshell encapsulates the vicissitudes of Afghan history down the ages.

Be that as it may Afghanistan neither had a constitution, nor had any semblance of political culture familiar in West in form of democracy. *Loya Jirga,* the tribal assembly only, gave some institutional mechanism for the ramshackle political structure to rule the area. Plethora of warlords and tribal heads, made lives of ordinary people too difficult. Oppression and exploitation was ever shadowing the day-to-day life of ordinary people, who had to begin with little to keep them economically afloat. As land for agriculture is just around 7 per cent, by default growing poppy is another alternative to earn some money. Here too drug lords rule the roost along with innumerable fixers, smugglers and middlemen. No surprise, Afghans have migrated elsewhere for job or joined some religious institution to keep body and soul intact. It is interesting to note that though Afghan soldiers are brave and courageous, British authorities in India employed few Afghan soldiers compared to the *Gurkhas.* Constant fighting within the country was never fully controlled and neutralized by the central military headquarter that sense, it was a bane, not a boon to the country at large. Even today there is nothing like Afghan military, which is strong enough to defend its borders or put down lawless elements within the country.

Democracy

The post Vasco-de-Gama age of Asian history, had seen the advent of European colonial powers to this continent. They conquered many areas by force of arms ostensibly with the stated objective of doing trade and commerce. Portuguese, Dutch, French, English and minor powers like Danes in due course, created and demarcated boundaries of Asian countries. Wherever English rule prevailed, they brought with them the English language and in garbled and distorted form tried to superimpose democratic practices and structures in their colonies. And a major spin-off was that, the colonial subjects were slowly allowed to persue higher studies in Britain. Thus, the percolation of democratic ideas came into the subjugated colonies through these students. That was just one important contributory factor. This situation was not prevalent in Afghanistan. No foreign European power had occupied it and there was "democratic deficit" to begin with. Election, free vibrant press, political parties, independent judiciary and executive responsible to legislature, were all something alien to the people of Afghanistan. It was only after 2001 American occupation of Afghanistan, that a democratically elected President Hamid Karzai became head of the state. A newly drafted constitution was approved by the Loya Jirga. Hamid Karzai had obtained a postgraduate degree in Political Science from the University of Himachal Pradesh in India. The US ambassador to UNO, former ambassador to Afghanistan Zalmay Khalizad, is Afghan-American, who migrated to USA, did his academic studies over there and became US citizen. The cream of Afghan student community has migrated to Western countries. By and large, it is accepted that democracy as one understandss has western origin. It is one of the most difficult form of government to introduce and operate. Further, as case of double jeopardy, it is questioned that in Muslim countries of Western and Central Asia, the tender plant of democracy had not bloomed. As one turns one's gaze to the Muslim world, one finds except for Turkey, most of the countries are not having democratic form of government in true sense of the word.

Afghanistan during its long two hundred years of history, with the benchmark of 1747, when Ahmad Shah Abdali created a new state from Kandhar as his capital, it had all forms of government like monarchy, theocracy, republic and communist regime. Today, it is called Islamic democracy. Husk of democracy is to be seen, when the writ of law does not prevail in 34 provinces, far-flung in its geographical expanse. Provincial capitals are inaccessible due to lack of infrastructural network and constraints of geographical topography. Afghan polity is rickety, dysfunctional and handicapped by endemic poverty, corruption, famine-cum-flood syndrome, poor transport, subjugation and seclusion of women and high rate of illiteracy. Women are just kept out of the picture. Naturally half of the population does not count politically. Woman are totally denied education and any work facilities. It is a deadly cocktail which has a toxic affect of insurgency, civil war, gratuitous killing, violent radical Islamic ideology and tribal separatism, with no industrial or agricultural base to the economy. Carpet woolen and silk industies could not become engine of growth for boosting exports because of continuous war and violence. Afghan economy has no stake in world economy. Poor gross domestic product and poor wages and salaries of ordinary Afghan worker do not facilitate growth of sturdy sense of national pride and identity.

Post 1992 rule of Taliban was put to an end by US forces when it drove out Mullah Omar and Al Qaeda head Osama bin Laden to across border of Durand Line into Wazirstan a part of the Federally Administered Frontier Area of Pakistan. Taliban rule was totally anti-democratic. Today whatever democratic edifice, the Americans have installed, is eroded through their attacks from within Afghanistan and from across their sanctuary in Pakistan. It has therefore become a joke, that President Hamid Karzai is a Mayor of Kabul and lives in his fortress, guarded by American marines. President Karzai is constantly chafing the indirect control and surveillance of the Americans and the NATO led coalition forces military commanders.

Then, there are certain traits in Afghan character, which militate against the normal functioning of a democratic government. Their penchant for double-dealing, aversion to obedience, tribal loyalty and identity, superseding national loyalty, prevents growth of democratic ethos and culture. The political culture, therefore, is highly fragmented, segmented and loaded with layers of stratification. Even Communist rule 1973-92 was littered with coups, assassination and break-up of Communist party itself into facts like Khalq and Parcham.One example will do. Sardar Mohammad Daoud, the close relative of King Zahir when he was vacationing in Italy, launched a coup and deposed him. The French educated former Prime minister grabbed all the power and the offices of the President, Prime Minister. But in a coup but in a coup engineered by Noor Taraki, he was killed. A nail was pierced in the coffin of Constitution of 1964. This is a continuing theme in political history of Afghanistan.

One important caveat is how democracy could strike roots, when it is a western importation with the country's coffers always empty. it invariably received funds from abroad. The founder Ahmad Shah Abdali and so his predecessors, the invaders Mahmud of Ghazni and Mohammad Ghori, brought wealth from India. Then British doled out some money to tribal chiefs just to humor them. During the post-1945 era, when Cold War was at its apogee, Soviet Union poured out lot of money plus gave lot of economic and military assistance. Now the USA and lot of NATO allies and the world at large including India has given help of one sort or another.

USA in particular after driving out Taliban from Kabul and the kingpin of Al Qaeda Osama bin Laden from his mountainous cavernous hideout at Tora Bora, across the Durand Line into Pakistan's Wazirstan, area poured out Millions of dollars to put up a governmental structure under the President Hamid Karzai. Loya Jirga approved this.

Angela Morkel President of Germany said Germany's frontier lies at the Hindukush. Thus, much fear was fear infused into the hearts of many heads of Western world. The list of international donors went on widening, but corruption and hemorrhaging of funds could not still bring vibrant democracy in war torn Afghanistan.

In fact, the war on terror widened divisions in Afghan society and put on backburner the development and reconstruction agenda, which provides muscular strength and wherewithal of democratic governance. Former Canadian Ambassador to Afghanistan Chris Alexander said thoughtfully that it would take five generations to make any difference to the conditions in Afghanistan. This becomes more intelligible, when in hindsight, one finds how even the faint flicker lighted by King Amanullah's (1919-28) reformist impulses, was smothered by the debilitating feudalistic culture. For democracy to flourish and get embedded in the political culture of Afghanistan, a dynamic civil society has to emerge. The jugular vein of civil society is throttled by constant war and lawlessness prevailing in society at large. No social compact, no social capital, no social cohesiveness is there. Instruments and mechanisms that could give legitimacy, responsibility and accountability to various organs of government both at centre and provinces and at grassroots level are non-existent. For example, various warlords with their militias, are constantly at daggers drawn or willing to offer their services to any foreign power for money or weapons. To cite one random example would substantiate this. In May 1992 Gulbuddin Hekmatyar launched his rocket attack on densely populated *bazaar* of Kabul, which not only took toll of human lives but also cut off electricity and water supply.[2] The weapons used were US made and financed by Saudi Arabia. The ubiquitous presence of the menace of landmines has blown off limbs of men, women and children.

Even the horrors perpetrated by the interregnum rule of Taliban 1992-2001, were a sordid tale of human savagery and cruelty. Noted Indian writer Khuswant Singh has said: "if you want to read a graphic description of the havoc caused by the Taliban, read the Afghan writer's two novels, namely, *The Kite Runner* and *A Thousand Splendid Suns*"[3]. Pakistan in quest for strategic depth had always desired Afghanistan to be under its protective wings and it was Benazir Bhutto who was instrumental in the installation of Taliban regime in Kabul. Taliban juggernaut had destroyed even the traditional tribal structure and radicalized the followers with new gusto of jihad.[4]

Civil society espouses equality, equity and fair play. Here, women and children had the worst of treatment, all through the history of Afghanistan. The patriarchal system, where polygamy is widespread and putting up of *burqa* from head to toe sequestered, secluded women folks from any activities of civil society. Their voice and views did not count. The much touted Pushtanwali – a code of Afghan societal behavior and norms do not accord any respectable status to women. In fact, it had high tolerance quotient for violence, revenge and resistance to authority. That meant more bloodshed and more mindless mayhem.

Civil society was weak and totally hallowed out of any developmental agenda for the welfare of one and all. There was never any dialogue with the government at level -centre, state and local. Citizen participation through debates and discussion was rare and very sporadic. Great paucity of NGO's (non-governmental organizations) opened, and run by indigenous people is a harsh commentary on idea of good citizenship and good governance.

Drug mafia and the culture, which spawned of illicit money and network of spies, agents, middlemen, and smugglers, polluted the environment of civil society. Civil society contributes to the total welfare of the nation by providing all sorts of services and amenities to residents living in villages, towns and cities. But unremitting violence and turbulence enfeeble everything. There is a question of two perspectives on civil society. Traditional and western in its orientation and conceptual dimensions. Traditional world view of civil society does co-exist in tension or conflict with western world view. Pukhtanwali the traditional code of social-cum-cultural behavior, has certain principles. Traditional words are there for it. Melmasta is hospitality, nanawati is right of fugitive to seek refuge, badal is right of blood dispute, tureh is bravery, sabat is steadfastness, inamdai is righteousness, ishteqamat is persistence, ghyrat is defense of property and mamus is defense of women. In the same breath, it has to be conceded straightaway that in actual reality, some of these precepts are blatantly violated. Then badal, the right of blood feud is barbarous and cruel. It is a sort of restorative justice or human rights where the victim gets woman, girl or money or goods or animals or any other thing from the perpetrator of the crime. Pushtanwali is a blend of custom and practice from a context of embedded conflict filtered through Islamic lens.

Then, Sufi network, mosque, local preacher and mullah also work in the background to settle disputes. However, ideologues and clerics from west Asian countries like Abdullah Azzam and Mohammad Ibn Abd al-Wahhab of Saudi Arabia have injected more radicalism and austerity in observance of Islamic practices and lifestyle. The former settled down in Peshawar, which became a nodal point of Afghan Diaspora. They glorified martyrdom and showed high indifference curbs to suicide bombing as a method to pulverize ones opponents. Use of human shield and more so of young children[5] did not meet moral censure of the ideologues and clerics, who veered towards the stance of Jihad against the Jews and crusaders in particular.

The violence, which generated out of this world view made mincemeat of civil society. Individuals, organizations showed stark capacity deficit. The peddlers of violence even became computer savvy and used all the media potential to get recruits to their cause, not only from within Afghanistan but also from neighboring Islamic countries as far away as Sudan or Chechnya. Vibrant forged passport industry mushroomed in the wake of collapsing authority of Army and Police. The legend of women fighters like Nazauna Shah Bori and of Malali of Maiwand was also resourced for purposes of violence. They retailed to the minutest detail all their gory deeds as self-appointed guardians of morality, justice and as guardian of people through blogs on websites. Also opened many websites and made full use of Al Jazzera, CNN, BBC and many other media outlets to get their message across to their opponents. The traditional norms and format of civil society were twisted, mangled beyond recognization by Taliban, warlords, insurgents and assorted malcontents. Liberty, which is the distinguishing hallmark of a robust civil society, was not there in Afghanistan during the time of monarchy, communist regime, during the civil, war time or under Taliban's dispensation.

In a functioning civil society, one could follow their own profession in unfettered way, within the bounds and parameters of law. Could form voluntary associations, professional associations, social service organizations, where education and pursuit of knowledge, arts and creative culture is given full scope and encouragement. This was muzzled and no room for any dissent or unorthodox views was allowed to sprout. It is no surprise that intellectuals and professional class have migrated to USA, Canada and many western countries plus Pakistan and Iran.

In British capital city of London there is place called Hyde Corner in St James Park, where you can stand and speak on any subject which you like and air your own views. It is a great safety valve, you can cry hoarse in advocating your cause. Of course, it is within bounds of propriety. You cannot bear any arm or weapon to annihilate or liquidate your opponent. France, which has a distinction of undergoing revolution in 1789, very thoughtfully presented to USA a Statue of Liberty. A noble gesture today, international society has been doing to its best in revitalizing the structures and institutions of civil society in Afghanistan. International donor agencies are pumping money, personnel, knowledge, skills and capacities in reinvigorating civil society in war ravaged country. Taliban diehards have killed many women workers. Recently, one has seen the plight of South Korean volunteer workers over there.

The free liberating spirit of freedom, enabled Vida Samadzai an expatriate Afghan beauty, studying in California U.S.A to participate in Miss Earth title competition in Manila, (Phillipines) in 2003. Same year; a Woman's Magazine by name Morsal (Rose) was published and also 10 Afghan women passed the driving test and started driving their cars. All this has happened with the American occupation of Afghanistan.

The international community including India, has extended lot of assistance to build its civil society. It has succeeded in Afghanistan's entry into SAARC grouping of states.

Under World Food Programme, New Delhi is providing high protein biscuits to 1 million children. It has helped in establishing transmission lines and built modernized telecommunication networks across Afghanistan. A technological feat looking to the geographical topography was seen. Then undertook *Salna Dam* project in Heart. Built a strategic Delaram-Zaranj road which, would give Afghanistan a landlocked country access to Iranian port Chah Bahar.So far, Afghanistan had depended on Pakistan for sea outlet. Indira Gandhi Hospital for women was built in Kabul providing women much needed medical facilities. Financial aid was also provided. In all projects, Afghan nationals are associated and given necessary training and skills. With all that help provided to Afghanistan in its reconstruction and nation-building, Indian Embassy in Kabul became a centre of terrorist attack on July 7, 2008.It is tragic that geopolitical compulsions and national rivalries between neighboring nations hamper work launched by India. To some it is an eyesore and irksome.

The building and nurturing of civil society in Afghanistan becomes a battleground, in which nations of the international community and nations in its neighborhood are locked in clandestine warfare. At times, terrorism is let loose on hapless country, compounding the problem of national development. It becomes more complex when the ruling elite and bureaucracy, instead of working wholeheartedly on national development agenda, work more to buttress their position and siphon off money given by the international community.

The upshot is that the enfeebled civil society could not combat financial misappropriation of money by those who are movers and shakers of the governmental machinery and its fledgling economy. The Afghan civil society is devoid of large number of lawyers, engineers, accountants, social workers, educationists, managers, agricultural -cum-livestock experts, bankers, business entrepreneurs, journalists and media specialists. All teachers, professors, scientists are building blocks of civil society and also for the lifeblood of it. It has also failed to raise its voice forcefully against violence, terrorism and drug mafia.

Human Rights

Human rights have taken a centre stage in any discussion or analysis that tries to probe the disintegration and horrible situation, which prevails in Afghanistan. Women, children, orphans, disabled segment of the population have born the brunt of horrible violation of their human rights. The multi-media both printed and electronic, plus the Internet have brought a qualitative change in dissemination of news. And what happens on the streets and bylanes of Afghanistan, are known to the world instantaneously. The ubiquitous TV screen has empowered good people around the world to lend a helping hand to the people of Afghanistan.

Terror, violence, mindless killings has been the running thread of Afghan history. Women, widows, orphans, disabled and poor people, do not count much before the mighty and powerful despots, military leaders, *mullahs* and clerics. Women are not supposed to work outside their homes. They need not drive vehicles, should always be in veil and draped from head to toe. Schools teachers become target of attack. Afghan alumni who had fought against the Soviet occupation and were also involved as mujahideen in civil war, are hardened peddlers of violence. They have not shown either any remorse or aversion to use children as shield or even as suicide bomber. Drugs, terrorism and religious extremism make for an explosive mixture.[6] Even a cultural heritage like *Bamiyan* -the Buddhist work of art has been destroyed with impunity, despite international protest.

Human rights, organisations of all those who differ with them politically, ideologically or religiously, are done to death. Religious extremism has seen Sunnis at throats of Shias.The warlords like late Ahmad Shah Massoud, Gulbuddin Hekmatyar, Abdul Rashid Dostum, Haqqani and others, had killed lots of people and made thousands flee to neighboring countries for shelter like Pakistan, Iran and even tried their luck in Central Asian Countries. The enterprising and educated lot immigrated to West. Even were farmers and children to the war front. The stories of atrocities perpetrated by Taliban, assorted insurgent Mujahideen groups, warlords and drug mafia syndicate have no end. Even women workers of many international charities and NGO's, had found their throats slit with great barbarity. The psychological profile of these merchants of death show high degree of morbidity and they drape themselves in clothes of martyrdom culture.

The morbidity and mindset show them as dangerous sociopaths. Jayant Prasad India's Ambassador to Afghanistan puts it succinctly that these people "do not accept democracy and political pluralism. Or do not believe in human rights and fundamental freedoms and those that don't operate within constitutional bounds. If you do it, then it is to accept that you can fry snowballs".[7] Even in Holy Book of *Quran,* it is clearly mentioned that killing of one person is like killing all mankind'[8]. But the bloodletting has remained unabated.

There is another unfortunate spillover affect of America's war on terror code named "Operation Enduring Freedom". Lot of innocent civilians have died due to bombing by the fighter planes, gunships, helicopters, missiles, grenades, etc. In targeting the terrorists, poor hapless innocent people too get killed. After all, 'they (Afghans) are only worth one tenth of an Alaskan sea otter rather than 40 camels'[9]. This collateral consequence of the war has aroused the ire of Human Rights organization all over the world. Human Rights Watch, Amnesty International, etc.

The loss of Human Rights means the death knell of civil society and democracy because there are backward and forward linkages of Human Rights with the other two. Freedom and liberty, equality and fraternity are all interdependent and indivisible.

Conclusion

The bottom line remains that Afghanistan was not only a failed state, but is also a fictive state. There were pervasive feeling of surrealism to the country which had become a killing field, in which macabre dance of death was seen. Taliban is no more on the rampage. If Afghanistan had Talibanised, then surely Pakistan, had come under the threat zone of Talibanisation. Only a Nostradamus can foretell the future scenario. However, at the moment the ground reality is, grim.

Monarchy has failed so did communism. Taliban rule was a failure and the rule of war loads in their turf was no currency for good government. Americans with NATO – led allies with irresolution have saved Afghanistan from

Anarchy tribal federalism in form of Loya Jirga had shown its inadequacies, all down the line to provide a semblance of good governance.

The predecessor of UNO, the League of Nations had a novel idea of Trusteeship Council for certain areas in Africa, which were unfit to govern themselves. Perhaps something to that effect under the leadership of UNO can give some respite to the nation from ravages of war, till it takes time to sort out the mess and take the reins of office all by themselves.

Afghanistan has natural resources and this could be made good use of in establishing industries. Much needed funds could be generated. Gas and oil is there in its neighborhood and Afghanistan could join in fruitful joint ventures. Both gas and oil pipelines could pass through its territory, taking the energy resources to different countries.

There is element of fragility all around, where death stalks everywhere and yet there are even ordinary men and women of Afghanistan and from many parts of the world, who have decided to work for its nation building and regeneration. Despite all the vicissitudes of fortune and turbulence, there has been a feeble effort by Afghans to have a democratic framework to see them through, for a better peaceful order. But it is a long haul. Western powers, principally USA is rooting for democratic form of government because they see it as a solvent to Afghanistan's problem of endemic instability. At the same time, war between US and NATO-led occupying forces and *Taliban* forces from their sanctuary in Swat and Wazirstan has resulted in loss of human lives and violation of human rights of civilians trapped in the ever widening arc of conflict. Future looks bleak for benighted Afghanistan and eliminatin of Baitulah

Mehsud through a missile attack has complicated the matter further at ground level.

Despite "troop surge" and appointment of Richard Holbrooke as special envoy to Afghanistan and Pakistan, President Barak Obama's "Aj-Pak" policy no way gurantees victory against Taliban. Thus the occupation of Afghanistan by USA and NATO-led forces would go on indefinitely for many years to come. It is like waiting for Godot.

References

1. "Dealing with Warlords," *Arab News*, (Editorial) February 26, 2005, Jeddah, Saudi Arabia.

2. Naom Chomsky, World Orders, Old and New (Oxford University Press, New Delhi, 1994, pp 97-98.

3. Khuswant Singh, "Taliban Menace", *The Hitavada*, December 9, 2007, Nagpur.

4. Sayyad Hasan Khan and Kurt Jacobsen, "Guarding the Guards", *The Statesman*, October 8, 2008, Bhubaneshwar.

5. Radhika Coomarswamy, "UN Special Representative for children and armed conflict", *Herald*, September 10, 2008, Goa.

6. K.Subrahmanyam, "Smash the Opium Trade", *The Times of India*, August 5, 2008.

7. Jayant Prasad (Interview), *Outlook*, November 10, 2008, Mumbai.

8. Quran 5:32.

9. Marc W.Herold, "Matrix of Death", *Frontline*, October 24, 2008.

2

Democracy and Human Rights in Bangladesh

Indra Mohan Jha

Introduction

Elections are a celebration of democracy. Democracy is best suited to the cause of human rights. It is in this context that the results of the elections (December 29, 2008) in Bangladesh augur well for the protection and promotion of human rights. This is the first general election in seven years, with the remarkable fairness and peace – a total contrast to the failed elections in 2007, which was marred by violence, leading to emergency rule in the country. The most striking feature is a huge turnout of about 80% of voters, expressing their desire for a stable government to herald Bangladesh toward an era of modern liberal democracy, having a clear focus on peace, prosperity and social harmony. Sheikh Hasina's Awami League (AL) pledged to build a digital (modern) Bangladesh, attracting younger generation who formed nearly one–third of the electorate. These young voters, with a new vision turned the tide against Khaleda Zia's Bangladesh Nationalist Party (BNP) and its Islamist ally *Jamaat – e – Islami (JI). Jamaat* had opposed the liberation by joining hands with Pakistan in 1971. They became powerful in collaboration with BNP, to bring Bangladesh back on Pakistan's track. However, voters rejected Jamaat's empty religious rhetoric. They could win only two seats in the 300–member parliament compared to 20 in 2001.[1] Thus, the as electoral verdict reiterated the values of liberation – to create a liberal society that espouses the traditional spirit of Bangladesh.

Bangladesh as a part of Bengal is deeply influenced by the glorious heritage of intellectual, political and social reforms and renaissance heralded by Raja Ram Mohan Roy, Ishwar Chand Vidyasagar, Ravindarnath Tagore, Kazi Nazrul Islam, Lalan Shah etc. Yet, it has its share of the sub–continental paradox of human rights violations on accounts of poverty, corruption and repression of various hues. Its existence as East Pakistan (up to December 16, 1971) was marked by untiring struggle against exploitation by parasitical ruling, elite (militarily–mullahs–feudal lords) of West Pakistan. Naturally, Bangladesh suffered worst birth pangs known in recent times. Rape and murder by Pakistani forces was the cornerstone on which their freedom struggle was built. Women as a symbol of purity, as representation of social honour were despoiled. The society and economy was devastated due to years of loot and plunder, unleashed by Pakistani butchers. Millions became refugees of lacs and thousands were killed and raped.[2]

In the night of March 25, 1971 about 90,000 well–trained and well–equipped Pakistani forces unleashed repression in Dacca. This heinous campaign was christened

"Operation Searchlight" with the declared goal to crush the liberation struggle of Bangladesh. That was the beginning of a well-planned Pakistan reign of terror with cunningness, surprise, deception and speed, combined with shock action.[3] Zulfikar Ali Bhutto himself (in Dacca) wrote of the night, in *The Great Tragedy*, of death and destruction to save Pakistan.[4] Reports of loot, killing and rape shook the conscience of humanity. Reacting to the tragedy of Bangladesh, Andre Malraux French Culture Minister bemoaned, "People of our generation have experienced enough horror to be, alas! No longer shocked, and human nature is such that it is rare that horror doesn't breed horror".[5] Sheikh Mujibur Rahman duly expressed the continuing tragedy of Bangladesh in a historic public meeting at Dacca Race Course on March 7, 1971. He lamented:

> *Today I come to you with a heavy heart. The streets of Dacca, Chittagong, Khulna, Rangpur and Jessore have been dyed red with the blood of our brethren. People of Bangladesh today want liberation, they want to survive, they want to have their rights ... the history of the last 23 years is the history of the dying cries of the people of Bangladesh, the history of pathetic bloodshed and the history of misery of oppressed people. We shed blood in 1952. We could not establish ourselves in power in 1954 even after wining the elections. In 1958 Ayub Khan promulgated the martial law in the country and made us slaves for 10 years. In 1966 the Six–point programme was launched and only for that many of our brothers were killed. Ayub had to step down in the face of a mass upsurge in 1969 and then came Yahya Khan. He said he would return power to the people and let the country have a constitution. We*

believed in his words ... But what did we get in return? Arms were used against unarmed people of Bangladesh.[6]

Yet, these unarmed suffering people of Bangladesh won their freedom from the jaws of notorious Pakistani Generals. Their sacrifices earned them international support and sympathy. They became a symbol of struggle to assert their rights. The leaders of Bangladesh had a vision of a modern state based on secular democratic principles. Mujibur Rahman in his broadcast to the nations on October 28, 1970, on the eve of the general elections pledged that his party Awami League was committed to make a total shift from the policies of Pakistan. He pleaded that,

> *"A real living democracy must be established, in which all the fundamental freedoms shall be constitutionally guaranteed... the present economic system, which has established an intolerable structure of injustice, must be radically altered. The entire land system has to undergo a radical reorientation in the interest of the actual tillers of land. The wage structure throughout the economy must be altered in keeping with the dictates of justice... we firmly believe in the equality of citizens. The members of the minority community should know that we have always stood against every from of communalism. They shall enjoy equal protection of the laws... it is imperative for us to avoid involvement in global power conflicts. We must, therefore, pursue a truly independent non–aligned foreign policy.*[7]

Thus, there was a commitment to turn a feudal–fundamentalist–military dictatorial Pakistan upside down to create a society based on the principles of welfare state and humanism. West Pakistan under military rulers did not tolerate this. Awami League strived for these values, even in a separate sovereign Bangladesh in erstwhile East Pakistan. Bangladesh Proclamation of Independence sought legitimacy in their "right of self–determination of the people of Bangladesh... whose will is supreme ... to ensure for the people of Bangladesh equality, human dignity and social justice,... Bangladesh to be a sovereign peoples' republic".[8] Guided by this spirit, Bangladesh became independent.

Unfortunately, things went wrong very soon. Sequence of events after independence led Bangladesh to the old path shown by Pakistan. After about four decades of independence it resembled another Pakistan. There was no place for democracy and human rights. Mullahs and military ruled the roost in all these years except for some intervals of weak elected governments managing anyhow to survive merely to remain in power. In their quest for power, respective governments had contributed to further weakening the values of liberation struggle. In such a situation human rights violations of the weak and marginalized was abominable. Perhaps, Bangladesh then had the lowest rating on human rights measurements. This is obvious from the observations of Amnesty International:

> *...Think of the metaphorical darkness from which the people of this country are seeking to escape. For decades, Bangladesh has been caught in a downward spiral of corruption, insecurity, political violence and organized crime in which human rights and the rule of law have been the first casualties... Repressive laws, including laws granting special or emergency powers, have been used and abused by successive governments. Police and other state officials have sided with the*

> *affluent and the influential, so that most vulnerable – women, minorities, the poor and the marginalized – have been the least protected. The declaration of the state of emergency and the installation of a caretaker government in January 2007 were desperate measures to save the country from ever – increasing levels of insecurity and political violence, further bloodshed and mayhem, and set on track free and fair elections for a democratic government. In a country where the state machinery – courts, police and military – not only fail to deliver justice and security but is often the instrument of persecution...*[9]

One wonders why did Bangladesh slide downward to the darkness of its existence today? Why it failed to consolidate its humanist historical heritage and social culture of Bengali Bhadralok? What happened to the stirring exhortation – *Joi Bangla* against exploitation and repression by West Pakistan? Why the legacy of liberation degenerated into the hell of today? To seek some answers to these questions, one needs to look into the political developments taking shape in Bangladesh in the aftermath of independence wherein the seeds of dictatorship and Islamic fundamentalism began to take roots. Commitment to secular–democratic polity seemed uncomfortable even for the new establishment. They too proved no better than any other political elites in the sub–continent.

Democracy Vs Islamic Dictatorship

The saying that "revolution devours its own children", goes well with the sequence of events in Bangladesh. The new nation adopted its constitution under the charismatic leadership of Sheikh Mujibur Rahman on December 16, 1972. The four pillars of the state policy were: nationalism, socialism, democracy and secularism. Amongst all secularism was more pronounced in the constitution and functioning of the state. Mujib tried to up hold the secular Bangla identity of the new nation— may be to emphasize separateness from Islamic Pakistan and proximity to India. Article 12 of the constitution upheld the principle of secularism to be realized by the elimination of (a) communalism in all its forms, (b) granting by the state of a political status in favor of any religion, (c) abuse of religion for political purposes, (d) any discrimination against or persecution of persons practicing a particular religion. Article 38, separately disapproved of use of religion for political purposes.[10] The intention was to eliminate communal forces from the body politic, by showing respect for every faith despite the fact that, Bangladesh remains predominantly an Islamic society with more than 88% Muslim population. It also recognized state's regard for people's sentiments and long–established traditions. As an example the daily sessions of the parliament opened with recitations from the holy *Quran* and also form the *Gita*. [11]

Like wise, *Parliamentary democracy* was an inspirational force for the people of Bangladesh to wedge the war of independence. The constitution provided democratic rights for people under a parliamentary government. People and elite were habituated to it since the British days. Yet, Mujib was designated as president in his absence. However, on his return from detention in Pakistan on January 10, 1972 assumed the office of President only to step down on January 12, 1972 to become the Prime Minster and undisputed leader of the people of Bangladesh.

Unfortunately, the new Mujib dispensation proved only a successor to the earlier regime under Pakistan. Revolutionary hopes and aspirations of the masses were belied. The bureaucracy and police remained undisturbed; and their role during the nine months of struggle was ignored. Mujib's condemnation of genocide and to hold a Neuremburg-type trial of war criminals, remained an empty rhetoric, never to be implemented. Instead, he began to appease the sentiment of Islamic forces. In 1973 he declared a general amnesty for all those considered as Pakistani collaborators. About 30,000 pro-Pakistani forces were released from jail. The Islamic academy that he had abolished in 1972 was revived and in March 1975, upgraded to a foundation. He also started visiting religious gatherings and gave up his famous valedictory exhortation – *Joi Bangla.*[12]

Not only that, Mujib wanted friendly and fraternal relations with Islamic countries. Article 25 of the constitution reflected close ties with Islamic countries in historical and cultural contexts. Islamic identify was emphasized by showing commitment to become an effective member of the organizations of the Islamic Countries (OIC) at Lahore summit on February 27 after Pakistan recognized Bangladesh on February 24. This significant achievement was possible through the good offices of Egypt and Kuwait.[13]

Rehabilitation of the *Mukti Bahini*, an unorganized army of about 1,30,000 to 1,80,000 youth, seemed a difficult task. The proposal to utilize their services for constructive works was ignored. On the other hand, liberation war commanders found it hard to surrender their arms and shed their freedom of action. As a result these armed youth found an outlet in anti–social activities. Loot, rape, gang warfare became their favourite pastime. Unscrupulous politicians used them to settle scores with rivals. Political violence claimed over five thousand victims during the four years of Awami League rule.[14]

Situation got further aggravated when in April 1973 about 28,000 Bengali military personnel were repatriated to Bangladesh. Their lack of commitment to freedom struggle and integration in the armed forces made them fodder to the cannons of ambitious generals and unscrupulous politicians in days to come. Their absorption further weakened the traditional supporters of Mujib. The raising of a new paramilitary force, *Jatiyo Rakkhi Bahini* (JRB) having exclusive allegiance to Mujib proved morally and politically disastrous. JRB became the target of anti–Mujib campaign. In January 1974 JRB got protection against any legal action and was allowed to arrest without warrant. JRB seemed to work as official goons for strike–breaking, chasing out slum–dwellers from Dacca, searching for rice hoardings in the countryside and fighting the underground guerrillas. They used brutal methods. Working at the behest of the Mujib regime, JRB was used against both political opponents and the army as a warning to them not to think of a coup. Favoured treatment for the JRB enraged the army since the beginning. Thus, JRB proved dangerous in the long–term for Mujib to have created suspicion and division in military, civilian administration and people at large.[15] Poor administration, problems of reconstruction and the food shortages, etc peaked in 1974. Rapid nationalization caused severe setback in production. Opposition to Mujib increased as problems mounted. Perceiving imminent dangers owing to his declining popularly, inefficient administration with rampant corruption and threat from the army, Mujib tried to consolidate his position. He revived the old three party alliance—Awami League, National Awami Party and the Communist Party of Bangladesh. He also tried to create a new political structure with pro–liberation parties, the armed forces, the bureaucracy and other sections of the society. On June 6, 1975, Bangladesh became one–party state with

Bangladesh Krishak Shramik Awami League (BAKSAL), as the sole legal political grouping. On January 25, 1975, the fourth constitution amendment was already passed to change from parliamentary to presidential form of government. This whole process was perceived as total centralization of power with one–party, one–president–Mujib. This move sharpened polarization in Bangladesh and painted Mujib as a total negation of his own self of the liberation days exuding democratic fervour. Some important members of parliament resigned in protest – making obvious, the cracks within.[16]

All this did not strengthen Mujib; instead weakened his moral authority. He did not have time to consolidate politically. Anti–liberation reactionary forces were already celebrating the ongoing mockery of liberation. Mujib had already made himself unpopular. Naturally, when he was assassinated on August 15, 1975, there was no serious public outrage to mourn his death. A stunned nation was groping in darkness of days ahead. Thus, began a series of coups– one after another. Between August and November 1975, three governments were installed. The Mushtaque government installed after August 15, 1975 massacre, was overthrown on 2/3 November by Major General Khaled Musharraf, only to be over thrown (killed). A new government came to power on November 7, 1975 under Major General Ziaur Rahman. He was respected as a war hero of freedom struggle and commanded large following in the arms force as well.

However, Zia began to undo the legality of liberation. He emphasized individual initiatives, pursuit of power, wealth, and orderly government against Mujib's democracy, egalitarianism and distributive justice. Most significantly, he removed Article 38, which disapproved of use of religion for political purposes. Nonetheless, he added "Bismillah–ur–Rahman–ur–Rahim" in the preamble. Socialism was replaced by "total faith and belief in Almightily Allah".[17] Islamisation of Bangladesh became complete when Lt Gem. HM Ershad made it an Islamic state. Ershad captured power on March 24, 1982 after Zia's brutal murder on May 30,1981, overthrowing Justice Abdus Sattar, the president. As the Chief Martial Law Administrator, he suspended the parliament, constitution, and political activities. Law courts were supplanted, censors introduced and all aspects of national life were guided and controlled by armed forces.[18] The two generals ushered Bangladesh in the age of Islamic dictatorship, skewing the roots of democracy. The Ershad dictatorship came to an end on December 6, 1990 due to mounting public pressure, generated by joint struggle of the (BNP) and AL. The ensuing March 1991 elections results brought BNP closer to *Jamaat – e – Islam* (JI) to from a government under the leadership of Begam Khaleda Zia. *Jamaat* used this opportunity to further its agenda of transforming Bangladesh into an Islamic state, to be governed by *sharia*. Over a period of time, these elements benefited from instability to garner their support base in different sectors in Bangladesh. They have filled sensitive civil service, police, intelligence and military posts with their sympathisers. It was estimated that the "fundamentalist sector of the economy" earned an annual profit of about $1.2 billion. They became so powerful that few dared to write against them at the cost of being targeted.[19] They built a strong nexus with Pakistani terror outfits to create havoc in the name of religion in the sub-continent as a whole. The situation in Bangladesh could well be described as a land reeling under political instability, militarism and fundamentalism. Natural victims were marginalized ones - poor, women, children and minority.

Poor, Women, Children and Minority

Bangladesh was described as the "basket Case" in the 1970s. The situation remained similar with some difference of degree. The marginalized ones suffer as this appalling life as a helpless lot. A country with 153.3 million people is still growing at the rate of about 2 per cent. As a result, it is one of the most densely populated (1083 persons per sq km) country in the world. 41.3 per cent of the population earn below one dollar a day to live in absolute poverty.[20] The Special Rapporteur on food highlights poverty in Bangladesh. The country is very disaster prone - not only susceptible to frequent floods, but also droughts, tornadoes, earthquakes and epidemics. Disasters often cause havoc in this predominantly agricultural country with 80 per cent population living in rural areas; half of them in abject poverty. Less than only 10 per cent rural populations have enough land to survive. More than two-third rural population is landless, leading to migration to urban centres to live in terrible slums. About half of the population is too poor to afford enough food to sustain a healthy and productive life. Levels of malnutrition are amongst the highest in the world. Every year, 30,000 children become blind due to vitamin A deficiency. Over half the population is affected by iodine deficiency, including 80 per cent children. Women are the worst victims. Far more girl children are underweight and stunted. This is due to the archaic custom that women eat last, which means that they often eat least.[21] This speaks of the traditional attitude of discrimination against women. This is also a major cause of problems related to underdevelopment of Bangladesh.

Women are the worst victims of human rights violation in Bangladesh due to the exploitative nature of law and society and its social institutions. Domestic violence, dowry deaths, rape, sexual harassment and trafficking are a well accepted fact of life. *UN Fund for Population, Annual Country Report 2000*, has identified Bangladesh as having the world's second highest rate of 47 per cent domestic violence. There is an increase of 68 per cent of rape cases, 78 per cent acid throwing, 49 per cent in dowry related violence and 82 per cent in domestic violence. A new fashion of dowry has become common among Muslims as well. About 50 per cent of married women suffered physical or mental torture on this account.[22] This prevails in every strata of the society. Hindu laws remain the same as before 1947 without any change. Polygamy is not illegal. There is practically no inheritance for women. Divorce is difficult and women cannot adopt children.[23]

Women's condition became more pathetic with the rise of Islamic fundamentalism. Muslim Personal Laws, governed by *Sharia* place women in subjugation to men in matters of inheritance, marriage-divorce, custody of children, etc. Wife inherits only one eighth of her husband's property, if she has one or more children and one-fourth, if she is childless. A daughter inherits only half of a son's share. If there are no male children, a daughter inherits only a fixed share and the rest goes to other agnatic relatives. However, as the per customs, daughters give up their rights in exchange for *naior* (the right to visit father's/brother's home). Thus, having no property to fend in time of crises, makes them more vulnerable in case of divorce or husband's death. The Muslim Family Law Ordinance, 1961, allows up to four wives, provided each wife is treated equally. Islam permits this under certain conditions, which are never taken into consideration.

Legal system remains archaic and discriminatory against women. This is more obvious in marriages and crimes like rape. Rape is hardly reported as physical examination puts women to shame and have to suffer social stigma. Reported cases are withdrawn, compromised or dismissed for lack of proof. There is almost no conviction. "Principle of burden of proof" becomes a vital factor for denial of justice, whereas the defendant assumes no legal burden of proof by merely denying the charge. In rural areas, where the Islamic laws prevail, the victim is required to produce at least three witnesses.[24] This discrimination is also there in the political domain. 30 women members are indirectly elected by the Parliament. The practice of additional seats for women is a carry over from Pakistan, where it was assumed that women were unlikely to win in a general election.

The case of Taslima Nasreen makes it amply clear that Islamic fundamentalists have become very powerful. Her book *Lajja* (1993) presented the atrocities against Hindu minority in the aftermath of Babri Mosque demolition in Ayodhya (India) on December 6, 1992. It is important to note that Taslima's crime, according to fundamentalists, was double. For one, she raised her voice for non-Muslims (Hindus in particular), and second, she pleads for women's equality, women to have uniform civil code and not to be suppressed by the religious laws of the Mullahs. She has distinguished herself as a champion of womens' rights not only in Bangladesh but whole of the sub-continent through her book *Narir Kono Desh Nei* (Women Have no Country).[25] Naturally, she earned the wrath of the Mullahs. Her life is in danger and she had to flee the country.

In this context, it is interesting to note a weird case of Islamic law being practiced in Bangladesh. A self–styled

Muslim cleric, Abdus Sattar (a retired soldier) calls himself a '*Pir*'. He has been guarding Bara Masjid road in Chittagong's Pirojpur town. Women are not allowed to use the road as there is a mosque on the road, which according to sattar is illegal in Islam. A woman cannot take even her sick child to hospital on this road. Administration does not care at all.[26] After all, women and children have hardly anything to protect. Their life is so painful that an estimated 10,000 to 20,000 women and children are trafficked every year to India, Pakistan, Middle East, etc, for sex trade, domestic work, beggars and camel race.[27] The government is least bothered about children's plight. Even there is no comprehensive data on the extent of sale of children, child prostitution and child pornography.[28] Ironically, Bangladesh is a party to International Covenant on Economic, Social and Cultural Rights, Covenant on Civil and Political Rights, Convention on the Rights of the Child, and Convention on Elimination of All forms of Discrimination against Women, with reservations though. The basic problem is that, the national legislation is not fully in compliance with the provisions of international obligations and there is inadequate implementation of existing laws. As a result, there is a massive violation of human rights overtly or covertly.

Such a drudgery of Bangladesh life drives people to other countries in search of livelihood. The most natural destination is India to work as low-end fitters, locksmiths, painters, cutters, welders, rickshaw pullers, domestic servants and labourers. They are mostly illegal migrants. Their number is said to be over two millions in last four decades. One estimate suggests that about four hundred Bangladeshi enter India every day that comes to about 1.5 lac every year. Now they have spread over to Delhi, Jaipur, Bikaner, Jaisalmer, Ahmedabad, Mumbai, Bangalore, Mysore, Hyderabad, etc besides the traditional destination. West Bengal, Tripura and Assam. Now a new phenomenon has emerged (i) They feed Jihadis recruitment. The important link is through *Harkat-Ul-Jihad-al-Islam (HUJI)*, the terrorist organization based in Bangladesh. Huji's main aim is to establish an Islamic state in Bangladesh and work towards formation of an Islamic caliphate. It has wide contacts with international Islamic terror groups especially in Pakistan.[29] These migrant workers have fallen prey to religious superstition and are being lured into the trap of terror, which is engulfing the sub-continent. This is an unfortunate paradox. Those who leave their homeland in search of livelihood, are being used to destroy the life of innocent people in the name of religion due to poverty, illiteracy and superstition. This is a painful case of poor human rights conditions. This calls for immediate remedial measures.

BNHRC

People of Bangladesh have suffered military regimes, suspension of constitution and fundamental rights. Law enforcement has been militarized, deaths in custody, arbitrary arrests detention and denial of justice are common. Even democratic regimes have failed to prove better, due to thoroughly corrupt and inefficient administration. Protection of human rights in such a situation needs a strong human rights institution. Several non governmental organizations have been raising their concern. The role of the Human Rights Council, which represents 200 activist human organizations, is praiseworthy. In April 1995, the Government approved a project, to assess the need for such a body and to make recommendations for its establishment. The project entitled 'Action Research Study' formulated initially on the Institutional Development of Human Rights in Bangladesh (IDHRB), was to start in July 1995. However, it was delayed due to prevailing political crisis in the country. It was revived in 1996, when an agreement was signed between the government and the United Nations Development Programme (UNDP). The project was to prepare the grounds for the eventual establishment of a viable institutional mechanism, to promote and protect human rights as guaranteed under the constitution of Bangladesh. The IDHRB project formulated a draft bill – the Bangladesh National Human Rights Commission Act 1999. The draft bill proposed that the NHRC be set up, for "the protection, promotion and creation of the conditions for the enjoyment human rights". The bill also stated that an effective mechanism for the protection, promotion and creation of the condition for the enjoyment of human rights should be evolved, to implement the constitutional commitment.[30] However, this draft bill was not implemented.

The Council of Advisors after coming to office the Council of Advisors on January 11, 2007 pledged to establish a commission. Foreign Ministry placed the draft to this effect before the Council of Advisors on September 8. Finally, the NHRC Ordinance was accepted on December 9, 2007.[31] The Commission is empowered to investigate complaints by individuals or may initiate on its own. In proven cases of violation, it can either settle the matter or pass it on to the court or relevant authorities.

The decision to establish the NHRC was widely appreciated though with apprehensions . There is a fear that this may prove yet another bureaucratic mechanism packed with subservient judges and bureaucrats. Moreover, defence forces are considered very sensitive and have remained beyond any public scrutiny. Therefore, without power to adjudicate and issue binding commands, it might prove a glorified cipher and promise of unreality. To convert it into a real human rights watchdog, there is enormous need for unity amongst humanist sections of Bangladesh, who are active in different ways. It is essential to channelise the energy of organizations in this area. A number of oganisations are working on the promotion of women's rights in association with Islamic religious leaders, who have helped to promote community awareness on women's issues such as elimination of child marriage, acid-throwing, and other acts of violence against women. Works of organizations such as Bangladesh Legal Aid and Services Trust (BLAST) and the Madaripur Legal Aid Association (MLAA) to provide legal aid to the poor and to improve access to justice and in arranging mediations to resolve disputes, are remarkable. Several grassroots NGOs are active with informal village courts to raise awareness of human rights and gender issues, where the precepts of Islamic laws are inconsistent with national law.[32] These examples are encouraging. These initiatives are bound to check Bangladesh from further sinking into the quagmire of inhuman insanity that crept in after Mujib's assassination.

Under the new democratic dispensation presided over by the Awami League, there is hope for a better condition in Bangladesh. However, endemic political/bureaucratic corruption, military dominance and all pervasive poverty, raise apprehensions. Can theses hopes and aspirations be translated in to practical terms? Will politicians think and work beyond their personal greed? Will battling Begams bury the hatchet? Answers may not be obvious, as patterns of politics take time to change. Politicians hardly reach at consensus in Bangladesh, even on serious national issues. Bickering has already begun. Khaleda Zia and BNP MPs-elect stayed away from swearing in ceremony in Parliament on January 4, 2009 without citing any valid reasons. BNP has alleged that the poll was "stage managed" and had a large scale rigging.[33] This is an ominous sign of probable shape of things to come. Begums must muster courage to cooperate because only a democratic set-up can serve their interests well. They themselves have suffered instability, Islamic fundamentalism and military dictatorship. Thus, political will in conjunction with people's will desperately requires protecting democracy in Bangladesh for the protection and promotion of human rights. Only this kind of commitment and conviction can convert what once Henry Kissinger called the "basket case" into *Sonar Bangla*.

References

1. *The Times of India (New Delhi)*, 30 – 31 December 2008.

2. *Bangladesh Documents, vol. II* (New Delhi), p. 75. An estimate by *The National Geographic*, September 1972 placed the death toll in East Pakistan at about 3 million.

3. Siddiq Salik, *Witness to Surrender* (Karachi: Oxford, 1978), p. 228.

4. See Md. Shamsul Huq, *Bangladesh in International Politics: The Dilemmas of the Weak State* (New Delhi: Sterling, 1993), p. 30.

5. Foreword by Andre Malraux to "How Pakistan Violated Human Rights in Bangladesh" (New Delhi: ICWA), in *Bangladesh Document*, n. 2, p. 7.

6. Sheikh Mujibur Rahman, *Bangladesh, My Bangladesh: Selected Speeches and Statement*, October 28, 1970 to March 26, 1971 (New Delhi: Orient Longman, 1972), pp. 92-3.

7. Ibid, pp. 3-11.

8. "The Proclamation of Independence", Mujibnagar, Bangladesh, April 10, 1971.

9. "Ending the Downward Spiral in Bangladesh", http://www.amnesty.org/en/news-and-updates/features-stories/ending-downward-spiral-bang.

10. J. N. Dixit, *Liberation and Beyond: Indo-Bangladesh Relations* (New Delhi: Konark, 1999), pp. 264- 65.

11. Md. Shamsul Huq, n. 4, p. 44.

12. Syed Anwar Husain, "Religion and Ethnicity in Bangladesh Politics", *BIISS Journal* (Dhaka), vol. 12, no. 4, October 1991, p. 428.

13. Huq, n. 4, p. 234 and J. N. Dixit, n. 10, p. 184.

14. Ishfaq Ilahi Choudhury, "Civilian Control of the Military in Bangladesh: Moving Towards a Democratic Tradition", *BIIS Journal*, vol. 20, no. 1, January 1999, p. 77 and Kirit Bhaumik, "Mujibur Rahman: Where he Faltered", *World Focus* (New Delhi), vol 3, no. 7, July 1982, p. 10.

15. See Md. Shamsul Huq, n. 4, pp. 51-54.

16. Baxter, Craig and Rahman, Syedur, *Historical Dictionary of Bangladesh*, 3rd edition, (Metuchen. N. J: Scarecrow Press, 2003.

17. J. N. Dixit, n. 10, pp. 243, 265.

18. Samar Sen, "Ershad in Control", *World Focus*, n. 14, p. 3.

19. Selig s. Harrison, "Bangladesh-New Hub for Terrorism", *Tribune* (Chandigarh), August 5, 2006.

20. See *HDI Report 2007-2008* (New York: UNDP) and *Economic and Social Survey of Asia and Pacific (New York: UN, 2008), Statistical Annex.*

21. *Report of the Special Rapporteur on the Right to Food*, Commission on Human Right, E/CN.4/2004/10/Add.1,29 October 2003.

22. *The Greenwood Encyclopedia of Women's Issues Worldwide: Asia and Oceania* (Westport: Greenwood Press, 2003), p. 73 and *Bangladesh Observer* (Dhaka), July 29, 2002.

23. Chanchal Sarkar, "Obsolete Laws Bane of Bangladesh Women", *National Herald* (New Delhi), November 13, 2000.

24. *Bangladesh Observer* (Dhaka), April 25, 2001and also see Habiba Zaman, "Violence against Women in Bangladesh: Issues and Responses", *Women's Studies International Forum* (New York), vol. 22, no. 1, January-February 1999, pp. 37-48.

25. *Hindustan Times* (New Delhi), March 25, 2007.

26. *Times of India* (New Delhi), January 14, 2009.

27. *The Greenwood Encyclopedia*, n. 22, p. 74.

28. *UN Committee on the Optional Protocol to the Convention on the Rights of the Child on the Sale of Children, Child Prostitution and Child Pornography*. CRC/C/OPSC/BGD/CO/1, June 8, 2008.

29. *The Times of India* (New Delhi), June 9, and July 30, 2008.

30. http://www.hurights.or.jp/asia-pacific/no_18/no18_bangladesh.htm.

31. http://www.hrcbmdfw.org/blogs/bangladesh/archive/2008/01/01/809/aspx.

32. *Report of the Special Rapporteaur, n. 21.*

33. *Times of India* (New Delhi), January 5, 2009.

3

Bangladesh: Assessing Democratic Consolidation and the Human Rights Situation Under the Civil Military Regime

Sreya Maitra

Introduction

The evolution of international politics has witnessed the development of governance and statecraft which provide sanctity to the principles of freedom, equality and integrity at the level of individual human existence. As the democratic political system subsumes the facilitation of these norms, the march towards democratization by states in the beginning of the twentieth century, has been hailed as the sine qua non of political maturity and modernization. Realist imperatives of political rule, have demanded the articulation of constitutional methods of constraining such actions, which subvert the authority and legitimacy of the state. But the rights of the citizens in their individual capacity as well as political, legal and socio-cultural entities have been considered as vital traits of a vibrant political system. It is to this end, that scholars have observed that fundamental human rights and the nature of government are organically linked.

For the post colonial states in the Third World, the transition to democracy and the adoption of its inherent patterns has not been a smooth. In many cases, the process is yet to be completed. The signature of turbulence is writ large. The absence of adequate political institutions and the continuance of inappropriate colonial structures and rules have acted as retarding forces. The prevalence of unstable governments being confronted by a host of political, socio-economic and military challenges in some of the post colonial societies, have rendered the democratic situation and the prospects of democratic consolidation questionable. The scope of practicing human rights has, consequently, been jeopardized. The analysis of the socio-political situation in Bangladesh may be made from this vantage point.

The collapse of democracy and the prolonged rule of the civil-military regime in Bangladesh has been the product of a range of complex yet inter-related factors. In terms of its impact, there can be little argument that the foundation of human rights has been grossly subverted. Scholars have unequivocally argued that the presence of a civil-military regime has been antithetical to the exercise of human rights, whereas the restoration of democracy in the near future would act as its legitimate safeguard. The present paper seeks to highlight the adverse correlation between the civil military regime in Bangladesh and the fabric of human rights as witnessed in the turmoil there. It argues that the consolidation of democracy after December 2008 elections, would be crucial for her socio-political stability. For this purpose, the paper would be divided into the following sections:

- Section One would provide the theoretical background to the requisites of democratic consolidation.
- Section Two would introduce the dimensions of the history of politics in Bangladesh in the context of the dilemmas of the post colonial states in establishing democracy.
- Section Three would highlight the rise of fundamentalism and the human rights situation in Bangladesh.
- Section Four would throw light on the legal system of rights and the impediments to its safeguard.
- Section Five would briefly trace the recent political tensions and the human rights situation and offer some concluding observations.

Democratization and the Constitutive Processes

Democratization in the 20th century and even a little earlier, has been underlined by the political-economic and social-cultural logic that on the whole, democratic governments are less prone to revolutions and other forms of civil violence and thus, less likely to make war with each other. There is a high priority accorded to equity, justice, civil liberties and human rights. The armed forces are unequivocally subservient to civilian rule. The citizens have the adequate means to access the governmental processes and have a real say in collective decision making via elected representatives in national and sub-national legislatures. The poor, minority, ethnic and religious groups, women and young people, also have avenues of airing their views on issues of national or regional interest.[1]

The process of democratization is inclusive of the dual stages of the transition to democracy (from another form of political system) and its subsequent consolidation and sustenance. The accomplishment of both steps crucially hinge on a set of contiguous factors. The transition to a more democratic political regime may be from an authoritarian or semi-authoritarian political system to partial or full democracy. Samuel Huntington defines a 'wave of democratization' simply as a group of transitions from non-democratic to democratic regimes that occur within a specified period of time and that significantly outnumber transitions in the opposite direction during that period.[Huntington, 1991,5] Huntington identifies three waves of democratization and notes that this global trend lost steam between 1962 and mid 1970s.[2] Scholars like Kraxberger point out that the process of democracy spread to most post-colonial societies following the third wave, that is from 1974. This resulted in a 'radically restructured map of global democracy and much optimism about the future diffusion of democracy'.[3] Democratic transition essentially entails the leaving of political office by a non-democratic government and the organization of relatively free and fair elections.[4]

The sustenance of democracy and its consolidation is propelled by some more structural and proximate factors. Evidence suggests that most political transformations away from once-stable non-democratic regimes do not end in consolidated democracies. Especially in the context of the nascent democratic regimes in the Third World, scholars largely opine that there is no straightforward progression from transition to consolidation.

Defining Democratic Consolidation : Scholars have variously judged the scope of the process of democratic consolidation and the requisites for its accomplishment. A wide and rich literature exists on the subject which may briefly be recounted here for illustration.

- Huntington assesses whether a polity has a consolidated democracy by a 'turn-over test', that is, a ruling party loses an election, an opposition party or a coalition wins it and next time, loses. This test has the virtue of being easy empirically to verify but it has the vice of not being nuanced enough. For example, following the introduction of democracy after the Second World War, Japan did not fulfill the criteria of Huntington's test until 1993, nearly fifty years later.[5]

- Mainwaring, O'Donnell and Valenzuela argue that democratic consolidation is not dependent on electoral tests per se, but should be perceived as a situation when 'all major political actors take for granted the fact that democratic processes dictate governmental renewal'. [Mainwaring, O' Donnell and Valenzuela 1992:3]

- For Bratton and Van de Walle, democratic consolidation is 'the more or less institutionalization of democratic practices, complete only when citizens and the political class alike come to accept democratic practices as the only way to resolve conflict.[Bratton and Van de Walle 1997:235].[6]

Scholars opine that democratic consolidation requires the fulfilment of the following conditions:

- Democratically-oriented actors must heavily outweigh non-democratically oriented actors.

- Elites and masses alike, must be comfortable with politics rooted in democratic norms and behaviour,

- Leaders of political parties agree to subordinate their strategies and divisions to the common goal of not facilitating a return to authoritarianism.

It is argued that with the development of these conditions, there is the growth of the genuine features of a democracy, namely; more open political competition, commonly accepted political rules, stable democratic institutions and a satisfactory range of state-guaranteed civil and political rights upheld by the rule of law.[7]

There is a wide agreement in the literature that to consolidate democracy is to create and sustain a novel kind of political environment involving, inter alia, new challenges to both civil society and political society actors. The collective aim that once sustained and encouraged them, namely, to oust the non-democratic regime, is no longer there. Instead the challenge shifts to two new areas:

- How to institutionalize democratic competition,

- How to balance interest and aspirations of various groups previously united in opposition, now in political competition.[8]

This novel situation clearly demands a different range of skills and commitment than those needed to engineer a transition from authoritarianism.

In an elaborate case study of democratization in the Third World, Jeff Haynes argues that three specific factors played a crucial role in helping to consolidate democracy in some of these nations. These have been enumerated as:

- Development of a democratic political culture,
- Colonial legacy of representative institutions which carried over into the post-colonial period.
- A strong civil society to provide countervailing power to that of the state and a high degree of consensus among political elites.

Haynes states that these factors laid the conditions for 'continuous democratization' in eight states namely Latin America, Caribbean, Jamaica, Trinidad and Tobago, Colombia, Costa Rica, Venezuela, Botswana and Mauritius and India.[9]

Another school of thought expounds that consolidated democracy cannot be solely characterized by; election of officials, free and fair electoral system, real possibility of opposition victory, universal citizenship and suffrage and civil liberties (including free mass media) and respect for minority rights. In fact, there are various regions where democratic consolidation could not be achieved despite the adoption of democratic principles. These are termed as 'procedural democracies' as opposed to 'substantive democracies' and maybe viewed only as a part of a just society. Countries like Pakistan, Brazil, Guatemala and Colombia, for example are replete with cases of human rights violation and other inequalities.[10] There is one variable, which cannot be glossed over in the debate and analysis on democratic form of government much fancied and adopted by new independent states emerging from the thralldom of colonialism. All erstwhile colonial powers were not the same.

The democratic ethos and legacy however flawed and jettisoned left by Britain, France, Spain, Portugal, USA, Belgium, Germany etc, differed from each other as chalk from cheese.

Bangladesh: Independence and its Aftermath

In the post colonial states of the third world countries, the process of democratic consolidation has frequently been impeded by structural and socio-cultural factors and poor rates of economic development. The case of Bangladesh can be introduced in this context.

As is well known, Bangladesh came into existence as a result of the secessionist movement in East Pakistan against the increasing discrimination and exploitation by the military government of West Pakistan. With the imposition of military rule and periods of martial law in 1958 under General Ayub Khan, resentment and alienation grew in East Pakistan.[11] The Bengali Awami League, which demanded substantial self-government won the local elections in December 1970. To suppress the growing secessionist movement, the Government in West Pakistan postponed the Constitutional Assembly and imposed martial law. East Pakistan retaliated with nation wide strikes and the call for non-violent resistance. Negotiations between the Government and the leaders in East Pakistan broke down, and the state deployed the central Army to restore law and order and pre-empt a potential rebellion by Bengali forces. The army made a concerted effort to weaken the Awami League.[12] Hostilities broke out in East Pakistan and Indian troops moved into Bangladesh on 4th December 1971. On 16th December 1971, Pakistan forces surrendered unconditionally and withdrew from East Pakistan.

Post-Independence: The pangs suffered by Bangladesh at its birth, were extremely painful. The havoc created by the Pakistan army and the dislocation that any war leaves behind in its wake, had to be handled by people, who had largely been agitators and not administrators. It is generally conceded that they did not do a good job.[13] However, Bangladesh embarked on its journey as an independent nation with commitment to the Westminster model of a liberal parliamentary democracy based on secular ideals. Scholars observe that the principal of secularism offered to the polity a sense of citizenship as opposed to that of religious sectarianism.[14]

Mujib-ur-Rahman became the first leader of independent Bangladesh in December 1971. The Constitution was adopted in 1972, providing for a Parliamentary democracy characterized by the separation of powers with a unicameral legislature, a strong Prime Minister and an independent judiciary. The Constitution proclaimed a State policy of nationalism, secularism, socialism and democracy.

The first few years of independent Bangladesh dominated by the Awami League was marked by administrative and economic chaos and increased authoritarianism. The consolidation of all parties into a single party augured ill for Bangladesh's democracy and was a sign of Mujib's growing unpopularity.[15] To bring unity of all nation building forces under a single command; to meet the formidable challenges of a war-ravaged economy and problem ridden new state, Sheikh Mujibur Rahman assumed total power. Totalitarian control was given legal-political sanction through constitutional arrangement. The power structure was altered and the single party, *BAKSAL*, now ruled Bangladesh.

Mujib started to use symbols of Islam in public to shore up public support. The deliberate use of 'Khuda Hafiz' by Mujib instead of his trademark '*Joy Bangla*' towards the end of his rule, while not undermining secularism, was an indicator that politicians believed that playing up to religious sentiments of the people was a substitute for good governance and gained them popularity. However, it did not help him survive. An army coup spearheaded by a few disgruntled army officers on August 15, 1975 assassinated Sheikh Mujib and his family members and overthrew the government. The constitutional arrangement of single party control was thus replaced by a military dominated civilian regime. The assassins were openly allowed to leave the country without facing trail. Thus by 1975, Bangladesh switched over to one-party Presidential system of monolithic character'.[16] From the vantage point of the theoretical precepts of democracy, the case of Bangladesh validated dual theses:

- Rupert Emerson's argument that new states starting with parliamentary democracy soon lose their way and settle back into authoritarian or dictatorial regimes.[17]

- The democratization thesis that nascent democracies often find it difficult to consolidate the democratic framework and experience 'democratic reversal'.

This was also the juncture when Bangladesh assumed the theoretical status of a 'collapsed state' which has been characterized by scholars like Rotberg as a tense, deeply conflicted, dangerous and bitterly contesting warring factions, which may consist of insurgencies, criminal gangs, militias and other groups which together indulge in persistent, internal armed conflict.[18]

Mujib's assassination marked the beginning of a period of chaos and a series of military coups that ended only with the Army Chief of Staff General Ziaur Rahman's ascension to power.[19] But the latter's authority lacked political legitimacy. It became imperative that for political longevity, he seek support from wherever it could be had. It was here that the fundamentalists, who had opposed the very creation of Bangladesh, demonstrated their survival skills. Allying with a General who was desperate for legitimacy and support but whose record during the liberation struggle was impeccable, they started to wipe their own slate clean to re-emerge in public life. From here to preaching their brand of Islam and the subsequent deterioration in the condition of the minorities was, by no means imminent but was certainly a distinct possibility. For Zia, distancing himself from the Awami League was extremely important if forces not allied to Mujib had to be mobilized. Therefore, he tried to create a Bangladeshi identity, as distinct from Mujib's Bangla identity, where Islam had a role.[20]

As Zia's credibility and popularity rose (due to his steps of liberalizing the economy, stress on agriculture and to peasantry and a certain extent of decentralization of power), to the legitimacy of the fundamentalists who had allied with him also increased. But given the fact that Zia left none in doubt about where real power actually lay. There was not really much that Islamic politicians could do.[21]

Ershad who succeeded Zia in 1982, followed the latter's path. Having deposed Abdus Sattar in a bloodless coup, he too lacked legitimacy. Hijacking Zia's constituency was out of the question, given the suspicions that exist till date, about his role in Zia's murder. Nor could he, given his background, hijack Mujib's constituency even if he was inclined to. It was he, who made Islam the religion of the state, legalizing the superiority of the status of Islam compared to the other religions. While this was a step in competitive populism with respect to Zia's Bangladesh Nationalist Party (BNP) and appeasement of the fundamentalists, who promised to establish an Islamic state. It laid the foundation of legalized unequal treatment of minorities, while not quite reinstalling 'dhimmitude'.[22] ("Dhimmitude" during Mujib's era implied the superiority of Islam as the religion of the State.) With the state behaving thus, the fundamentalists became more audacious. Mass organized attacks on minorities began during Ershad's regime. However, support of the Islamic groups proved to be counter productive for Ershad. The radical Islamic group, Jammat, launched an anti Ershad movement in 1991, which finally restored democracy in Bangladesh. The Jammat gained further legitimacy in the times to come, and it thrived by its judicious alliance with the Bangladesh Nationalist Party (BNP). BNP won the election in 1991 and Begum Khaleda Zia became the Prime Minister of Bangladesh.

After the prolonged political crisis since 1994, the Awami League was voted into power in 1996, with Sheikh Hasina Wazed, daughter of Mujib, as the new Prime Minister. In October 2001, a coalition of the Bangladesh National Party and three other parties formed a new government under Prime Minister Begum Khaleda Zia.

The politics of Bangladesh in the 1990s have been vividly characterized by the deep political hostility between Sheikh Hasina and Khaleda Zia. It is observed that the animosity is largely personal, as it stems from the differences over who played a greater role in the country's independence struggle-Hasina's father Sheikh Mujibur Rahman or Khaleda's husband General Ziaur Rahman.[23] On assuming power in 1991, Khaleda's party pushed the idea that her husband was an equally key player in the independence struggle as Mujib. The latter had been recognized as the 'Father of the Nation' in Bangladesh's Constitution in 1972. Khaleda's government amended the Constitution in 2004 to delete this reference.[24]

Caretaker Government: Bangladesh introduced the caretaker system in 1991 after military President Hossain Mohammad Ershad was toppled through a people's uprising led jointly by Khaleda and Sheikh Hasina. Though the leaders cooperated in the movement to oust Ershad, their ways parted with the latter's departure. Their uncompromising attitudes and the refusal to trust each other for organizing fair elections necessitated the institutionalization of the caretaker system. In the last few years, during the course of which, the two parties have ruled alternately, the outgoing government has had to hand over to an independent caretaker government three months before the poll was due.[25] Article 58 of the Constitution stipulates that parliamentary elections be conducted by an independent Election Commission during the three month tenure of a neutral, non-party caretaker government.[26] However, this system in itself has become susceptible to a host of corrupt practices. These maybe pointed out as follows:

- The personal animosity of the two opposition leaders has led the political parties to politicize the institutions, especially the judiciary, from which the caretakers are drawn. In fact, the BNP brilliantly succeeded in this. One electoral commission appointed by the caretaker government had sought a BNP nomination for the election.

- Observers have argued that the caretaker arrangement, designed to bolster a failing democracy, has eased the intervention by the army. Fearing a murderous the Western diplomats did not issue any rebuke. The United Nations (UN) did nudge the army to intervene with the warning that the UN might reconsider its peacekeeping contracts with the army, if it participated in biased polls.[27]

It is due to the complex interplay of these factors, that some scholars have opined that Bangladesh has gradually veered to its own version of '*home grown democracy*'.[28] The major features of the home grown democracy have evolved out of the so-called practices since 1991:

- Parliamentary democracy has been largely ineffective.
- Religion has become part of the democratization process under the BNP-alliance government, compromising and in some case destroying the liberal process.
- Power has been concentrated in the hands of the Prime Minister due to the incompetence of some ministers.
- Civil and police administration have been politicized creating a major crisis for maintaining law and order.
- The armed forces have a role in keeping election related violence under control.
- Minorities and political opponents have been persecuted and stripped of their rights and in some cases even assassinated.[29]

Scholars argue that the seeds of Bangladesh style home grown democracy were sown during the BNP regime of Khaleda Zia when the latter manipulated the outcome of by-elections at Magura, Mirpur and Manikgonj to prevent the Awami League from gaining electoral victory. But on assuming power in 1996, the Awami League government also turned the whole process of by-election farcical.[30]

Since 1975, therefore, the political system of Bangladesh has consistently worked in an authoritarian environment and bred a non-democratic political culture. It has been argued that crime, cadre and corruption (triple C) are synonymous with Bangladesh's democracy.[31] Under this democracy, a minister never loses his/her job even when caught red-handed as a godfather in disguise or as looter of the nations' wealth in broad daylight.[32]

Fundamentalism and Human Rights

The prolonged political turmoil and the rampant intervention by the military to maintain order has adversely affected the human rights situation in Bangladesh. Fundamental rights have been violated and basic freedoms curtailed at every step. The fabric of human rights is further weakened by the fundamentalist assaults and assassinations. Fundamentalism has been used as a tool by the civil military regime to prolong its political survival and suppress opposition. This has spawned the subversion of human rights on politico-religious grounds, perpetrated through the unfair utilisation of the administrative, judicial and legal systems. As the authoritarian rulers continue to hold fort in Bangladesh, the saga of violation of human rights has been documented by the reports of the "Human Rights Watch" in the recent decades.

Prior to highlighting the complex dimensions of the gross atrocities, being committed in Bangladesh, it would be pertinent to understand the reasons for degeneration of the country into the present state of authoritarian Islamization.

Rise of Fundamentalism: Bangladesh was declared as a secular country in 1971 which guaranteed fundamental rights to all its citizens. It was thus, expected that the significant Hindu minority constituting 20% of the population and the small Buddhist minority would be well protected in the new born state. Secularism was one of the four fundamental principles of state policy enshrined in the constitution of Bangladesh which was written within a year of the country's liberation and passed on 4th November 1972.[33] The Constitution also indicated the means by which this was to be established. Article 12 read as follows:

The principle of secularism shall be realized by the elimination of: [34]

- Communalism in all its forms,
- Granting by the state of political status in favour of any religion,
- Abuse of religion for political purposes,
- Any discrimination against or persecution of persons practicing a particular religion.

Article 38 provided inter alia that no person shall have the right to form or to be a member or otherwise take part in the activities of, any communal or other association or union which in the name or on the basis of any religion, has for its object, or pursues a political purpose.

The reign of terror unleashed in 1971 and the consequent persecution of the Bengali masses in the name of defending Islam and Islamic bond between the provinces of Pakistan had already made the future of Islam as a basis of state policy, uncertain in the new state. The obvious and widespread public hatred against the fanatics who collaborated with the Pakistan military junta and denominational politics were also clear indicators that Islam would have no place in the formulation of state policy. However, academics point out that secularism in Bangladesh was understood more in the sense of neutrality among the religions or equal treatment of all religions and their followers rather than a total separation of the Church and the State. People expressed ceaselessly that secularism did not mean absence of religion or religiosity.[35]

But starting from the mid 1970s, Islam made a definite comeback in Bangladesh politics. While the political regimes responsible for fanning the Islamic identities and fundamentalist groups for political ends have been discussed, in the previous section, it would be pertinent to observe that the degeneration of commitment to secularism in the political system had a direct impact on the escalation of violence and human rights violation. As experts note:

"Bangladesh's tryst with Islamism appears all the more surprising given its experience with Pakistan; especially the genocide that took place in the early 1970s. The Pakistani officers as well as mullahs supporting the Pakistan state to motivate jawans from West Pakistan to carry out the massacres used religious sentiments. Thus, Bangladesh's adoption of secularism was consistent with its experience with Islamic reaction in the early 1970s. Yet, before the decade was over, Mujib was dead and secularism was no longer a part of the Bangladesh's constitution. From this to the entry of fundamentalism in public life, was a short step that was duly taken by fundamentalist groups. What inevitably followed was the deterioration of the treatment of minorities."[36]

During Mujib's phase, some modest efforts were made to provide security to minority groups. But soon after his brutal assassination in August 1975, his successor Zia-ur-Rahman was not so reassuring to the minorities. President Ershad and Prime Minister Khaleda Zia were equally non-committal to the protection of the Hindus and Buddhists in Bangladesh. Their persecution went on increasing.[37] The Awami League government of Sheikh Hasina had once been leftist and secular. It had the largest following among the Hindus and other minorities but it did not succeed in giving them a sense of security. In December 2000 it made a pact with the radical Islamists due to her political compulsion.[38] During that period, sporadic attacks on the religious minorities continued and the Hindu temples were regularly looted and desecrated by the fundamentalist terrorist outfits, with the civil service and police by large remaining apathetic.[39]

Scholars opine that like many Muslim countries, Bangladesh has moved towards a more bigoted Islam in recent decades, propelled partly by its politics.[40] The rising influence of the Jamaat-i-Islami bears testimony to this trend. With around 7% of the popular vote, the Jamaat has never increased its following. But through shifting alliances, it has certainly increased its influence. It had its first two ministers in the last government and 18 seats in the Parliament. [41] Scholars have even warned that given the centre stage which Jammat occupies and the power and legitimacy it enjoys, an unavoidable consequence is the acceptance and practice of militant Islam, by a growing number of Bangladeshis. [42] This has been amply demonstrated in recent times, by the extensive processions launched in Bangladesh in favour of Osama Bin Laden, Mullah Omar, Al-Qaeda and the Taliban with significant participation.

The religious radicalism has fomented violent militant attacks and subversion of the rights of the minority population. Since 1999, 19 bomb and grenade explosions by religious extremists belonging to militant organizations such as the Jam'tul Mujahideen Bangladesh (JMB), Harqatul Jehad and Ahle Hadith have left 181 people dead and over 1700 injured. In August 2005, there were synchronized bombings in 63 districts which seized the government with panic. There were a series of investigations and between December 2005 and October 2006, over 30 alleged militants were arrested (including 6 leaders of JMB), 241 cases were filed and 29 people were sentenced to life imprisonment or awarded capital punishment.[43]

Since the handing over of power to the caretaker government in 2007, observers fear that Islamists, both in the mainstream and the radical margin will profit from the hiatus. The JMB campaign gave Western countries a fright and brought a slew of unsubstantiated reports that Al Qaeda leaders were in Bangladesh.[44]

Human Rights Violation: While religious hatred fuels human rights violation in itself, in a majority of the cases, political vendetta acts in conjunction with the former. The subversion and downright trampling of rights (as claimed by human rights activists) is manifested at various levels of political and social life. These may be enumerated as follows:

Intolerance to Political Opposition: Bangladeshi political regimes have displayed a singular lack of tolerance. Major opposition parties register dissent through violent demonstrations and enforced strikes. But the party in power usually takes advantage of state resources to suppress opposition activities. The latter are portrayed as anti-state and treasonable activities and the state policy machinery is used for making politically motivated arrests and repression of opposition members. Consistent reports demonstrate that various governments have used the police to crackdown on their opponents, sending the message that anybody who is challenging the government is exposing himself/herself to the risk of torture. Consistent and credible reports, attest to the widespread if not systematic practice, of using torture and ill-treatment as a means of suppressing political opposition.[45]

Journalists had also faced violence and assaults on several occasions, particularly during the times of public unrest. There was a marked increase in institutional violence against journalists, strikers, students and members of the political opposition.

In 2006, in Kushtia (South West Bangladesh), a BNP member of the Parliament assaulted and threatened a journalist for reporting his illegal activities. There were also reports of three journalists being killed allegedly for their reports on corrupt syndicates or religious militants. Gangs allegedly belonging to the ruling party alliance, fundamentalist groups and powerful business houses assaulted 72 reporters. Criminal and defamation cases were filed against 63 journalists.[46]

Religious Intolerance: Religious minorities are not well represented in selected boards of government services and agencies. They have very poor access to bank loans and other opportunities. Also, they are often troubled by thugs and extortionists with little active measures of redressal by the state. Land grabs from religious and ethnic minorities have become common phenomena. The Hindus have complained that the repeal of the Vested Property Act in 2001 has not helped in the recovery of properties appropriated by powerful individuals. In 2006, village gangs aligned with the BNP were reported to have attacked temples and demolished Hindu deities. The Buddhist '*Ras Mela*' had to be cancelled in a few villages because of the intimidation. The Ahmaddiya sect had also been threatened with expulsion, violence and occupation of their mosques by religious zealots under the banner of 'Khatme Nabuwat' movement. The government had neither revoked its ban on Ahmadiya literature nor it prosecuted persons who attacked Ahmadiya mosques. In 2006, however, under international pressure, it was able to prevent large-scale violence.[47] The case of writer Taslima Nasreen encapsulates the syndrome of religious zealotry: were she was hounded out of the country. Her writings proscribed and voice muzzled.

Police: The police in Bangladesh are known to be corrupt, partially as a consequence of being misused as party functionaries by the ruling government. Long practice of using violence for political ends, the high levels of corruption, the poor training of police forces and almost complete immunity for the perpetrators, are considered to be the reasons for the prevalence of torture. Police related human rights abuse are plentiful. Unlawful detention, excessive use of force, torture, deaths in custody, repression against women are still widespread.[48] The practice of torture is also facilitated by the lack of safeguards. For example Section 54 of the Code of Criminal Procedure allows for arrest and detention without a warrant or an order from a magistrate on nine different grounds for up to 24 hours. The detainees are denied access to lawyers, relatives or doctors. Also the Special Power Act of 1974 allows for preventive detention.[49] In 2001, the police committed a number of extra-judicial killings and some persons died in police custody under suspicious circumstances. The police routinely used torture, beatings and other forms of abuse while interrogating suspects. In 2006, 51 prisoners, of whom 32 were standing trial, were reported to have died from various causes, including violence by guards, fellow prisoners and delays in medical treatment. Prison conditions are extremely poor for a majority of the population.[50]

The Public Safety Act (2000) gave even greater opportunity to the police to abuse its powers by affording them immunity from prosecution and public scrutiny and allowing them to detain those suspected of having committed any of the crimes defined in the Act. But this was repealed in 2002 under pressure from the press and leaders of opposition political parties, who voiced for its immediate repeal based on a sharp reminder of specific cases where it was grossly misapplied as an instrument of political vendetta.[51]

In 2006, the Rapid Action Battalion (an elite anti-crime, anti-terror unit) and the police were responsible for hundreds of extra-judicial killings. These were however, euphemistically dubbed as 'cross-fire killings'. Many of these were of criminal suspects but some also had a political taint. RAB and other security agencies also perpetrated torture during custody and interrogation. The public display of the tortured and executed victims appeared to be a RAB tactic to instill fear among criminals and the population. Security forces used mass arrests as means to suppress demonstrations.[52]

***Judiciary*:** Much of the judiciary in Bangladesh is subject to executive influence and suffers from corruption. A large case backlog slowed the judicial progress and lengthy penal detention was a problem. Reports reveal that after a suicide bomber killed 2 judges in 2005, the judiciary had operated in a climate of fear and uncertainty. This was exacerbated by political interference and pressure at the national and local levels. On November 12 2006, the Judges' Association in the Lower Courts asked the government for additional protections from.[53]

Women: Women still remain in a subordinate position in society, though they had been heads of the State. They remain ignorant of their rights because of continued high illiteracy rate and unequal educational opportunities. They face strong social stigmas and lack economic means to obtain legal assistance. Thus, they are incapable of seeking judicial redressal. Moreover, rape of female detainees in prison or other official custody has been a perennial dimension of human rights abuse.[54] Further, reservations to Articles 2 and 16 (c) of the Convention on the Elimination of All Forms of Discrimination against Women (CEDAW) have not been withdrawn. Even by 2006, the Bangladesh Parliament had not amended citizenship laws to enable women to pass their nationalities to their partners and children as recommended by CEDAW. [55]

Administrative Arbitrariness: The government, on its part rarely convicts and punishes those persons responsible for torture and unlawful deaths. It continues to arrest and detain persons arbitrarily and to use the Special Powers Act and Section 54 of the Code of Criminal Procedure, which allow for arbitrary arrest and preventive detention to harass political opposition and other citizens by detaining them without formal charges. The Human Rights Watch argued that the government encourages violence by urging retaliation against opposition members who attack government supporters. The government has also filed numerous criminal cases against opposition leaders and activists.

In 2001, the government limited freedom of assembly, particularly for political opponents and on occasion, limited freedom of movement. It allowed a wide range of human rights groups to conduct their activities but continued to refuse to register a local chapter of Amnesty International.[56]

Workers' Rights: The government had also continued to limit workers' rights, especially in the Export Processing Zones. Domestic servants in many cases, work in condition that resemble servitude and lead to high incidents of abuse. Following the collapse of the garment factory in 2004 and fire in another factory in Chittagong in 2005, workers became more vocal in their demands for minimum wage, maternity leave, overtime pay, safe working conditions. But by 2006, over 2 million workers who contributed to exports from 4000 factories did not see improvements in their labour conditions. Consequently there were strikes in several factories in Gazipur and Savar. But the strikers were attacked by gangs allegedly hired by the management and police. A tripartite 'Minimum Wage Board' recommended an income that fell short of the workers expectations.

Workers migrating out of Bangladesh to countries like the Persian Gulf states in many instances they have their passports withheld.[57]

Abuse of children, child prostitution and child labour remain widespread problems.

Trafficking in women and children for the purposes of forced prostitution and at times for forced labour are also examples of human rights abuse.

Legal System of Rights in Bangladesh

Bangladesh is bound by certain international principles to ensure the safeguarding of human rights. These international treaties are ratified by authorized state representatives but it is not fully clear whether approval by the Parliament is required as the executive has in several cases, ratified treaties without such an approval. International treaties do not automatically become part of national law and consequently have to be incorporated by a legislative act. Bangladesh has not yet adopted any specific implementing legislation incorporating the provisions of the United Nations Convention against Torture or the International Covenant for Civil and Political Rights, despite its ratification of these treaties that constitute customary international law.

The treaties of human rights or humanitarian laws, which it has ratified or acceded so far may be enumerated as follows[58]:

- Four Geneva Conventions of 1949 (1971) and Additional Protocol I and II to the 1949 Geneva Conventions (8th September 1980).

- International Convention on the Elimination of All Forms of Racial Discrimination (1979).

- Convention on the Elimination of All Forms of Discrimination against Women (1984)

- Convention on the Rights of Child (1990)

- Convention on the Prevention and Punishment of the Crimes of Genocide (1998)

- International Covenant on Economic and Social Rights (1998)

- Convention Against Torture and Other Cruel, Inhuman or Degrading Treatment or Punishment (1998)

International Covenant on Civil and Political Rights. (2000)

Bangladesh, however, has not committed to accept the competence of the Committee against Torture or the Human Rights Committee to receive individual complaints against torture. In the absence of regional mechanisms individuals who have suffered torture only have recourse to national remedies and there is only limited review by international bodies of the compatibility of Bangladesh's practice with its international obligations. [59]

At the level of national law, neither the Constitution nor any Statute contains any express right to a remedy for injuries caused by public officials or for torture in particular. However, as a matter of Constitutional law, victims may seek redress through a writ application to the High Court Division of the Supreme Court.

At the national level, the Constitution of Bangladesh provides adequate safeguards from physical violation of an individual and freedom from fear. The 1972 Constitution of Bangladesh promulgated the supremacy of the 'rule of law'. A few relevant laws maybe enumerated at this juncture for illustration:[60]

- Article 27, Part III reads: "All citizens are equal before law and are entitled to equal protection of law."
- Article 31: "To enjoy the protection of the law, and to be treated in accordance with law, and only in accordance with law, is the inalienable right of every citizen, wherever he may be and of every other person for the time being within Bangladesh and in particular no action detrimental to the life, liberty, body,

reputation or property of any person shall be taken, except in accordance with law."

- Article 32: "No person shall be deprived of life or personal liberty save in accordance with the law."
- Article 33 (1): "No person who is arrested shall be detained in custody without being informed, as soon as may be, of the grounds for such arrest, nor shall he be denied the right to consult and be defended by a legal practitioner of his choice."

However, the clause of preventive detention limits the above mentioned Constitutional provision. The existence of the 'Special Power Act' of 1974 under which a person can be kept in detention for indefinite period is an indication of bad rule of law situation in the country.

Article 35 constitutes the right to protection in respect of trial and punishment. But these rights, guaranteed by Part III of the Constitution are not absolute. They have too many restrictions. There is no guarantee against arbitrary legislation threatening or suspending fundamental rights. Also, the provision of declaring a state of emergency (Article 33) by the President provides scope for abrupt derogation of rights.[61] Under Article 141C, the President further has the power to suspend the right to move the courts for the enforcement of any of the fundamental rights.[62] Thus, scholars observe that too many restrictions and exceptions have rendered the fundamental rights hollow and eventually it is difficult to understand how much is left with the people by way of fundamental rights.[63]

The Law for Speedy Trial (Droota Bichar Ain, 2002) had created the process of implementation and investigation.

The court system is beset with the overwhelming backlog of cases and this situation, factored along with corruption encountered in the judicial process at the lower level, ultimately prevent many people from obtaining a fair trial.[64] The critics thus, point out that the Constitution has played a trick with citizens; what it gives with one hand, it takes away with the other.[65]

Thus it maybe argued that the lack of a democratic culture, the prolonged rule by the military and the politically motivated constitutional amendments have chaffed the sanctity of the legal system and its 'teeth' to redress the abuse of rights of various sections of the society being perpetrated by the political and religious forces.

Recent Political Tensions and Human Rights Situation

Bangladesh was at the threshold of a new phase of political rule with the end of the 5 year mandate of Khaleda Zia's government in October 2006. The caretaker government assumed political leadership. The Awami League and its 14 party alliance renewed their longstanding demands of [66]:

- Appointment of neutral persons to the caretaker government,
- Reform and restructuring of the Election Commission
- Withdrawal of officials seen as partial to the outgoing government.

Widespread violence between the supporters of Khaleda Zia and Sheikh Hasina was responsible for the cancellation of the general elections slated to be held in January 2007. An emergency was imposed after which the Interim government again assumed authority. Fakhruddin Ahmed headed this and the administration has the responsibility of preparing the country for elections, which, took place at the end of 2008. It has the backing of the military, but Dr Ahmed has said that it is his administration, which is in charge. The Interim government had promised to clean up corruption before the election and had set up fast-track courts to prosecute dozens of high profile figures.

The Awami League and the BNP had called for the polls to be held by June. But the Election Commission said that some 50 million voters (out of an estimated 80 million) were yet to be registered. So, the election date could be set till September. Both parties had called for the release of their detained leaders who were facing corruption charges.

Meanwhile, the void in political leadership and the present state of emergency had heightened the hopes of the military for another prolonged period of rule. Fundamental rights of citizens are being curtailed at the alter of political expediency. Political analysts argue that the longer the emergency persists, the less likely a graceful, timely exit by the army becomes. In the absence of other leaders, the army had the option of trusting the judges to convict the two Begums and barring them contesting in the elections so that civilian military rule continues and democracy is not restored.[67]

It has been argued previously that there are certain specific requisites of a democracy and its genuine consolidation. Unless these are established, human rights cannot be practiced to any effective degree by the nation.

It was imperative that in the 2008 elections, Bangladesh resumes its political journey on the path of a parliamentary democracy. It is only then that the abrasion of human rights in the country can be redressed to some degree. Despite the travails of experimenting with democracy and the interregnums of military rule, the Constitution of Bangladesh remains avowedly committed to the idea of parliamentary democracy. The steps taken by the caretaker government to ensure political stability and the organization of free and fair elections with the systematic registration of all bona fide voters, augurs well for the future of the nation. It maybe hoped that the continuation of such positive political trends facilitate the restoration and the consolidation of democracy and the prevailing democratic institutions in Bangladesh and render improvements in the human rights situation. The bottom line remains that as Bangladesh has been a new entrant into the comity of nations only in 1971, as an aftermath of Indo-Pakistan conflict. The shadow of its bloody beginning has been totally eclipsed or eradicated. Not surprisingly, human rights story in the benighted once derisively dubbed as "breadbasket" case is a chequered one.

References

1. Jeff Haynes; 'Democracy in the Developing World; Africa, Asia, Latin America and the Middle-East', Blackwell Publishers Incorporated, 2001, p. 10.

2. Larry Diamond, 'Is the third wave of democratization over: an empirical assessment', Working Paper # 236, March 1997 as

cited at: http://www.nd.edu/~kellogg/publications/workingpapers/WPS/236.pdf.

3. Brennan M Kraxberger, 'Failed States: Temporary Obstacles to Democratic Diffusion or Fundamental Holes in the World Map?' Third World Quarterly, Volume. 28, No. 6. Rouledge 2007, p. 1055.

4. Jeff Haynes; 'Democracy in the Developing World; Africa, Asia, Latin America and the Middle-East', Blackwell Publishers Incorporated, 2001, p. 10.

5. *Ibid*, p. 11.

6. Bratton and Van de Walle, 1997:278 as cited in Jeff Haynes; 'Democracy in the Developing World; Africa, Asia, Latin America and the Middle-East', Blackwell Publishers Incorporated, 2001, p. 11.

7. *Ibid.*

8. Jeff Haynes; 'Democracy in the Developing World; Africa, Asia, Latin America and the Middle-East', Blackwell Publishers Incorporated, 2001, pp. 11-12.

9. *Ibid*, p. 12.

10. Howard Handelman, 'Third World: The Challenge of Third World Development', Princeton Hall Incorporated, 1996, Chapter 10, pp. 245-249.

11. "Redress: : Torture in Bangladesh ; 1971-2004, Making International Commitments a Reality and Providing Justice and Reparations to Victims", The European Initiative for Democracy and Human Rights, August 2004, p. 5.

12. *Ibid.*

13. Dipankar Sengupta and Sudhir Kumar Singh (ed), 'Minorities and Human Rights in Bangladesh', Authors Press in Association with SPANDAN, Worldwide Circulation through Authorspress Global Network, 2003, p XV

14. Megha Guhathakurta and Suraiya Begum, "Bangladesh: Displaced and Dispossessed" in Paula Banerjee, Sabyasachi Basu Ray Chaudhury and Samir Kumar Das (ed), 'Internal Displacement in South Asia, Sage Publications 2005, p. 188.

15. Dipankar Sengupta and Sudhir Kumar Singh (ed), 'Minorities and Human Rights in Bangladesh', Authors Press in Association with SPANDAN, Worldwide Circulation through Authorspress Global Network, 2003, p. XV.

16. Gyasuddin Mollah, 'Democratic Institution Building Process in Bangladesh:South Asian Experience of a New Model of Caretaker Government in a Parliamentary Framework', Working Paper No. 3, December 2000, South Asian Institute, Department of Political Science, University of Heidelberg, Germany, p. 3.

17. *Ibid.*

18. R. I. Rotberg, 'Failed States in a World of Terror', Foreign Affairs, 81(4), 2002, pp. 127-141 as cited in Brennan M Kraxberger, "Failed States: Temporary Obstacles to Democratic Diffusion or Fundamental Holes in the World Map', Vol. 28, No. 6, 2007, p. 1057.

19. Dipankar Sengupta and Sudhir Kumar Singh (ed), 'Minorities and Human Rights in Bangladesh', Authors Press in

Association with SPANDAN, Worldwide Circulation through Authorspress Global Network, 2003, p. XV.

20. *Ibid.*, pp. XV- XVI.

21. *Ibid.*

22. *Ibid.*

23. Information accessed electronically at http://news.bbc.co.uk/1/hi/world/south_asia/country_profiles/1160598.stm#facts

24. Information accessed electronically at http://news.bbc.co.uk/1/hi/world/south_asia/country_profiles/1160598.stm#facts

25. 'Everybody but the Politician is Happy', Economist, February 10th-16th 2007, pp. 27-29.

26. Human Rights Watch, 2007 accessed electronically at http://www.unhcr.org/cgi-bin/texis/vtx/refworld/rwmain?docid=45aca2992f

27. 'Everybody but the Politician is Happy', Economist, February 10th-16th 2007, pp. 27-29.

28. Moazzem Hossain, 'Home-Grown Democracy', Economic Political Weekly, March 4-10th 2006, Volume XLI, No. 9, p. 791.

29. *Ibid.*

30. *Ibid,* p. 792.

31. *Ibid*, p. 793.

32. *Ibid.*

33. Krishna Gopal, 'The Politics of Communalism and Secularism in Bangladesh', in Dipankar Sengupta and Sudhir Kumar Singh (ed), 'Minorities and Human Rights in Bangladesh', Authors Press in Association with SPANDAN, Worldwide Circulation through Authorspress Global Network, 2003, p. 5.

34. *Ibid.*

35. Krishna Gopal, 'The Politics of Communalism and Secularism in Bangladesh', in Dipankar Sengupta and Sudhir Kumar Singh (ed), 'Minorities and Human Rights in Bangladesh', Authors Press in Association with SPANDAN, Worldwide Circulation through Authorspress Global Network, 2003, p. 5.

36. Dipankar Sengupta and Sudhir Kumar Singh (ed), 'Minorities and Human Rights in Bangladesh', Authors Press in Association with SPANDAN, Worldwide Circulation through Authorspress Global Network, 2003, p. XV.

37. *Ibid*, p. 128.

38. 'Everybody but the Politician is Happy', Economist, February 10th-16th 2007, pp. 27-29.

39. Dipankar Sengupta and Sudhir Kumar Singh (ed), 'Minorities and Human Rights in Bangladesh', Authors Press in Association with SPANDAN, Worldwide Circulation through Authorspress Global Network, 2003, p. 128.

40. 'Everybody but the Politician is Happy', Economist, February 10th-16th 2007, pp. 27-29.

41. *Ibid*, p. 29.

42. Dipankar Sengupta and Sudhir Kumar Singh (ed), 'Minorities and Human Rights in Bangladesh', Authors Press in Association with SPANDAN, Worldwide Circulation through Authorspress Global Network, 2003, p. XX.

43. Human Rights Watch, January 2007 accessed electronically at http://www.unhcr.org/cgi-bin/texis/vtx/refworld/rwmain?docid=45aca2992f

44. 'Everybody but the Politician is Happy', Economist, February 10th-16th 2007, p. 29.

45. "Virtual Bangladesh: Human Rights" accessed electronically at http://www.virtualbangladesh.com/humanrights.html

46. Human Rights Watch, January 2007 accessed electronically at http://www.unhcr.org/cgi-bin/texis/vtx/refworld/rwmain?docid=45aca2992f

47. Human Rights Watch, January 2007 accessed electronically at http://www.unhcr.org/cgi-bin/texis/vtx/refworld/rwmain?docid=45aca2992f

48. "Virtual Bangladesh: Human Rights" accessed electronically at http://www.virtualbangladesh.com/humanrights.html

49. Country Reports on Human Rights Practices-Released by the Bureau of Democracy, Human Rights and Labour, February 23, 2001. accessed electronically at http://www.state.gov/g/drl/rls/hrrpt/2000/sa/692.htm

50. *Ibid.*

51. Dalem CH. Barman, M. Golam Rahman and Tasneem Siddiqui, 'State of Democracy in Bangladesh', International IDEA and

Department of Peace and Conflict Studies, November 2002, p. 29.

52. Human Rights Watch, January 2007 accessed electronically at http://www.unhcr.org/cgi-bin/texis/vtx/refworld/rwmain?docid=45aca2992f

53. *Ibid.*

54. Virtual Bangladesh Human Rights" accessed electronically at http://www.virtualbangladesh.com/humanrights.html

55. Human Rights Watch, January 2007, accessed electronically at http://www.unhcr.org/cgi-bin/texis/vtx/refworld/rwmain?docid=45aca2992f

56. Country Reports on Human Rights Practices-Released by the Bureau of Democracy, Human Rights and Labour, February 23, 2001. accessed electronically at http://www.state.gov/g/drl/rls/hrrpt/2000/sa/692.htm

57. "Human Rights Watch, World Report" January 2007 accessed electronically at http://www.unhcr.org/cgi-bin/texis/vtx/refworld/rwmain?docid=45aca2992f

58. "Redress: Torture in Bangladesh; 1971-2004, Making International Commitments a Reality and Providing Justice and Reparations to Victims", The European Initiative for Democracy and Human Rights, August 2004, p 13.

59. *Ibid*

60. Dalem CH. Barman, M. Golam Rahman and Tasneem Siddiqui, 'State of Democracy in Bangladesh', International IDEA and

Department of Peace and Conflict Studies, November 2002, pp. 27-28.

61. *Ibid.*, p. 27.

62. *Ibid.*, p. 39.

63. *Ibid.*, p. 27.

64. *Ibid.* p. 28.

65. *Ibid.*

66. http://news.bbc.co.uk/1/hi/world/south_asia/country_profiles/1160598.stm#facts

67. 'Looking For Exit', The Economist, February 9th-15th 2008, p. 30.

References

1. Jeff Haynes; 'Democracy in the Developing World; Africa, Asia, Latin America and the Middle-East', Blackwell Publishers Incorporated, 2001.

2. Dalem CH. Barman, M. Golam Rahman and Tasneem Siddiqui, 'State of Democracy in Bangladesh', International IDEA and Department of Peace and Conflict Studies, November 2002.

3. Dipankar Sengupta and Sudhir Kumar Singh (ed), 'Minorities and Human Rights in Bangladesh', Authors Press in Association with SPANDAN, Worldwide Circulation through Authorspress Global Network, 2003.

4. Paula Banerjee, Sabyasachi Basu Ray Chaudhury and Samir Kumar Das (ed), 'Internal Displacement in South Asia, Sage Publications 2005.

5. Gyasuddin Mollah, 'Democratic Institution Building Process in Bangladesh:South Asian Experience of a New Model of Caretaker Government in a Parliamentary Framework', Working Paper No. 3, December 2000, South Asian Institute, Department of Political Science, University of Heidelberg

6. The Economist, February 10th-16th 2007.

7. The Economist, February 9th-15th 2008.

8. Economic Political Weekly, March 4-10th 2006, Volume XLI, No. 9

9. Human Rights Watch, World Report 2007 at http://www.unhcr.org/cgi-bin/texis/vtx/refworld/rwmain? docid=45aca2992f

10. Country Reports on Human Rights Practices at http://www.state.gov/g/drl/rls/hrrpt/2000/sa/692.htm

11. Human Rights Watch, Asia at http://www.hrw.org/doc?t=asia&c=bangla

12. Virtual Bangladesh: Human Rights at http://www. virtualbangladesh.com/humanrights.html

13. Official website for BBC: http://news.bbc.co.uk/1/hi/world/south_asia/country_profiles/1160598.stm#facts

14. Third World Quarterly, Volume 28, No. 6, 2007.

15. 'Redress: Torture in Bangladesh; 1971-2004' at http://www.redress.org/publications/Bangladesh.pdf

16. Larry Diamond, 'Is the third wave of democratization over: an empirical assessment', Working Paper # 236, March 1997 as cited at http://www.nd.edu/~kellogg/publications/working papers/WPS/236.pdf

4

Bhutan: - Monarchy and Simulated Democracy in the Amphitheatre of Hills

Dharampal Singh

The Dragon's Dreams: "The state of Bhutan is sometimes spoken of as a mini yam between two rocks or the land of the thunderbolt, or world's last Shangri-La", [1] observes L S Rathore. In fact British novelist James Hilton who wrote a novel in 1933 titled "Lost Horizon" coined the word. Subsequently, these phrases and metaphors represent the importance of Bhutan as a convenient buffer state between India and China as also its utterly vulnerable position vis-à-vis imperialist China. With the forcible occupation of Tibet by China in 1959, the entire trans-Himalyan border became hot and volatile. China's rapacity began to grow and it began preaching its imperialist doctrine of 'blending the five colours"[2], viz., China, Nepal, Sikkim, Bhutan and Tibet.

Indeed Sikkim, Nepal, Bhutan and Laddakh, were described as "the four teeth with which the Chinese will grind their way to the southern seas."[3] The first stop in the direction of extending Communist China's hegemony over Bhutan was the forcible occupation of eight Bhutanese enclaves in Tibet, which were under Bhutan's control for over 300 years. The Chinese goal is complete absorption of these trans – Himalyan States into Chinese territorial fold.

Drukyul - The Land of Thunder Dragon: "Embedded within the snow white folds of the high Himalyas, the ancient kingdom of Bhutan has preserved its independence from time immemorial, untainted by the baser aspects of the outside world. Although today it is classified as one of the poorest and a least developed country in the world, it has, unlike most others, retained its integrity and distinctive way of life virtually intact,"[4] observed Peter Collister. It was under the control of British government of India and obtained its independence in 1949 from New Delhi.

There are few countries in the world whose history has been influenced so much by geography as the state of Bhutan. The great natural barrier of this land – the Himalyas has provided geographical isolation from the rest of the world. The ruggedness of the terrain has made the Bhutanese self-supporting, traditional, determined, brave and intrepid fighters. But whereas the rugged mountains and thick forests have provided relative inaccessibility to the land, the river valleys of south have contributed to the partial opening of land to outsiders, particularly India. But porous borders have conduced to massive illegal immigration of Nepalese who overtime have become a source of great discomfort and alienation. Having captured Sikkim, the Nepalese set their gaze firmly on Bhutan and aspired to do another Sikkim here but timely vigilance shown by the monarch has prevented the eventual absorption of Bhutan into Nepalese fold. The illegal Nepalese hordes of immigrants tried to spread their tentacles far and wide but the Bhutanese monarchs could foresee the demographic subversion of these immigrants and drove away much of the Nepalese who came without valid passports and other papers.

Political Transformation-Modernity of Tradition: As has already been pointed out, the relative isolation and inaccessibility of the region has fostered among Bhutanese a longing for hoary tradition of submission to the God king and showing unflinching loyalty to him. However, some of the monarchs of Bhutan were farsighted people who knew that winds of change would one day transform their tiny kingdom and turn the people away from hereditary monarchy. Sensing that in the not so remote future, the docile people of Bhutan shall turn hostile and dismantle all outmoded and archaic institutions and breathe the spirit of democracy and equality, the forward looking monarchs themselves took initiative and decided to transform Bhutan into a modern, democratic state. This is called revolution from above. All political initiatives came from deeply entrenched monarchs and not the people who were will tradition-bound and exhibited great deference to their age-old institution of monarchy.

National Assembly: The third monarch Jigme Dorji Wangchuck established the National Assembly in 1953, consisting of 150 members, elected for 3 years term. Till 1968, it did not possess legislative supremacy and laws passed by it were subject to gubernatorial veto by the king. In 1968, the king surrendered his power of veto and the National Assembly was given full legislative supremacy. More importantly, all officers of the government, including the king would be forced to resign if a vote of no-confidence is passed against them. There could be rarely be a country where the hereditary monarch himself subjected himself to some self-denying ordinances and agreed to abdicate on being directed by the National Assembly.

Council of Ministers: The same year 1968, administrative system underwent a momentous change and a cabinet headed by the king was constituted. The cabinet is responsible to the National Assembly and can be voted out by a no-confidence motion.

Royal Advisory Council: It consists of nine members – six representing the people, two, the clergy and one is a nominee of the king. It holds office for three years. It offers advice to the king on all matters of national importance. It may report direct to the National Assembly of any act of commission or omission by the cabinet or even the king, which proves its democratic credentials fully. It has also to ensure that courts act according to the law of the land.

Revolution From Above: Bhutan is a country, which is undergoing a period of swift transition and transformation. Monasticism gave way to monarchy in 1907. Since then there have been several changes and absolute monarchy has been converted into a benevolent constitutional monarchy. It has been verily a revolution from above. The Bhutanese monarchs themselves took bold initiatives to relinquish absolute authority and constitutionalise themselves. History records instances of absolute rulers being defanged either through a violent revolution or through a process of prolonged constitutional struggle, but it is rare for a monarch to willingly and voluntarily subjecting himself to some stringent self-denying ordinances and clipping his own wings and that too, without a vocal demand from people. And the person who initiated reforms and brought about this change of transforming absolute monarchy into a limited, constitutional one, was none other than partially British educated king Jigme Dorji Wangchuck. His efforts were faithfully emulated and continued by his successor King Jigme Singye Wangchuck, who publicly declared that he would abdicate if he failed to solve the issue of immigrant Nepalese settlers of southern Bhutan.

This is truly surprising for a country, which was a Lamaist theocracy between 1616 and 1907. Power was vested in the Shabdrung Ngawang Namgyal (1616-1651) who exercised powers in consultation with fellow Lamas of high rank. In 1907, theocracy was replaced by hereditary absolute monarchy and in the second half of 1960s, king Jigme Dorji Wangchuck initiated far reaching constitutional reforms to put restrictions on his own powers. In 1968, he surrendered his power of vetoing legislation. Even more startling was, the king's declaration that if a vote of no confidence was passed in the National Assembly called Tshogdu, the king would abdicate. Initially the Tshogdu refused to accept this recommendation of the king but when he insisted on it and repeated it in 1989, the National Assembly accepted it. New king is now under a constitutional obligation to abdicate, if a two-thirds majority in the Tshogdu passes a no-confidence motion. This shows that the surrender of power by the monarch is real and genuine and not cosmetic. How many examples can one furnish of a monarch voluntarily offering to quit if his people so desired. It is the sincerity of the monarch's feelings and not a window-dressing. Bhutanese royalty has set a precedent for other living monarchs to ape and emulate this example and take a leaf or two out of this to survive. It is self-sacrifice at its highest and best. Kudos to Bhutanese rulers who could get past the hang over of earlier governance by Lamas and their own hereditary forefathers and usher into a truly democratic dispensation.

Migrations – A Silent Invasion And A Biological Trap: By far the most serious problem plaguing Bhutan is the one caused by the unchecked, undocumented migration of illegal hordes of Nepalese settlers which is threatening the demography of Bhutan. The Bhutanese are undergoing a serious trauma of being converted into a minority in their own habitat.

The Nepalese entry into Bhutan is over a century old. It is said that one Kazi Ugyen Dorji was authorized to bring contractual Nepalese labourers, called *tangyas* or forest labourers, to clear the sub-tropical forests in southern Bhutan and cut the timber. Their number was obviously limited. The first group of Nepalese arrived in the year 1863 when Ashley Eden wrote in his report that at a village called Sipchu, he had sighted two grass huts of Nepalese people, whose number rose to twenty after two years. Rennie reported this. This process continued and Charles Bell in 1894 and John Claude White in 1905, again referred to the sighting of small Nepalese settlements on the Bhutanese soil in southern Bhutan. They originally came in small driblets. It was a trickling rill that became a torrent as time passed by and acquired tidal dimensions to submerge large territorial tracts in southern Bhutan with infiltrators, unmindful of national boundary barrier, which Dasho Jigmi Thinley described as a "necessary evil"[5] to be accepted and honoured.

Lure of gainful employment always induced Nepalese to go in for newer pastures such as in Darjeeling, Kalimpong,

Sikkim and elsewhere in India as domestic helps and security guards/watchman. They began tracking into Bhutan as unsuspecting labourers, settled here and began easing out the original settlers, Lepchas, from their hearths and homes. Arthur Foning, a Lepcha from Kalimpong wrote a book entitled "Lepcha, My Vanishing Tribe" in which he bemoans the loss of habitat for his tribe on account of unchecked entry of illegal Nepalese, who were once brought by the British as indented contractual labourers. In his striking language, "The British may have done this for our good but, as seen later, the result proved to be complete disaster and a sort of curse for us Rong-folk".[6] This was the beginning of a long track and its real effects were seen in Sikkim where the three races of Lho-Mon_Limbos (Bhutias, Lepchas and Limbos) were outnumbered by illegal hordes of Nepalese.[7]

Nepal and Lebansraum: Nepalese can call themselves the children of mountains. In the mountaineous ruggedness lie their innumerable settlements, mostly on the hilltops and the slopes both. Verily they have to maintain a delicate balance between men and mountains to survive. Failure to maintain this, may invite the wrath of each other in a destruction spree. Unfortunately, this has happened in Nepal where man's reproductive capacity far exceeded the productiveness of land and forests. Between 1930 and 1961, the populations of Nepal nearly doubled from 5.532 million to 9.753 millions,[8] registering an annual increase of about half a million hungry mouths to be fed, which is roughly equivalent to the entire population of Bhutan. Since nature abhors vacuum and Bhutan had more vacant land than what its inhabitants can occupy, the Nepalese began settling in southern Bhutan, illegally and clandestinely. Being a porous and almost undefended border, Bhutan offered no resistance to people's nocturnal migration during night hours. The maximum work force of Nepalese is in India, followed by other neighbouring places such as Sikkim and Bhutan. Having overtaken the Lepcha-Bhutia combine in Sikkim, their eyes are firmly fixed on Bhutan where they want to repeat a Sikkim, an eventuality most dreaded by the Bhutanese.

As stated earlier, terrified by the exaggerated claims of Nepalese settlers of their majority, the Bhutanese belatedly swung into action and started making enquiries about the actual status of migrants according to the provisions of their Citizenship Act, 1985. Though the government had given 1958 as the cut off year to determine the legal status of migrants, those who could not measure up to its stringent provisions and were actually staying in an illegal manner, took to heels to escape detection while others were expelled for their failure to fulfill citizenship norms and qualifications. The Nepalese government is not taking back its citizens and is keeping them in temporary camps to parade to the world the unfair treatment and human rights violations allegedly being meted out to them. The irony of these camps is that several poor Nepalese, famished by hunger, trickle into these camps, pretending to be refugees, but a larger segment consists of genuine fugitives or expatriates. The point is what is the status of these refugees so called and how for the Bhutanese government is responsible for this human tragedy? It needs a little deep delving and soul-searching. Certainly the Bhutanese government cannot be exonerated from the blame of not keeping its borders under proper vigil and allow the festering growth of Nepalese settlers. But though belated, Bhutan government is well within its rights to safeguard her territorial integrity and sovereignty. Even if the government makes the claim of Bhutan for Bhutanese, it is not wrong. Where will the Bhutanese citizens go if they are squeezed by Nepalese illegal influx? An infiltrator can seek neither legal compensation nor any humanitarian aid and deserves to be expelled forthright. He is a trespasser liable to be punished. There is a paradox. Nearly 137,263 Bhutanese refugees are also living in camps in Nepal managed by UNHCR. That is about 14 % population of Nepal.

In Retrospect: In conclusion it can be asserted that Bhutan has verily witnessed a revolution from above. The constitute is a gift from the monarch. Perhaps his British education has something to do with it. The Nepalese illegal immigrant have unsuccessfully tried to raise the question of breach of human rights but no country in the world has accepted their plea. The country has an enlightened monarch and a fully democratic system, which augurs well for it. It has been hailed as a land of demigods: "the gandharvas who have eloped with princesses to sport on mountain tops; Yakshis with their arms entwined with overhanging branches; Kinnars practsing steps in an amphitheatre of hills."[9] The future portends problems for the only Buddhist state in the world from both internal and external challenges, which are bound to erupt. If Bhutan does overcome the problems then it would graduate from simulated democracy to real authentic functioning democracy.

References

1. L.S.Rathore, the Changing Bhutan, Jain Brothers (New Delhi) 1974, p.1.

2. *Ibid.* p. 2.

3. *Ibid.* p. 3.

4. Peter Collister, Bhutan and the British, UBSPD, Reprint, 1996, p. 1.

5. Dasho Jigme Thinley, The Current Situation in Bhutan, in Rama Kant and R.C. Misra, edited, Bhutan: Society and Polity, Indus Publishing Company, New Delhi, 1996, p. 222.

6. *Ibid*. p. 224.

7. *Ibid.*

8. *Ibid*. p. 226.

9. Quoted in L.S. Rathore, Op.cit., p. 87.

5

Women and Violation of Human Rights

Flavia Agnes

Introduction

The preamble to the United Nations (UN) Charter of 24th October 1945 assures equal rights to men and women. In pursuance of this assurance, in 1946 the UN Economic and Social Council established the *Commission on the Status of Women* to recommend and report on the promotion of women's rights in the political, economic, social and educational fields. The culmination of the Commission's work is the Convention *on the Elimination of All Forms of Discrimination against Women* (CEDAW) adopted by the General Assembly in 1979. It is the most comprehensive legislation, which awards recognition to the rights of women for equality, and mandates elimination of all forms of gender based discrimination. The CEDAW has the potential to generate the sensitivity on women's issue. The six-part, thirty-article convention addresses various measures that need to be taken by ratifying States to eliminate discrimination against women in various fields, including political and public life, nationality, education, employment, health, marriage, and family life. India ratified the convention with certain reservations. In 1997, the Supreme Court of India in *Vishaka v State of Rajasthan*[1] for the first time, recognized sexual harassment as a human rights violation and invoked the provisions of CEDAW and thereby rendered it part of the domestic statutes through an innovative process of judicial law making.

On December 10th, 1948, the General Assembly of the United Nations adopted and proclaimed the Universal Declaration of Human Rights (UDHR). Ever since, this has become the *magna carta* of human rights.

At the Second World Conference on Human Rights, held in Vienna in 1993, women's rights were recognized as human rights. The UN General Assembly on 20 December in 1993 unanimously proclaimed a *Declaration on the Elimination of Violence Against Women.* The Declaration recognized "that violence against women is a manifestation of historically unequal power relations between men and women which have led to domination over and discrimination against women and to the prevention of their full advancement, and that is one of the crucial social mechanisms by which women are forced in to subordinate position compared to men."

The various UN conferences have also served to highlight the plight of women and violation of their rights. The UN General Assembly proclaimed the year 1975 as Interna-tional Women's Year and convened a conference in Mexico City. The conference adopted as its principal decisions, the 'Declaration of Mexico on the Equality of

Women and their Contribution to Development and Peace and the World Plan of Action for the Implementation of the Objectives of the International Women's Year'. Acting on recommendations of the conference, the period from 1976 to 1985 was declared as the "United Nations Decade for Women: Equality, Development and Peace". The mid-decade conference was held at Copenhagen, Denmark in 1980 to assess the impact of the UN intervention on the lives of women. The end of the decade conference was held at Nairobi, Kenya in 1985. The UN General Assembly endorsed the 'Nairobi Forward-Looking Strategies for the Advancement of Women'. In the resolution, the General Assembly pointed out that implementation of the forward-looking strategies should result in the elimination of all forms of inequality between men and women and in the complete integration of women into the development process. A decade later, the fourth UN Conference was held in Beijing, China in 1995.

The various treaties or conventions, declarations and resolutions passed by the UN are reflective of a sustained struggle and a measure of success on the part of the women's movement – global, regional and national. The greatest victory of the movement came when the UN declared that violence against women is a violation of human rights.

While this is the global scenario, at the national level, the Constitution of India, which was drafted roughly around the time of the UDHR contains several principles such as equality, freedom, liberty and due process of law and renders them as justiceable fundamental rights, which can be enforced through the intervention of courts. The Indian government has set up several special statutory institutions to give effect to the constitutional provisions of human right of all persons including those of the disadvantaged and weaker sections of the society. The National Human Rights Commission (NHRC), the National Commission for Women (NCW), the Minority Commission and the National Commission for Backward Classes, The National Commission for Scheduled Castes and Scheduled Tribes are examples of this trend.

Despite these efforts, violations of basic human rights of women persist both in the developed world as well as the developing countries. The situation in India is in keeping with this general trend. The problem of analyzing the status of human rights violations of women in India is the invisibility of women in statistics related to human rights; especially those complied by the NHRC. Also, the human rights violations against women are often subsumed in the wider concerns about caste violence, custodial harassment, state terrorism against civilians, etc. There are very little analyses of the cumulative violence suffered by women in both domestic and public spheres.

This essay analyses the struggle of the Indian women's movement to foreground issues of violence against women and bring violation of rights, both by the State and civil society actors on the plane of human rights. Though at various points, the movement did experience a sense of victory and a measure of success, but overall it has been an uphill task with the gains constantly being set off by the losses, as is reflected in this essay.

The demand for legislative reforms had received a prompt and positive response from the State, which had given the movement a sense of achievement. But the trends within the judiciary, as reflected in law journals revealed that, the legislations were, in fact, ornamental in nature and had given the movement a false sense of success. It was then, that many of us started probing into the pitfalls of the campaign and the loopholes within the reformed laws.

Domestic Violence and Dowry Deaths

The issue that received wide publicity in the early eighties is domestic violence and dowry deaths. It seemed that a plague was spreading across most Indian cities and an increasing number of urban, educated, middle class women were falling prey to it. The ultimate manifestation of the decease was a charred body of a young bride. The cause of death was being identified as 'dowry'.

In the wake of the public protests against these deaths, it came to be accepted, both nationally as well as internationally, that women in India were being subjected to a culture specific violence termed as 'dowry violence', which eventually culminated into a 'dowry death'. Further, it was explained that increasing consumerism and avarice by husbands and in-laws were the root cause of this problem. Dowry deaths were providing the husband a convenient outlet to get rid of one wife and find another, with even more dowry. But rather fortunately, society is not divided into two clear and mutually exclusive categories of parents – those of the boys, the dowry takers and the other of girls, the dowry givers. On the contrary, in most cases, the boy's parents, the dowry takers also happen to be the dowry givers, the girl's parents. This renders the theory of consumerism, avarice and greed as the root cause of dowry and dowry related violence seemed a little too far fetched.

But since the blame for domestic violence, a more universal problem related to women's subordinate status within marriage and their powerlessness, was laid squarely in the custom of 'dowry'. It was presumed that a more stringent law against dowry would, in effect, prevent marital murders. Accordingly, the Dowry Prohibition Act of 1961, which had stipulated that 'giving and taking dowry was an offence', was amended twice during the campaign, in 1984 and again in 1986 to make it more stringent.

The 1961 legislation defined dowry narrowly, as property given '*in consideration of marriage*' – and did not include anything given after the marriage, as this was held to be 'not in consideration of marriage'. The offence was non-cognizable (N.C. and bailable) and prescribed a mild sentence of a maximum punishment of six months. The complaint had to be filed within one year of the offence. But through the amendments of 1984 and 1986 the scope of 'dowry' was widened to include anything given in connection with marriage either before, at the time of, or after. But customary and traditional gifts were excluded. The offence was made cognizable and non-bailable. The prescribed minimum punishment was five years of imprisonment and a fine not less than Rs.15, 000 or the equivalent of the value of such dowry, whichever was more.

In addition, newer provisions were added on to the Indian Penal Code (IPC), which specifically laid down offences related to dowry – *dowry death* (Section 304B) and cruelty to wives and *dowry harassment* (Section 498A). In addition, rules of evidence were amended to shift the burden on the husband and his family, in cases of suicides by married women (S 306 – abetment to suicide) and dowry deaths. Despite these legal reforms the problem continued.

The campaign against 'dowry' and 'dowry deaths' artificially linked dowry, which is property, related, to 'death' which is a criminal act of violence. The complexities of the two separate issues - domestic violence and women's property rights were not probed into. The Dowry Prohibition Act did not take into account the vulnerability of a girl, not only in her marital home but also in her natal family. It did not address the issue that parents would go to any length to get their daughter married and keep her married at all costs rather than face the stigma of having an unmarried or a divorced daughter at home.

The protests against 'dowry demand' and 'dowry harassment' were articulated in most cases, not at the time of marriage, but only after the death of the girl. The parents who had sent the daughter back to the husband's home despite the impending danger to her life and had met all demands of dowry while the girl was alive, were now willing to stage a public protest against the in-laws, in order to retrieve their property and to cause the husband's family public humiliation.

The protests were organized through active support of women's organizations. Since the law against 'giving and taking dowry' was premised upon superficial and erroneous presumptions that a stringent law against dowry would curb domestic violence, it is not surprising that the law did not have the desired effect. But even the newer provisions within the Indian Penal Code meant for curbing domestic violence were saddled with the 'dowry' premise and hence proved to be inadequate to meet real life situations of victims of domestic violence. The demand for a law to prevent only dowry related violence turned out to be a narrow, shortsighted and a wrongly formulated strategy. By placing the dowry violence on a special pedestal, the routine violence faced by women across class, community and urban-rural divide, was denied recognition and legitimacy. The police refused to register a 'simple' case of domestic violence as according to them, this did not amount to cruelty under Section 498A of IPC. In order to access the criminal justice system, violence faced by women within homes had to be superficially and falsely attributed to dowry. This in turn resulted in screwed statistical data in police records, which conveyed an erroneous picture that all reported cases of violence were dowry related.

Vague allegations of dowry demands were added on to genuine complaints of physical violence, mental torture, sexual abuse and economic depravation. This cast aspersions on the credibility of the entire complaint since the trumpeted charges of dowry demand could not withstand legal scrutiny in a criminal court and resulted in either quashing of the complaint at the initial stage itself or acquittal even in the most genuine cases of domestic violence. This in turn led to an erroneous presumption that women were misusing legal provisions and were harassing innocent husbands. In some cities, the so-called 'harassed husbands' launched a counter campaign to curb this menace.

While the cause of 'harassed husbands' was being projected, women kept on dying in their homes and the alleged murderers went scot-free. Within a system afflicted with police apathy and corruption, irregularities and delays in investigations, unscrupulous medical professionals willing to doctor medical and forensic reports, inefficient, indifferent and corrupt public prosecutors and a gender-biased judiciary, conviction rate was dismal. In most cases of wife murders, the prosecution failed to prove the offence 'beyond reasonable doubt' and the accused husbands and relatives were acquitted by invoking the legal premise of 'benefit of doubt', which an accused is entitled to, under the criminal justice system. With such low conviction rates, the deterrent value of the enactments was totally lost.

The ingredients of the lofty and much applauded offence of dowry death (Section 304B) made it impossible to prove this offence. Earlier a case of wife murder would be registered under Section 302 – murder – plain and simple. The prosecution would have to prove that the death was homicidal and relate the offence to the accused in terms of his / her physical proximity to the scene of offence and the motive for murder. But after the amendment, a wife murder ceased to be 'murder' and was relegated to 'dowry death'. To meet the stipulations of the section, the woman had to die within seven years of marriage, and that prior to her death; she had to be subjected to dowry harassment by her husband and his relatives. Only once these ingredients were proved, the onus would shift on the husband to prove that he did not commit the offence. But most cases never reached this stage. The provision just appeared progressive on paper, since complaints regarding earlier demands for dowry are never registered, and the actual impact of this provision was practically nil. Similarly the provisions of abetment to suicide, with its positive rules of evidence, also failed to bring redressal as the courts interpreted the newer provisions in the most technical manner.

More recently, the Domestic Violence Act of 2005 has tried to address the problem of domestic violence. This law provides for protection orders and civil injunctions to protect the rights of women. The state appointed protection offers are bound to help women to secure their rights of a dignified and violence free domestic environment. Hopefully, this new enactment will provide women with better statutory armour against domestic violence. This enactment sets free the movement from the malice that has plagued it, of attributing all categories of violence suffered by women within their families to 'dowry' and widening the scope of the term 'domestic violence'.

In Conclusion

As this essay reveals, human rights of women continue to be in a deplorable condition in India, despite the international conventions and declarations and domestic statutes and Constitutional protection. The campaigns initiated by the women's movement and the statutory reforms, which were affected as response, have helped to bring public attention to the issue. But they have not served as a deterrent. The reported cases of rape and dowry murder continue to be on the increase. In 2005 the official statistics brought out by the National Crime Record Bureau (NCRB) revealed that 1 rape occurs every 29 minutes, 1 molestation every 15 minutes. 6000 women are killed in their homes every year for dowry. This relates to only official figures. The unofficial figures are staggering. And the worst scenario is during communal and caste violence where there are hardly any reported cases and hence the ground level reality is blurred and remains hidden beneath official statistics. This ought to be a grave cause of concern for all human rights activists and ordinary citizens of the country.

Reference

1. AIR 1997 SC 3011.

6

Attack on Minorities and Minority Commission in India

Ram Puniyani

Introduction

India's tragic partition (1947) left a deep scar on the South Asian polity. While Pakistan was formed on the basis of Islam, India was formed on secular grounds. That time undivided India had 25% Muslim population. Of this India was left with 11.6% Muslim population, while 13.4 were in Pakistan. Meanwhile a large affluent section of Muslims left for Pakistan. Today Muslims constitute 13.4% of India's population and are 138.18 millions in total population. (2001 Census) The sporadic but regular occurrence of the violence against this community, has left it with a feeling of insecurity and has resulted in ghettoization. A large section of this minority was on the lower rungs of socio-economic levels, which went on worsening with time, due to the social and political discrimination. This has been put forward by various indices as presented by Gopal Singh Commission in 1982 and by Sachar Committee, 2006. The findings of this committee are very disturbing as this section of India's population has been constantly sliding down.

Muslims have not been able to take advantage of various government schemes one of the reason being that they are mainly small farmers, marginal farmers, agricultural labourers, landless labourers, city based artisans and petty workers. Amongst other reasons, one of the main causes for this, is the discrimination and indifference on the part of planning and implementation authorities. "Consequently, the limited progress that some sections of Muslims have been able to make in recent years, owes almost wholly to their own efforts. Overall, the economic conditions of most Indian Muslims are unenviable, to say the least. Most of them eke out a hand-to-mouth existence, either by way of self-employment in petty trade, or by working in the unorganized sector. They are engaged mostly as construction laborers, rickshaw, taxi and truck drivers, handcart pullers, coolies, barbers, tailors, carpenters, pavement hawkers, or at best as mechanics, fitters, plumbers, electricians or welders." [1]

"As far as education is concerned, figures of Sachar Committee suggest that Muslim men and women are less educated than their non-Muslim counterparts. In fact, a large number of Muslims do not even possess basic reading and writing skills. At the national level, the number of literate Muslims is less than non-Muslims. Based on the figures of the 2001 census, only 55 per cent Muslim males are literate as compared to 64.5 per cent non-Muslims, while only one among 41 male graduates as opposed to one among 19 non-Muslims. The condition of the Muslim women is much worse, with only one among a hundred being a graduate." [2]

Their representation in the jobs in the government offices, public sector and private sector is abysmal, more the higher jobs, lower their representation.

Since the decade of 1980s, India has seen the unprecedented political phenomenon, the one related to Communalism, i.e, religious identity based politics. This phenomenon uses the religious identity for political mobilization, which in turn forms their route to coming to political power. The agenda of communal formations is essentially to suppress the human rights of weaker sections of society. It begins by spreading hate against the people of 'other religion', this hate propaganda in turn vitiates the social atmosphere and aids in the precipitation and intensification of communal violence, This violence over a period of time intimidates the minority communities, ghettoizing them.

On the other hand, the second biggest minority, the Christians have been facing the violence from 1997. This violence has been gradually stepped up and the worst of it has been seen in Orissa from August 2008. This is happening mostly in *Adivasi* areas, where the poor sections of society have been deprived of social facilities.

Minorities

Today, India is seeing this ghettotisation of Muslim minorities, and an equal intimidation of the Christian minority. Muslim minority has been subjected to repeated communal violence followed by arrest of large number of Muslim youth on the pretext of their being terrorists, while the Christian community has been intimidated due to the attacks on the nuns and priests in remote places and due to the horrific violence, which is gradually becoming more intense. Globally, we are witnessing a period of Islamophobia, which has increased the insecurity of the Muslims, World over, more so after the events of 9/11 2001, the attack on Afghanistan and Iraq. In South Asia, one has witnessed this as a simmering problem right since 1940s, the partition of India, and migration of Hindus from the then West and East Pakistan. To add to the problem, the issue of Kashmir over a period of time has come to be seen, as a Hindu-Muslim issue while it is the result of ultra nationalism of India and Pakistan and the US design to keep a foothold on this strategically important region, through its proxy, Pakistan. The result is aggravation of the anti Muslim sentiments, constructed around the memories of partition and the imbroglio, which continues in Kashmir. Christian minorities have been living in fear of violence more so in remote places.

Genesis of Problem

As such the Hindu Muslim conflict as it is known, began during the colonial British rule, when the declining classes of feudal lords, resorted to politics in the name of religion, duly backed up by the British policy of divide and rule. The mis-representation of history and distortion of demographic and other issues went on, aggravating the 'hate other' from both the sides. In India, Muslims were the bigger victims. No sooner had the partition riots subsided, the communal violence began in 1961 and went on increasing in intensity over a period of time. By late seventies, its threat as an obstacle to realization of democratic principles started becoming obvious.

The politics of Hindu right, intensified its onslaught in the decade of eighties, *Rath Yatras* (chariot processions) and community mobilization of sections of Hindus around *Ramshilas*, use of religious platforms for communalization, went on throughout this decade. The central veering point of this mobilization was the *Babri Masjid*, which was claimed as the place where lord Ram was born. It was asserted that there was a magnificent temple, which was destroyed by *Mughal* invader Babar. So, the idea was to reclaim the birth place of Lord. This intensified into the campaign for demolition of *Babri* mosque. The demolition led to riots all around, more severely in Mumbai.

From 1987 in particular, Vanvasi Kalyan Ashram, became active in the far-flung places spreading the hate against Christian missionaries. The charge leveled was that, the service of the poor was a mere pretext to covert gullible *Adivasis* into Christianity. The culmination of this hate propaganda, was seen in the burning alive of Australian Pastor Graham Staines and then sustained attacks on the nuns and priests in remote areas.

By 1990, the adverse effects of globalization started affecting the average people and while on one side the relatively affluent sections started emerging, the deprived sections were brought under the influence of identity based politics, which stood on the ground of hate other. And parallel to this there was a rising impact of identity based politics and the communal mobilization, around religious issues shot up drastically.

Communal Violence

The two drastic programmes, the one of 1992-93 (Mumbai) and the one of Gujarat (2002) left a heavy trail of blood and gory tales of violence of unimaginable proportions. Earlier studies had been pointing out that, the victims of this violence are predominantly Muslims to the extent of 80 per cent.[33] The Gujarat carnage witnessed the percentage going much adverse to the Muslim minority.

Anti-Muslim Violence

The violence in India on communal grounds has been going up in intensity from the last more than two decades. As such, the rise of sectarian politics during the end of nineteenth century, saw a respite for few years after the independence of the country. But it did return in a sporadic manner, since 1961 Jabalpur riots. Later Jamshedpur and Rourkela riots broke out. "Of the bloody programs in sixties, the ones at Ranchi, Bihar (1962) and Ahmedabad, Gujarat (1969) stands out as the major events. In seventies, the Turkman Gate massacre of 1976, perpetrated by police, the riots in Moradabad (1980), Nellie, Naogaon, Assam (1983), Bhiwandi (1984) and Meerut (1987), have been the major ones in which, more than a thousand lost their lives" (Khalidi, 1995). The Ramjanmabhumi campaign left a big trail of blood in which more than thousand people lost their lives in 1989. The massacres of Bhagalpur, Hyderabad and Aligarh heralded the onset of bloody 80s, which has seen the peak of communal violence. Advani's rath yatra (1990) and post Babri demolition riots were one of the worst, the country has suffered so far. The post demolition riots, gripped Mumbai, Surat, Bhopal in a major way and many other places in a significant way. From 1960 to 1995, the incidences of riots have been on an upswing. A big proportion of these have been taking place in six states UP, Gujarat, Rajasthan, Bihar, Madhya Pradesh and Andhra. So far, these riots' occurrence is mainly in cities, but involvement of villages is also there, and has been in the rise but lately even the small towns and villages are also being drawn in the vortex.

The demolition of Babri Mosque in 1992, in a way can be called as a watershed in the political profile of the country. From here on, the violence changed qualitatively and its adverse and long term effects, started taking the toll of community psyche, leading to ghettoization of Muslim minorities and the intense anti minority sentiments amongst a vast section of middle classes and sections of other parts of society.

Anti-Christian Violence

The attacks on Christians began especially from last 1997onwards. These attacks are being orchestrated by different communal organizations and a general hysteria is being created against the Christian Missionaries. During the year 1998-99 many a priests were humiliated (Fr. Christudas being paraded naked in Dumka), one of them being burnt alive along with his two sons aged 11 and 7, many a churches have been damaged in these attacks, Bibles have been burnt and nuns have been raped in interior places. This has occurred in the backdrop of anti-Christian propaganda that Christianity is considered as a foreign religion, their missionary activities are a mere ploy for inducing people for conversions to adopt Christianity and their schools and Hospitals are mere mistaken as tools for the same. Most of the inquiries by social activists, National Human Rights Commission and National Minorities Commission have shown that different organizations affiliated to SP are behind these attacks, and the attacks. The taking place by communal organizations. The most dreaded of this rocked Orissa during the period of December 2007 and then from August 2008, killing over 500 Christians, dislocating over a lakh of them and also involving the rape of a nun.

Anti-Sikh Violence

The major anti Sikh pogrom took place in 1984, in the aftermath assassination of Prime Minister Indira Gandhi by her Sikh bodyguards. The Sikh bodyguards who pumped bullet into the chest of the late Prime Minister Indira Gandhi, at point blank range were no way part of the Khalistani outfit but were enraged by the entry of Army soldiers into the holiest of holy Sikh shrine, the Golden temple at Amritsar. In this massacre nearly 3000 Sikhs were killed right under the nose of the central government and with the police force looking the other way around. This led to a deep sense of insecurity amongst the Sikhs at large and most of the victims of the violence are yet to receive justice or suitable redressal.

Myths about Christians:

Christian missionaries have been setting up Churches, seminaries and schools wherever and whenever possible. They learnt Indian Languages, set up printing presses and published religious as well as secular literature, to spread literacy and their faith. In the process they adopted Indian languages for their communication and the Church adopted number of native practices. Despite 2000 years of Christian presence and 200 years of British rule the population of Christians in 1971 was 2.6 %, which in 1981 stood at 2.44%, in 1991 it was 2.32% and in 2001 it is 2.3%.

Despite this the threat of 'their' population overtaking the Hindu population, has begun only few years ago. This anti-Christian bogey comes at a time, when the anti-Muslim pogroms have more or less 'achieved 'the target 'of permanently intimidating and ghettoizing them. Also SP realizes that if it has to break the electoral jinx, to be able to come to power on its own, it needs a newer vote bank and for this, adivasis have been seen as the ones having best potential. There is also a growing realization in SP, that after conversion to Christianity the adivasis become more educated and aware of their rights taken as this is a big threat to 'status quo', which is the base line of SP politics. These two factors seem to be the major ones in the current SP strategy of intimidating the missionaries. Their calculation is that, after this type of 'treatment', they will be reluctant to go to the remote places and that will make the SP's job of wooing Adivasis to its fold comparatively easy.

Christians Today

Orissa has witnessed unprecedented violence against the tiny Christian minority. On August 23, 2008, Swami Laxmananand along with his four followers was killed, probably by a group of Maoists. Immediately, anti-Christian violence began on big scale. The way it began it seemed as if preparations for it were well afoot. It was systematic and widespread. It sounded as if preparation was already there, just the pretext was being waited for. So far many innocent Christians have been killed, wounded and rendered homeless apart from many Churches having been torched. It is alleged that Christians killed Swami or there is collusion between Maoists and Christians. It is unlikely that there is any such alliance between the two. Any way, what is important is that the crime of murder of Swami must be properly investigated and guilty must be punished as per the law of the land

The anti Christian tirade was also launched in December 2007, around Christmas time.

The most ghastly of this was seen in the burning alive of Australian Pastor Graham Staines along with his two innocent sons, aged 11 and 7 years. This was immediately followed by the murder of Fr. Arul Das. The violence kept the religious atmosphere a bit explosive. But though Christians form a miniscule minority, it pushed them into a heightened sense of insecurity and anxiety. It is immaterial that Christian missionaries are working in India from first century A.D. itself. It is immaterial that despite the allegations from communal groups, the population of Christians as per the census figures has been declining constantly. In the face of these facts the argument proffered was that since the converts to Christianity don't want to loose their privileges and that they don't declare their true religion and are crypto Christians.

It is not a mere coincidence that maximum violence in Adivasi areas has been seen in the poorest regions. Dangs in Gujarat is the poorest district of Gujarat, and Orissa is amongst the poorest states of the country. The insensate hatred translates into communal violence if not checked right at its incipient stage. Communal violence in Indian context gets assistance from the communalized state apparatus, sections of police in particular leading to polarization of communities and rise to political power of the communal party.

'Secular' Parties: 'Secular' State

The political outfits, the secular ones have shown tremendous weakness in the face of communal onslaught. Many of them have compromised with the communal politics, directly or indirectly. Some of them have shamelessly allied with them. The state apparatus has also been infiltrated to a great extent by the trained communalists. In addition, due to overall pressures of the communal offensive at all the levels, different wings of state machinery cannot be relied upon to protect the secular constitution and the accompanying social values. That leaves the civic society, which has to take the whole responsibility of the protecting and nurturing the principles and values; emerging from our freedom struggle, the values of secular democracy, and values of Liberty, Equality and Fraternity.

Affirmative Action

Prime Minister Manmohan Singh did state in the National Development Council that we need "to devise innovative plans to ensure that minorities, particularly the Muslim minority, are empowered to share equitably the fruits of development, these must have first claim on resources". This was backed up by the statement in Parliament by the minister of minorities' affairs that Government will implement the recommendations of Sachar Committee. It has acted as the ray of hope for the 'discriminated against' Muslim minorities.

In sum and substance, Muslim community is under-represented in most of the arenas of society, barring the jails. One also recalls the report of Gopal Singh commission of 1982 which also had found the poor status of this minority. Gopal Singh commission report was kept lying in the deep freeze, while the issues like Ram Temple kept hogging the national attention. To add up, one can say this community's representation as riot victim is way above its percentage in population. The commission had recommended that an Equal Opportunity Commission should be set up, a national data bank should be started, a nomination procedure should be started to ensure their participation in public bodies, in order to promote religious tolerance by a procedure to evaluate text books for appropriate social values, so on and so forth.

It is a matter of conjuncture, whether this Govt is really serious about it or is it a mere replay of the earlier broken promises during last several decades. During the last several decades, while Governments after Governments, have been promising to look after the problems of Muslim minorities, nothing much came out. This includes not only the longest reign of Congress party but also one of the formations, in which BJP was an important component or supporter. Amongst multiple reasons of the neglect of this minority one was the aggressive propaganda of rightest Hindus, that Government is out to 'appease' the Muslims, so that they can be used as vote banks. One does not know whether this aggressive anti minority propaganda did contribute to the policies of the government, but one can say for sure that this 'appeasement of minorities' had become a part of 'social common sense' in the face of the worsening situation of Muslims.

What is being called rank communalism is essentially a bit of affirmative action. Surely even the reservations, which were brought in for *Dalits* have improved their conditions slightly. Now a full fledged opposition to those polices in different language, has been unleashed. While in the case of minorities, not only the condition is bad as of today, the bigger worry is that, it is sliding towards worse very rapidly. We need to distinguish abuse of community identity for politics, and the bowing to the institution of religion from the concrete economic steps and social actions to support the weaker sections of society. Will the community identity become strong due to this? Will the community become crippled due to this?

Constituting Minority Commission: In order to protect and safeguard the minorities in India, the government of India has taken a step to constitute a Ministry of Minority's Affairs in Central government. At the time same a commission has been constituted by the government of India to look into the matters of minorities in India. National Minorities Commission was formed in January 1978 through a Government Resolution, which stated, "Despite the safeguards provided in the Constitution and the Laws in force, there persists among the Minorities a feeling of inequality and discrimination. In order to preserve secular traditions and to promote National Integration, the Government of India attaches the highest importance to the enforcement of the safeguards provided for the minorities and is of the firm view that effecting institutional arrangements are urgently required for the enforcement and implementation of all safeguards provided for the minorities in the Constitution, in the Central and State laws and in Government policies and administrative schemes enunciated from time to time. The Government of India has therefore, resolved to set up a Minorities Commission to safeguard the interest of the Minorities whether based on religion or language."

The Central Minorities Commission, which was set in 1978, consisted of a Chairman and two other members for three years. A Parsi and two members from Christian and Muslim headed the first Minorities Commission. The appointment of Parsi was greatly resented by the Muslim who constituted the biggest minority in the country. Therefore, the Commission was reconstituted on July 28,1978. While a Muslim was appointed as its Chairman its four members were taken from the Buddhist, Christian, Parsi and Sikh Communities.

The Janata Government of Morarji Desai, wanted to confer the constitutional status on the Central Minorities Commission. It introduced the 46th Constitutional Amendment Act, 1978 in Lok Sabha which was to abolish the office of Special Officer for Linguistic Minorities provided for in Article 350-B and to add Article 338-A to make room for a constitutionally sanctioned Minorities Commission. The amendment said "The Government are of the view that appointment of a commission to safeguard the interest of all minorities, whether based on religion or language, would provide a more satisfactory institutional arrangement for achieving the desired objective. A Minorities Commission was, therefore, set up by an executive order. Such a Commission would, if set up in pursuance of Constitutional provision, inspire greater confidence among the Minorities". In 1979, the bill was again introduced in the Lok Sabha as 51st Amendment Bill, but the it again fell due to lack of necessary support.

In 1984, the Commission was detached from the Home Ministry and placed under the Ministry of Welfare. The Commission suffered another setback in 1987 when it was robbed of its jurisdiction over the Linguistic Minorities of the country. Thus, the commission was reduced to the position of a helpless caretaker for Religious Minorities only. The non-implementation of the provision of 1978 Resolution that the Special Officer for Linguistic Minorities would act as the Secretary of the Commission also rendered the Commission less effective. In 1988, the Congress Government constituted a new Commission. It firmly turned down the suggestion that the commission should be given either constitutional or ordinary legislative status, or conferred powers exercisable under the Commissions of Inquiry Act, 1952.

After the overthrow of the Congress Government and emergence of a non-Congress government under VP Singh, a fresh demand was raised for according constitutional status to the commission. However, VP Singh government could not make necessary constitutional amendment in this regard, because the government had been formed with the support of BJP, which was not willing to permit him to equate the status of Minorities Commission with the scheduled castes Commission.

The Congress modified its stand on the Minorities Commission, after the assassination of Rajiv Gandhi and promised to accord it constitutional status. But when it came to power in 1991, it decided to accord statutory status to the Commission instead of constitutional status. In May 1992, Sitaram Kesari, the Welfare Minister introduced National Commission for Minorities Bill in the Lok Sabha. He said, "The Minorities Commission with a statutory status would infuse confidence among the Minorities about the working and effectiveness of the Commission It would also carry more weight with the State Governments/ Union Territory/ Administrations and the ministries/ departments and other organizations of the Central Government," But the bill was strongly opposed by the opposition in the House. Despite this opposition, the Lok Sabha eventually passed the Bill. Subsequently it was passed by Rajya Sabha and the President gave his assent on May 17,1992.

National Commission for Minorities Act, 1992

The National Commission for Minorities Act, 1992 provided for a seven-member Commission. The Government from amongst persons of eminence, ability and integrity appoints. Five members of the Commission, including the Chairman are taken from the Minority communities. The procedure for selection of the chairman and members of the Commission has been left to the discretion of the Government. The Chairman and other members of the Commission hold office for a term of three years. They can resign earlier by addressing the Central Government. The Chairman and member can also be removed from office if he (i) becomes an undischarged insolvent; (ii) is convicted and sentenced to imprisonment for an offence which, in the opinion of the Central Government, involves moral turpitude; (iii) becomes of unsound mind and declared so by the competent court; (iv) refuses to act or becomes incapable of acting; (v) absents himself from three consecutive meetings of the Commission without leave or absence; (vi) has in the opinion of the Central government abused his position and his continuance in office is detrimental to the interests of the minorities or public interests. When a person is to be removed he must be given a reasonable opportunity of being heard in the matter.

For the smooth working of the Commission, the Central Government provides a secretary and such other officers and employees as are necessary for efficient performance of the function of the Commission. These employees and officers are given such salaries and allowances, which are prescribed from time to time. The salaries and allowances of the Chairman, members and administrative staff are paid out of grant provided by the Central Government.

The composition of the National Minorities Commission was modified in September 1995 through an amendment in the Act. A new post of Vice-Chairman was created, even though he still continued to be counted as a member.

In May 1992 the National Commission for Minorities Act, 1992 was enacted giving statutory status to the erstwhile Minorities Commission and thus making it a more effective body to safeguard the interest of Minorities.

The Commission submits an annual report to the government, which is tabled by the government before each House of Parliament along with a memorandum explaining the action taken or proposed to be taken on the recommendations relating to the Union and the reasons for non-compliance, if any of such recommendations. How far this commission is able to protect these minorities attack, by majority community is a million dollar question before the Commission. The commission should evaluate its work and take effective measures to protect the minorities' interests. It requires more teeth to protect the minorities in India.

Endnotes

1. Report AA, JMI, ISIS, Indian Social Institute, New Delhi, 2006.
2. DNA 4th October 2006.
3. Study by Nirmala Niketan, College of Social work, 1993.

References

1. Asghar Ali Engineer, "Some thoughts on pluralist model of Nation Building", Minorities in India, Conference papers, Rajiv Gandhi Institute For contemporary Studies (RGISS), 1996, p. 27.

2. Imtiaz Ahamd, 'Indian Minorities', Minorities in India, RGISS, 1996, p. 27.

3. Iqbal A. Ansari, Readings on Minorities: Perspectives and Documants, Institute of Objective Studies ,New Delhi 1996.

4. Vinayak Damodar Savarkar, 'Hindutva, Who is a Hindu?', Nagpur, 1923.

5. M.S.Golwalkar, 'We or Our Nationhood Defined', Bharat Publications 1939.

6. Chritophe Jaffrelot, *The Hindu Nationalist Movement and Indian Politics, Viking,* New Delhi 1996.

7

Dalit and Law in India

Subhash Gatade

Introduction

Does the cost of a 'goat' equal that of a human being? Whether drinking water from a public lake, where even animals are free to visit, should lead to a riot like situation or the very interpersonal decision to marry a girl/boy of one's own choice, should culminate in the killings of the couple at the behest of the community elders?

Any person who bears humane sensibilities and sensitivities, would rather decry these 'mediaeval' style responses towards fellow human beings.

The person would rather find himself at wits end, if he probes further and discover that people affected by Tsunami engaged themselves in systematic discrimination against dalits, who were similar victims. He would be aghast to know that the upper caste perpetrators of the Killevenamani massacre (1969) of 35 plus Dalits, were allowed to go scot free by the judiciary on the spacious plea that the 'Upper Caste Gentry would not have gone walking to the place'.

In any normal country, all such exposures in the media would at least lead to uproar at the national level, lead to fresh stirrings within the nation's conscience, culminating in a process of self-introspection and possibly self-correction. But India presents itself as a peculiar case in the comity of nations. Here all such covert and overt violence against a part of the citizenry has received not only legitimacy; thanks to the purity and pollution based caste order-but has been sanctified by the religious scriptures also.

Thus India, a country of billion plus people, which is itching to get a superpower status, and takes pride in its ancient tradition and culture and whose elite goes gaga over the booming sensex, rather presents a strange spectacle of a nation. If one decides to go by economic indices alone, then we may get a rosy picture, but a close look at the goings on within the society makes it clear, that there is a disjunction between the world of economics and the life worlds of its people. The core of the society bears its encounter with barbarism in abundance.

But before raising the follies of the nation and its people in a haphazard manner, it would be opportune to take a close look at the alleged theft of a goat, which got exchanged by snuffing out the life of a man in his teens sometime back.

Not Playing a Goat !

" Lucknow : A teenaged dalit named Mukesh was beaten to death in Ferozabad district for daring to participate in Bhagwat Paath organized by the local Lodh Rajput community. The victim's brother and

some relatives who came to the rescue of the teenagers were also assaulted. The incident took place on Tuesday night.

Though the police confirmed that the provocation behind the murder was caste bias, the accused alleged that they had caught the victim while stealing a goat. The police could arrest only two of the twelve named accused.

The above news had appeared in the Lucknow edition of the *Times of India*. Of course, there was no follow-up of the incident in the print or the electronic media. Rather, it received the same fate as scores of other news, which are considered unimportant.

Imagine of one of those intrepid journalists would have decided to follow the story to see for her/himself, the way the event unfolds itself. What would be her/his observations?

To be very frank, the journalist would have discovered not single but multiple versions of the whole incident. For all practical purposes, one would decide one's presentation of the 'truth' depending upon one's own location in the caste matrix in the area.

The Lodh Rajputs, who come under the resurgent OBCs and who form backbone of local power structure in different areas, would have been hell-bent upon proving the 'crime' of the deceased. Perhaps to garner further community support to the inhuman act, committed by their own caste men, they might have presented a fresh slew of charges against him and would have also vouched that he also harassed ladies of the community. They would be loathe to listen to any counterview to their argument which would try to raise the issue of 'punishment' commensurate with 'crime' and the role of the institutions of justice delivery established by the republic more than 59 years ago to do the same.

The hapless dalits would have shared the way in which, they came to know about the tragic death of one of their dear ones, the way the police adopted a dilly dallying tactics in this particular case and how it itself became a party in the stigmatization of the whole dalit community. It does not require much of a genius to prophesise that in the absence of some powerful voice/s joining the grief of the dalits, the brutal murder of Mukesh by the *Lodh* Rajputs, slowly led to the blind alley of a 'closed file.'

The tragic prognosis of this incident may appear disturbing to any civilized person, but the fact of the matter is that, the way the troika of state-judiciary- (rest of) civil society unfolds itself in any of such cases of dalit atrocities, the fate is not dissimilar. May it be the case of 'traditional' atrocities where the dalits are denied any rights whatsoever in the Hindu society or may it be the case of 'modern' forms of resistance put in by the dalits or a caste Hindu response to the changing situation of the dalits, the picture is same everywhere.

It was only a few years back that a dalit basti situated in Gohana (a town, which is hardly 100 kms from the National capital) was attacked by a few hundred strong mobs of mostly *Jat* youth. The marauders burnt down scores of their houses and looted their property in daytime in the presence of two hundred strong police force posted near the *basti* with senior officers in attendance. The immediate provocation for the attack was the murder of a *Jat* youth allegedly by a few dalits who felt agitated when the murdered man along with his friends had passed obscene remarks against dalit women.

It was clear to any impartial observer, that the main 'grievance' of the *Jats* against the dalits was the way many among them had refused to follow the 'community profession' of cleaning *(safai)* and had charted an alternate path of life and were now refusing to tolerate humiliation any more.

Some of us who had visited the town after the attack and met a cross-section of victims there (and duly prepared a report of the incident) found to our utter dismay, in our second visit a year after, that out of 23 upper caste accused in the case, (while the actual number was in hundreds) only three could be apprehended and they were also released on bail immediately. During our second visit also we found that the CBI enquiry ordered into the case was moving at a snails pace and seven dalits were still languishing in jail without any sign of bail, supposedly for being party to the death of the Jat youth. It was also learnt that in one of their interim reports, the CBI officials had also stated that 'it also seems that few of the dalits have themselves burnt their houses to demand compensation.'

Way to Injustice Paved With "Good Laws"

Social Justice Minister, Government of India, Meira Kumar, pointed out that the conviction rate in cases registered under the Protection of Civil Rights Act is a mere 3.75 per cent. Besides, 75 to 77 per cent cases of crimes against Dalits remain pending despite the existence of special and designated courts. Union Home Minister Shivraj Patil, who was also present at the conference, acknowledged that the system was

> not delivering justice and existing laws safeguarding the rights of backward classes may have to be changed or tightened.

January 12, 2005, *The Telegraph*

The first Prime Minister of India Jawaharlal Nehru always sang paeans to the Unity and Diversity of the country. But he forgot to add that the institution, which 'unites' the Indian people who are spread over a subcontinent, is their strict adherence to the age old 'caste system'. It is a system based on exclusion and graded hierarchy and the only 'diversity', which it allows in it the nature of violence which is unleashed against the people, who are considered at the bottom of the Caste Matrix.

Perhaps the plight of the dalits in Gohana or in Ferozabad would lead us to a query about the presence/absence of appropriate laws to curb such offences against them. A person unaware of the way Indian polity functions, may presume that spurt in atrocities against dalits is mainly due to absence of laws. S/he is sadly mistaken.

The founding fathers of the Constitution had solemnly resolved :

> *to secure to all citizens Justice: Social, Economic and Political, Liberty of thought, expression, belief, faith and worship. And equality of status and of opportunity, and to promote among them all fraternity, assuring the dignity of individual and unity.* It also emphasised that : *The state shall not discriminate against any citizen on grounds of religion, race, caste, place and birth or any form.*

The Directive Principles of the Constitution underlined

> *The State shall promote with special care the educational and economic interest of the scheduled castes/tribes and shall protect them from social injustice and all forms of exploitation.*

It is worth noting that in accordance with these Constitutional provisions, Government has a number of measures, initiated for providing protection to untouchables (Scheduled Castes or SCs) and the tribals. These measures can be categorised into two broad themes: protective and developmental. Under the 'protective' sphere untouchability was legally abolished and its practice in any form forebidden by the Protection of Civil Rights (Anti-Untouchability) Act of 1955, Article 17 of Indian Constitution states:

> *"Untouchability" is abolished and its practice in any form is forbidden. The enforcement of any disability arising out of "Untouchability" shall be an offence punishable in-accordance with law.*

To protect the category of SC and ST in a more effective and comprehensive manner, a few other legislations were introduced. Policies of reservation and representation were adopted to improve the access and participation of these sections in the economic, educational and political spheres. The enactment of the bonded labour (Abolition) act, 1976 or laws to curb child labour were part of the other major measures taken to make the protection for these sections more stringent and effective. The year 1989 witnessed the government enacting another Act, namely the Scheduled Castes and Tribes (Prevention of Atrocities Act of 1989), an Act to prevent atrocities against SC/STs. The necessity for enactment of this act had arisen, because under the existing circumstances, the Protection of Civil Rights Act (1955) and normal provisions of the Indian Penal Code were found to be inadequate to provide safeguards. The SC and ST (POA) Act, 1989 was pioneer in many ways. It provides for not only appointment of special courts, punishment for neglect of duties to officials, forfeiture of property of the perpetrators, confiscation of arms from the dominant castes in the area, declaration of a particular area atrocity prone, and even asks for distribution of arms to the downtrodden, etc.

But as Justice V.K. Krishna Iyer, the legendary human rights activist and a former Supreme Court Judge puts it, all such 'half hearted legislation has proved to be impotent and ineffectual in practice'. He also added that the aim behind these attempts was to have a 'more effective, more comprehensive and more punitive provisions of law'. However 'the ruling classes saw to it that, at the functional level, the legislations were paper tigers' (All quotes from The Foreword by Justice Iyer to a book '*Dalit Utpidan aur Vidhik Upchar*, by P.L. Mimroth, Nov 2000, Delhi)

There have been innumerable reports detailing how the local police in connivance with the perpetrators themselves; sabotages implementation of laws, basically meant to protect the dalits and the tribals. It is noticed that instead of filing cases under the POA act, it prefers filing cases under normal provisions of Indian Penal Code, which facilitates release of the accused on bail easily. It also facilitates filing of 'counter cases' against the victims, so that a compromise could be reached. The Third Report of the NPC (New Delhi: Government of India, 1980, p. 31) had rightly underlined how: "Many false criminal cases are sometimes engineered, merely for the sake of making arrests to humiliate and harass some specified enemies of the complainant, in league with the police for corrupt reasons".

A related phenomenon is the way in which the powers that be, take steps to deter enlightened people to fight for constitutionally granted rights of the dalits and the tribals. *Human Rights Watch Report* (Vol. 4, no. 15, June 1992) shares details of how *Criminalisation of Social Activism* in India takes place. In its much acclaimed report 'Broken People - Caste Violence against India's "Untouchables" (1999) *Human Rights Watch* repeats how 'State agents have acted directly and forcefully against those attempting to claim their rights. Dalit activists throughout the country, face charges as "terrorists", "threats to national security" and "habitual offenders.." (p. 153)

The 'Report on Prevention of Atrocities against Scheduled Castes' (NHRC, 2004,Delhi) rightly underlined the way,the 'state has failed in this respect' on 'several fronts'. According to the conclusions of the report, the state has failed on 'several fronts'. These are 'failure to effectively implement the laws relating to atrocities against SCs and STs', which is 'reflected both in respect of preventing violence from taking place' as well as in the 'inability to punish perpetrators of violence after the crime is committed'; 'failure to act against its own agencies involved in the commission of violence;' failure to strengthen the watchdog institutions', etc. 'The failure of the state vis-à-vis mobilization of caste Hindus in favour of social democracy embedded in the constitution and various laws and state policies' can also be considered palpable which, has 'created ambivalence in its intentions and contradictions in its actions'.

The Sixth Report of the National Commission for SCs and STs (1999-2000 and 2000-2001) had expressed its deep sense of dissatisfaction over the way all these measures are implemented. While commenting that "The number of cases registered under Prevention of Civil Rights Act and SC and ST (Prevention of Atrocities) Act has been showing downward trend as a healthy development". It exposes the way this reduction in number of cases is achieved. According to the preface, "But from its reviews with various state governments the commission is of the view that a large number of cases go unregistered, mainly because of the reluctance on part of the police officers to register the cases and also because of lack of awareness among the members of these communities about the provisions of these acts.

"In addition, there are delays in investigation, collusion with offenders and manipulation of witnesses and evidence which all contribute to reduce the effectiveness of these protective legislations". (See Preface Page II). In the same vein, it tells us that in most of the states, neither the meetings of the monitoring and vigilance committees are held regularly nor any special courts are set up to deal with cases of dalit atrocities.

It also adds: "The question of setting up exclusive special courts, particularly in the states having large pendency, needs serious consideration of the government. The rate of convictions in various states ranges from 5 to 10 percent and it is necessary to examine the reasons for such low convictions rates and for taking urgent corrective action,"(Ibid). According to the commission. "The apex court has held that the Special courts cannot directly entertain the cases under these acts, without following committal proceedings. It is, therefore, necessary to amend these acts suitably to authorize the special courts to admit cases under these acts directly." (Ibid).

One can go on mentioning the various schemes or the affirmative action programmes run by the government, supposedly for the empowerment of the dalits and also give details about the systematic manner in which a conscious attempt is on to deny what is due to them. One would be surprised to know that not only thousands of posts, which are meant for them especially from the upper class category have been lying vacant for years together, but there are thousands and thousands of people belonging to the non dalit category, who have manipulated jobs meant for these sections by procuring 'false certificates' and the concerned authorities are sitting over this, despite repeated complaints by the aggrieved people. The seriousness of the phenomenon of false certificates can be gauged from the fact, that the last two annual reports of the National SC and ST Commission (since bifurcated) have devoted a chapter each to discuss the gravity of the situation arising out of this.

This makes it crystal clear that the state has to show firm political will, get ready to make amends to ameliorate the situation and move beyond pious rhetoric, if it is serious about the commitments it made with the 'other people' exactly 58 years back while promulgating the constitution. But one cannot expect that there would be any radical departure from the way, in which the state has been functioning.

Of course, before moving on to the unholy alliance between the state and (a section of) civil society, it would be opportune to take a close look at the Gujarat experience.

A Close Look At the Gujarat Experience

The Gujarat Earthquake in the year 2001 and the consequent relief and rehabilitation programme was an eyeopener to the outside world regarding the deep seated caste bias in the Gujarati community apart from the much talked about bias against the minorities. There were reports that at, places the relief and rehabilitation work bypassed the dalits and the Muslims. There were also reports about the siphoning of the relief material to the relief camps inhabited by the non-dalit or upper caste Hindus and how consciously the dalits as well as the Muslims were deliberately left out in many cases.

Of course, when one comes to the way the Atrocities act unfolds itself in the state, and then one comes across the same shocking pattern, which is evident at the national level. A conclusion of a detailed and systematic study of 400 judgements done by Vajibhai Patel, Secretary of Council for Social Justice corroborates this. It tells us that utterly negligent police investigation at both the higher and lower levels, coupled with a distinctly hostile role, played by the public prosecutors is the main reason for the collapse of cases filed under the atrocities act. It is worth noting that he has meticulously documented these judgements, delivered under this act since April 1, 1995 in the Special Atrocity Courts set up in 16 districts of the state. The study also blasts the common perception, that the inefficacy of this law is due to false complaints being lodged or compromises between the parties. In actuality, it is a complicit State that has rendered the Act toothless.

A write-up in the '*Communalism Combat*' (March 2005) by Teesta Setalvad presents in a nutshell the main findings of the study:

> *In over 95 per cent of the cases, acquittals have resulted due to technical lapses by the investigation and prosecution, and in the remaining five per cent, court directives are being flouted by the government. Often while crimes under the IPC against the accused have been proved, offences under the Atrocities Act*

have not, suggesting a systemic bias against recording and establishing crimes under this law.

As a result of the attitude of the state police and the state public prosecutors, those accused under the Act for criminal acts like murder (for which life imprisonment is the sentence) and rape are being allowed to go scot-free.

Numerous judgements of the special courts set up under the Atrocities Act in Gujarat — which due to lapses in investigation and prosecution, have led to the acquittals of the accused —have passed strictures against the negligence demonstrated by both the police and the public prosecutors and even summoned time-bound 'action taken' reports. Often policemen have even resorted to giving false evidence to protect the accused while prosecutors have attempted to mislead the courts by arguing that the provisions of the Atrocities Act are not mandatory.

Under section 4 of the Atrocities Act, "Whoever, being a public servant but not being a member of a Scheduled Caste or a Scheduled Tribe willfully neglects duties required to be performed by him under this Act, shall be punished with imprisonment for a term which shall not be less than six months but which may extend to one year". In 95 per cent of the judgments studied by the CSJ, courts have passed strictures against errant police officials invoking provisions of section 4 under the Atrocities Act, but the government of Gujarat, instead of taking action against the erring officers, has honoured them with promotions.

The deliberate manner in which the state machinery connives with the perpetrators of the crime, is evident in very many ways.

Acquittal due to investigation by a lower officer: The atrocity rules of the 1995 make it mandatory that, either a Dy SP or an officer above his rank, who is supposed to send his report directly to the state DGP, should carry out investigations of an offence. In 95 per cent of the cases, it is observed that the accused are acquitted merely on the ground that the investigation of the offence was done by an officer below the rank of Dy SP.

Acquittal due to non-inclusion of caste certificate by the police: The Act makes it clear, that the caste certificate of the complainant issued by a competent authority be annexed to the complaint and produced by the police before the court. There have been several judgments, when rape accused was allowed to go scot-free merely because the investigating officer did not annexed the caste certificate of the complainant.

Negligence by public prosecutors: The appointment of special public prosecutors to try cases is mandatory under the act but the hostile role played by such SPPs to prosecute cases destroys the case. It takes years to reach the stage of trial and when the victim/complainant enters the witness box to depose, he does not know who the PP is. The CSJ has studied several judgements in which, the courts have passed severe strictures against deliberate attempts by the special public prosecutors to avoid implementing the special provisions under the Act thereby vitiating the prosecution case itself.

The CSJ study rightly notes that 'an utter lack of commitment to this legislation and lack of political will by state governments to prosecute the atrocities committed under this Act, have rendered this legislation meaningless.' It also tells that 'the Scheduled Caste Welfare Department of the state government, created with the objective of providing social justice to Dalits and Adivasis, has glaring vacancies in key posts making the implementation of social justice measures even more difficult. There are over 300 vacancies in this state department, from the rank of district officer downwards in Gujarat alone.'

(Un) Civil Society and its Silences

It is possible that all these details where the state comes out in rather unflattering terms could be brushed aside as a story repeated ad nauseam. All the talk of dalit atrocities could be presented as another extension of the way, in which 'state in the third world' unfolds itself. But the key point worth emphasizing is that, caste atrocities much like gender oppression or racial atrocities have a specificity, which transcends the binary of 'state as perpetrator' and 'people as victims'. In fact they implicate the partisan role played by the people themselves.

Indian Express (A Dalit? Go find a Dalit society, DP Bhattacharya, June 17, 2008) had carried a story detailing how dalits are forced to live in 'only Dalit' residential societies. It demonstrated the deep biases and prejudices that work even in an urban milieu.

Ahmedabad, June 17: In a recent trend, Ahmedabad is witnessing "only Dalit" residential societies — around 300 of which have come up in the last few years. However, for most Dalits, it is not a matter of choice, but of compulsion.

"Even if a Dalit can afford a flat in areas dominated by the upper castes, they are often denied by the builders or the seller", retired IAS officer P K Valera, who lives in one such Dalit society in Ramdevnagar, says. Some social scientists say the alienation started since 1982, after the anti-reservation agitation, but agree that the caste and class distinctions have become more serious in recent years. This trend can be seen not only in the walled city but also in the posh areas of west Ahmedabad like Satellite, Vastrapur, Bodakdev, Ambavadi. Socio-political scientist Achyut Yagnik says, "There are more than 300 Dalit societies in the city."

(*Indian Express,* June 17, 2008)

The 'Report on Prevention of Atrocities against SCs 'prepared by NHRC (2004) presents details of the way in which the civil society presents itself:

- Civil society becomes a distinct beneficiary of caste based order and how it helps perpetuate the existing unequal social reactions and frustrates attempts to democratize the society because through the customary arrangements the dominant classes are assured of social control over people who can continue to abide by their commands without any protest.

  In fact, it represents the deep divide in social values, where people themselves wish to enjoy all rights and privileges which a democratic liberal society offers them, but are vehemently opposed to their being granted to the scheduled castes.

  Civil society effectively undermines the authority of the state by obstructing the effectuation of rights and entitlements to all citizens and attempting to perpetuate caste based inequalities, indignities and violence against SCs.

- Civil society reflects a deep-seated ambivalence between obscurantism and modernity.

Of course, the uncivil nature of the civil society presents before us a unique challenge, where the need then becomes to rise above a mere discourse on civil and constitutional rigths and address the failure of the largest democracy of the world to go beyond mere form. We have to appreciate that it concerns the greater hiatus that exists between constitutional principles and practice and corresponding ethical ones based on a diametrically opposed ideal. Everyone has to see that under the purity and pollution based paradigm, which is the cornerstone of our caste system, inequality receives not only legitimization as well as sanctification. As inequality is accepted both in theory and practice, a legal constitution has no bearing on the ethical foundation of caste based societies.

It was a manifestation of this real hiatus that when Bhanwari, a Saathin from Women's Development Programme, Rajasthan was raped by the villagers, the trial judge acquitted the accused on the reasoning that "rape is usual" and 'upper—caste man could not have defiled himself by raping a lower-caste woman.'

In Lieu of Conclusion

In his recent Hiren Mukherjee lecture (12 August 2008) organized by the Lok Sabha Speaker Dr Amartya Sen made very interesting observations about the whole idea of social justice. He said: 'In probing the idea of social justice, it is important, I would argue, to distinguish between an arrangement-focused view of justice, and a realisation-focused understanding of justice. Sometimes justice is conceptualised in terms of certain organisational arrangements — some institutions, some regulations, some behavioural rules — the active presence of which indicates that justice is being done. The question to ask here is whether the demands of justice must be only about getting the institutions and rules right?'

Perhaps the sixty plus year trajectory of India's democracy has demonstrated that we have focussed ourselves more on 'arrangement focused view of justice' and rather neglected 'realisation focused understanding of justice'. If we are keen to deliver justice to the downtrodden, is not it high time that we revisit our priorities till date and reboot ourselves to address (to quote Prof. Amartya Sen) 'problems of chronic deprivation and continuing inequity with adequate urgency' with a 'perspective of realisation of justice', which is central 'for the practice of democracy.'

8

Civil Society, Polity and Human Rights in Maldives

Joseph Benjamin

Introduction

Maldives archipelago lying between Tropic of Cancer and Tropic of Capricorn consist of 26 major atolls. It is located about 700 miles Southwest of Sri Lanka in Laccadive sea of India Ocean. It encompasses a geographical area, which includes small low lying 1,192 coral islands. Only 250 islands are inhabited out of which 4 islands have population of over 5000 people. 77 islands have population ranging between 1000-5000 and 118 islands have people less than 1000.

This smallest Asian nation with a population of just 3,70,000 people has a chequered political evolution. It came under British protection since 1796 and was converted into a British protectorate in 1887 and later on obtained complete independence on July 26,1965. But before British occupation Portuguese and Dutch had this palm fringed coral islands, under their yoke. Under the shadow of British protectorate rule, it experimented with republican rule under Muhammed Amin Didi followed by Ibrahim Nasir. Finally power came into the hands of Asia's largest serving President Maumood Abdul Gayoom 1978 – 2008. In October 2008 election, the first democratically elected President Mohamed Nasheed replaced Maumoon Abdul Gayoom. It also ushered in new members in unicameral legislative body *Majlis*. The country has 20 administrative districts; a Governor and local chief (*Katheebum*) to administer each district, modeled on British district collector office.

The people is Maldives mainly depend for economic survival on fishing, coconuts, handicrafts, boat building, boat repairing and garment production. The staple foods are imported. The islands are covered with coconut palms and the equatorial sun-drenched land yields millet, cassava, yams, melons and other typical fruits. All in all, dry land constitutes measly 115 sq miles of surface area. The Gross Domestic Product has grown at an annual rate of around 6 % from 1992-93. The Maldives economy generates foreign exchange through fish export, largely tuna and from thriving tourism industry. Also till 1965, United Kingdom had an airbase at Gan, which was economically a bonanza for the country.

Civil Society in Maldives

According to current estimates, a population of Maldives is approximately 370000.[1] Maldives was a caste based society well into the 1920s.[2] This was the result of its pre-Islamic historical legacy. But with advent of Islam it acquired a homogeneous identity as the population is 100 % Muslim. No doubt, there has been gap between the elite living in Male.[3] There have been three conflicting kinship systems, the Dravidians the North Indian, and the Arab. Efforts have helped to make Maldives more homogeneous in early 1990. Now, Islam, therefore, is important component of Maldivian religious identity but economic disparity and migratory pulls creates tensions and fissures in society. The capital city Male, is the magnet, which draws migrant for jobs. It provides other avenues for self-advancement. It is presumed that President Gayoom made some effort to reduce the gap.[4] Male, the capital of Maldives differs from other island communities also because as many as 40 percent of its residents are migrants. Maldives is pre-dominantly Sunni Muslim and has one common language Dhivehi (Sinhalese dialect) with fairly good literacy rate.[5] Being a very small country, it has 96% literacy rate.[6] Small Shia expatriate community too is there which is engaged in trade and commerce. Young brilliant students are given all help to go abroad for higher education studies. Women are encouraged to have higher education, which facilitates their empowerment. With great gusts and enthusiasm, women clad in traditional dress join others in Independence Day celebration, 26th September every year. Marriage rites and patterns are Islamic-centric, but some ideas have been syncretistic Dravidian to importation. Interestingly, enough divorce rate is rampant as per the United Nations Statistics.[7] In 1965 Maldives became a sovereign nation and joined the United Nations.

Islam in the Maldives

Islam made its entry in 1153 A. D. and soon it became a state religion. Islam permeates the society, culture and polity of state. The traditional Islamic law code of *Shariat*, forms the basic law code of Maldives. Friday being the most important day for Muslims, they attend prayer in mosque at 12.30 p.m. All shops and offices are closed at 11 AM to listen to the sermon.

Most inhabited islands have several mosques. Male, the capital city has more than thirty mosques. In mid 1991, Maldives had a total of 724 mosques and 266 women's mosques. With regards to *Namaz*, the people are very particular. Prayer sessions are held five times daily. Most shops and offices close for fifteen minutes after each call made day *Mudimu*, the caretakers of mosques.

During the ninth month of *Ramazan*, cafes and restaurants are closed during the day and the working hours are limited. The Isolation of Maldives from historical centers of Islam in the Middle East and Asia has allowed some pre-Islamic beliefs and attitudes to survive. This is for the simple reason that Buddhism had dug its heels in the cultural fabric topped by European overlay of Portuguese Dutch and British influences. There is some ethnic minority found in Maldives, among trading community, of Indian origin who settled in Maldives in around early nineteenth century. Besides this, there are also religious minorities belonging to the *Shia* branch of Islam. There are some Sri Lankans who have come to Maldives to work in tourist resorts and in this way Maldives is home to many ethnic minority groups.

Maldivian Government and its Constitution

The Maldivian politics is in the framework of a Presidential form of government, where the President remains both the Head of State and the Head of Government. This was deliberate choice by referendum of 2007 to have US pattern of government rather United Kingdom's Parliamentary form of government. The President heads the executive branch and appoints various official including members of the Maldivian cabinet. The term of president is five years. The President derives additional influence from his constitutional role as the "supreme authority to propagate the tenets of Islam. The *Majlis* is basically unicameral consist of 50 members. The unicameral legislature, the People's *Majlis,* chooses a single presidential nominee who is selected or rejected in a national referendum. Voters approved President Maumoon Abdul Gayoom for a sixth five-year term in 2003. In 2005 the government held parliamentary elections, which a Commonwealth Expert Team commended. The Dhivehi Rayyethunge Party (DRP), led by President Gayoom, is considered the governing party, although the current government came to power before the implementation of the party system in 2005. The Special *Majlis*, elected in 2004 to consider constitutional reforms, held a referendum in August to decide whether the country should have a presidential or parliamentary system of government. According to official figures, more than 60 percent of voters backed the presidential system endorsed by President Gayoom.

Each atoll elects two members in *majlis* by universal adult suffrage. Besides this, the President appoints eight members. Till 2005, parties were not allowed. In 2000 the political party was outlawed when a group of people applied to form a political party. The Maldivian legal system is mainly derived from traditional Islamic law. But secular official appointed by the President administers.

The Presidential and *majlis* election were held on a non-partition basis because there are no organized political parties in the country. Candidates contest as independent candidates based on their personal qualification.[8] The peaceful ouster of the Maldives's long serving dictator, Maumoon Abdul Gayoom, could be seen in the month of October 2008 and election was a political triumph not just for the tiny country of 320,000 populations, but also for the entire subcontinent.[9]

After 1978 election, there was a hope of having some democratic system but this could not happen. The constitution of the Republic of Maldives has mentioned some basic rights of people of Maldives. The Constitution of the Republic of Maldives came into existence in 1968 for the first time. But this was amended in 1970, 1972 and 1975 subsequently. Again this was repealed and replaced by a new constitution, assented to by the president of the Republic on 27 November 1997. The new constitution came into force on 1 January 1998. The President of the Republic proclaimed in assenting to the constitution, that it was a written constitution and the basic tenet of it was equality and fraternity.

A Maldives parliamentary resolution passed on 2 June 2005 allowed political parties for the first time since 1953. Now people can apply to register a party for the election. The constitution guarantees individuals rights. Constitution comprises of thirteen chapters on the administration of state, two chapters that define general terms and one chapter that deals with individual rights.

There are number of articles which talk about the administration of Maldives. Article 33 of the constitution talks about the powers and function of President. It stated that President of Maldives should be head of state, Head of Government and the commander in chief-of-the Armed forces and the Police of Maldives. Article 72 states that there will be three regular sessions of Parliament every year. The speaker of parliament would decide the dates of sessions. The President can convene an extraordinary session. The chief justice and other judges will be appointed by the President of Maldives and may be removed from their office pursuant to Article 117 and 123at his own discretion. The President of the Republic of Maldives has also authority to propagate the tenets of Islam in the Maldives. So in actual practice, Human Rights in Maldives was a farce. It is no surprise that there were attempts of coups in 1980, 1983 and 1988. Total clampdown on media, muzzling of dissent, rampant corruption and nepotism, kept the potboiling of popular discontentment ever on the boiling point. Maumood Abdul Gayoom multimillion-dollar palaces yacht, luxury and cars were an eyesore to ordinary people. The opposition Maldives Democratic Party had to operate from Sri Lanka in exile. It naturally drew international attention. USA state department made a scathing criticism, so did other countries like UK and save Asian neighbours. USA in its report has mentioned the violation of Human Rights in Maldives.[10] Interestingly enough, USA has no embassy in Maldives, yet its watchful gaze is all pervasive on this tiny sized nation.

Due to geo-political considerations India, had to bale out President Gayoom government perforce more than once. For example, Prime Minister Rajiv Gandhi sent 1600 troops on non-stop flights from Agra airbase in November 1988, which saved the President from possible ouster. Health facilities are abysmal. Just two hospitals are in the capital city Male and barely five regional hospitals in entire country. It fails to meet health needs. There is highly prevalent genetic disorder disease Thalassaemia, which takes toll of 1/6 of the population who have no medical treatment to save themselves from it.

Constitution and Individuals Rights

The inherent dignity, equality and inalienable rights of all members of society is the foundation of freedom, justice and peace in society. The principles of justice serve to ensure that any government by providing that at least some human rights, so fundamental and inherent that an individual's rights will supersede and invalidate any state act or treaty that endeavours to ignore them does not infringe human rights. The Universal Declaration of Human Rights, December 10, 1948, is not country specific. It is a universal law binding on all human beings across the globe, only because all are human beings.

The constitution of 1997 deals with fundamental rights and duties of citizens at a very general level. It provides certain fundamental rights, with ratchet clauses that those rights can not be guaranteed except as provided by the law. The article 15 of Constitution states that:

> *"No act detrimental to the life, liberty, body, name, reputation or property of a person shall be committed except as provided by law."*

The constitution provides guiding principles for lawmakers. One would expect to see clauses such as no one shall be subject to torture or cruel, inhuman or degrading treatment or punishment and no one shall be subject to arbitrary arrest, detention or exile, similar to those found in the document of Universal Declaration of Human Rights.

The constitution is subject to the law, including the regulations that effectively means that not only are practices of government, whether or not they result in barbarous acts, which would outrage the conscience of mankind, are protected by the Constitution but also the fundamental rights that should have been protected, are not guaranteed for the citizens.[11] Sometime a number of individual's rights can be abused by the legislation, enacted by the Parliament from time to time.

As per the amnesty international Report form 1992-2001, the National Security Service of Maldives, continues to detain several prisoners of conscience and possible prisoners of conscience and condition of detentions amounted to cruel inhuman and degrading treatment. The National Security Service has an open warrant, as a matter of practice, for arrest, search and seizure and to censor, intercept, read, listen or to divulge all forms of private communications among the members of the public including letter, message, telephone conversation electronic mail, data and so on.[12] The constitution provides individual rights but law being supreme, the individual's rights can be abused by the parliamentary legislations.

Constituting the National Human Rights Commission in Maldives

The Constitution of Maldives is subject to laws, enacted by the government and the parliament. Hence, there can be a possibility of individual's rights violation. Following the custodial death of five prisoners, the people came out on the streets and protested against government apathy towards prisoners. The protest led to stone throwing on some government buildings and the burning of the High Court premises. A special decree was issued by President Maumoon Abdul Gayoom in 2003 and subsequently, the first step to constitute a human right commission of the Maldives was through under the Presidential decree. The commission will have the "right to charge and receive charges/ allegations.[13]

In February 2004, a bill for creating a Commission on Human Rights was placed before Parliament. The bill was passed in 2005 and it was known as the Human Rights Commission Act (Law No. 1/2005). But complete strength of the Commission was not filled up, due to the some question about the law's compliance with Paris Principles. Again in mid-2006, the Parliament amended the Human Right

Commission Act 2005. The new law provided for power of inquiries on cases that occurred subsequent to the enactment of law, and cases that occurred prior to the enactment of the law but not before 1st January 2000 (with exception). Such cases may involve government officials or private persons. The Commission will have the power to summon witnessess and persons related to complaints filed, obtain their statements, and ask them not leave the country without prior permission. The Commission may try to seek amicable settlement of cases, may refer to court too. The citizens are asked to co-operate with Commission and whenever summoned respondents had to respond. Failure to follow the order of the Commission may either result in house arrest or dismissal from governmental office, in the case of public officials.

The Parliament of Maldives appoints the five members of Commission. In October 2006, the Parliament confirmed the members in the Commission. Again in November 2006, the Parliament confirmed Mr. Ahmed Saleem as the Chairman of the commission. The Commission funded from the annual budget approved by the Parliament. The Commission took up the cases of the detention of protestors in 2004. The Commission also took the cases of police brutality of various members of the families. The Commission was empowered to hold independent inquiry and may consult the legal experts. Since there were many legal hurdles with regard to public inquiry, the Commission could not functioned properly. There were many cases of obstruction of Human Right Commission work. The Chairman of the Commission resigned in less than two years out of five-year term. Following this, the other two members also left the Commission. The Commission was literally defunct and could not carry out any of the activities.

Again with regard to the Maldivian detainee, the Commission was unable to do anything. A major issue that arose in Maldives was the government proposals for the amendment of the Human Rights Commission Act of 2006 that subjects to dismissal from employment, any government official who withholds or distorts information requested by the Commission. The government proposed that the law be changed from terminating the employment of such individuals to simply punishing them with a fine. This amendment was formally adopted in the law after much debate, with Member of Parliament, Mr. Ibrahim Ismail opposing it. He argued that "the main reason we fought so hard to have the Law (Human Rights Commission Act of 2006) endorsed in the first place; was to prevent people in authority to hide information from the National Human Rights Commission and Human Rights NGOs".[14] The future of Human Right depends on people's awareness. The people should be vigilant about implementation of Human Rights law of 2006 in Maldives.

The Human Rights Commission of Maldives was very much influenced by International Human Rights NGOs, such as the Asia Pacific Forum of Human Rights and was supported by international community. On the Human Rights Bill, OHCHR and UNDP have provided the government with a number of recommendations to ensure that the institution becomes Paris Principle compliant. President Maumoon Abdul Gayoom announcing the Commission, in his press conference affirmed that it would function in accordance with "Paris Principle."[15]

As there were many Human Rights violations in Maldives, the UN and other development partners of the Maldives for constituting the Human Rights Commission in

Maldives made many interventions. They have noticed the violation of individual's rights and supported for the formation of the Commission. In January 2004, UNDP raised a Preparatory Assistance project to support the Human Rights Commission in Maldives. The project was implemented with the support from the governments of Canada and Norway. This proposal follows the successfully implemented Preparatory Assistance phase where key stepping-stones for Human Rights Commission where laid. The success of the preparatory phase includes:

- *Commenting by human Rights International experts on the Draft Bill, to ensure its alignment with the Paris Principles. This was implemented with the support of the* OHCHR;

- *Key workshops to advocate to the public to create a culture of Human Rights in the Maldives including workshop supported by* UNICEF *and* UNFPA *on* CRC *and* CEDAW.

- *A five-year action plan for the Human Rights Commission.*

- *A knowledge and attitude survey on Human Rights.*

With the support from the UNDP, a strategic Action Plan was prepared. At the same time, it consulted Government stakeholders, NGOs, the private sector, the UN agencies and a draft was prepared. The draft was finalized and adopted by the Commission. The strategic plan described three main functions for the Human Rights Commission of Maldives:

- *awareness raising on human rights issues both amongst the general public and the Government.*

- *to receive and investigate complaints of human rights violations and if the complaint is upheld by the Commission, to resolve the complaint between the parties; and*

- *to undertake research to provide policy advise to the Government where its practice and policies on human rights issues are weak, and analyze legislations for compliance with national and international human rights standards.*

Under the overall mission "to lead the promotion and protection of human rights under the Constitution of the Maldives, Islamic *Sharia'ah*, and regional and international Human Rights Conventions, ratified by the Maldives." The Commission identifies five long-term goals.

The project would support the implementation of Strategic Action Plan. The UN bodies like UNDP, UNISEF, UNFPA and WHO with other UN agencies will support key activities for the project. These UN bodies would assist in advancing, the human rights needs of the most disadvantaged groups. But the key beneficiaries would be all the people of Maldives. The whole project would be co-ordinated by OHCHR and UNPFA. The Maldives has very few NGOs and that is why, the project would make every effort to advocate for the establishment of human rights NGOs in the country. The whole country would be made aware of the human rights project. The national project manager and human rights advisor, are project staff, attach to the Commission who will be recruited by the UNDP in consultation with the Commission and Government of Maldives. In this project three parties are involved:

The Steering Committee will consist of following members-representatives from:

- *The Attorney General's Office*
- *Ministry of Justice*
- *Representative of the private sector*
- *The High Court of the Maldives*
- *Parliamentarians*
- *The Law Society*
- *Relevant NGOs*
- *Ministry of Planning and National Development*
- *Department of External Resources*
- *Supreme Council for Islamic Affairs*
- *Ministry of Home Affairs*
- *Commissioner of Elections*
- *Ministry of Education*
- *Ministry of Information and Arts.*

The annual report would be submitted to UNDP. There will be tripartite meetings.

Inspite all these, the US in its report has found violation of Human Right in Maldives. On various sections of Human Rights, the US has found that there is sheer violation of right of individuals in Maldives.[16] USA in its report has noticed violation of various sections of Human Rights of Universal Declaration of Human Rights.[17] These are: Respect for the Integrity of the Person, Including Freedom From Arbitrary or Unlawful Deprivation of Life, etc. There were cases of detention of protestors in August 2004. In August 2004, the police severely beat and arrested over three hundred protestors having a peaceful gathering at Republic Square in Male. Among the victims of police brutality were children and women. Some people were in critical medical condition due to the police beating.

There was no report of an official investigation in the case of National Security Service Captain Adam Mohamed, whose conviction related to three custodial shooting deaths in 2003 at Maafushi prison, which was overturned by the High Court in December 2006. The law prohibits torture and inhuman or degrading treatment to prisoners. There were reports of occasional mistreatment of persons by security forces. In January, the MDN reported that during widespread protests at Maafushi prison three prisoners received serious injuries from police. Ahmed Shabeer was temporarily paralyzed from his waist down, Hassan Manik bled heavily from his ears and Mohamed Ibrahim's wrists were badly cut. The victims or their families requested but there were no investigations.

Prison conditions generally met international standards, although pre trial detainees were not held separately from convicted prisoners. The law prohibits arbitrary arrest and detention, but it gives the government broad authority to conduct arrests and detain suspects. In practice there were reports that police arrested and held persons arbitrarily.

On the Section of Arrest and Detention one can see violation of individuals rights. The constitution provides for an arrestee to be informed of the reason for arrest within 24 hours and provides for the right to hire a lawyer. In addition, regulation requires, that a detainee be informed of the right to a lawyer at the time of arrest. The court does not appoint legal counsel. There is no legal requirement for search or arrest warrants. According to the AG's office, an arrestee's family is normally informed of the arrest within 24 hours, although the law does not require that police inform the family of the grounds for the arrest. Detainees are generally permitted to have counsel present during police questioning. A prisoner has the right to a ruling on bail within 36 hours;

however, there were reports that bail procedures were not publicized adequately, explained, or implemented consistently.

The constitution provides for freedom of assembly. However, in practice the government imposed limits on this right. The government permitted members of political parties, including those in the opposition, to hold public meetings and rallies with prior notification to the government. The police banned night rallies. Some rallies and demonstrations passed without incident and with minimal arrests. However, several rallies led to police, arresting and detaining demonstrators on unlawful assembly charges. Members of the opposition stated that their right to peaceful protest was restricted, while government officials countered that demonstrators gathered late at night and violated reasonable time, place and manner of restrictions on assembly. Most demonstrators arrested were later released without formal charges.

The law provides for freedom of association, but the government imposed some limits on freedom of association in practice. The government registered clubs only and other private associations if they did not contravene Islamic or civil law. In 2005 parliament unanimously voted to allow political parties to register and function. This followed a 2005, legal opinion from the AG, who interpreted the constitution as permitting political parties. According to the opposition, the government dismissed some MDP members who were civil servants. Government officials responded that the political beliefs of those dismissed, created a conflict of interest and made it impossible for them to function.

There were some reports of discrimination against various Islamic sub groups. In early June, police raided a mosque using batons against the congregation. The worshipers were suspected to be followers of Wahhabi Islam and had insisted on conducting Friday prayers at 12:00 noon. instead of 12.35 p m , as required by law.

The law prohibits children less than 14 years of age from paid or hazardous work. Guidelines prohibit government employment of children under 18 and employment in hazardous jobs such as construction, carpentry, welding, and driving. According to a 2003 report by the International Confederation of Free Trade Unions (now the International Trade Union Confederation), child labour was a problem in agriculture, fishing, small commercial activities, and family enterprises. The Child Protection Unit of the Ministry of Gender and Family is responsible for monitoring compliance with the Child Protection Act. The Ministry of Higher Education, Employment, and Social Security received complaints of child labour, conducted inquiries, and initiated legal action where necessary. As the Constitutional philosophy and institutions is Western in origin, the grafting of it the country has been patchy and intellectual. As a consequence, civil society never could engaged itself with the governmental machinery for good governance and transparency minus corruption. Even the concept of multi-parties, a precondition for functioning of a healthy democracy came into effect only as late as 1008. Some thing was witnessed in emergence of voice of society in response of Maldives. Indian Express reported, Mohamed Nasheed, who beat odds to take over as Maldives' new President, after languishing as a political prisoner, is considered a latter day Nelson Mandela and most prominent pro-democracy face of the archipelago who ended the 30 year reign of Asia's longest serving leader. [18]

Conclusion

The Commission has the power to visit and observe any authority, jail or any organization in the Maldives and submit necessary recommendations on the reform to be made, on the functions, procedures and physical facilities which may be made necessary for such an organization for the protection of Human Rights in the country. In order to protect human rights, Commission is empowered to investigate and take appropriate action, on the findings of complaint received from a person who suspects of his/her human rights having been violated, or from another person or entity to that effect, or when the Commission notices such an act is being performed. The Commission has been given much power to protect the rights of individuals in Maldives but it is noticed that various governmental bodies vehemently violate human rights. The newly elected President has now the responsibility to take serious step in protecting the rights of individuals. The UN and other international bodies must also monitor the law and its Implementation in Maldives. One should not consider it as the interference of International bodies in the internal matter of the country. After all, the Human Rights Act, based on Paris Principles, the UNDP and other international bodies automatically comes into the loop.

In passing, it has to be mentioned that former President Maumoon Abdul Gayoom was successful in lobbying before the Human Rights Councils that threat to survival by any climatic change is tantamount to violation of Human Rights. The havoc caused by Tsunami on 28th December 2004 is a sort of warning signal that any rise in sea level due to global warming may swallow up the entire cluster of coral Islands in the Indian Ocean including the Maldives archipelago.[19]

The UN predicts that the sea is likely to rise by up to 59 cm by 2100, drowning this smallest Asian country.[20] Maldives today was at the cutting edge of new turning-point, when a new President Mohamed Nasheed was ushered into office on November 11, 2008 and being a member of UNO (1965), Commonwealth (1982), SAARC (1985), which has given it an international profile though small in terms of size and demography it has to turn a new leaf on front of better governance, vibrant civil society and human rights. The new millennium goals of 21st century beckon it.

Endnote

1. See, *Manorama* Year Book, Kottayam 2008, p. 381.
2. Rashmi Sharma (2008) Encyclopaedia of SSARC and Member Country, Maldives and SAARC, Regal Publication, New Delhi, p. 65.
3. Male is the capital of Maldives.
4. There has been three conflicting kinship system; the Dravidians, the North Indian, and the Arab. Even the people of Kerala also have been migrated to this tiny country. Country has mixture of many ethnic groups).
5. five times a day finds nation expressing religious devotion in prayer at one of the many mosque.
6. *See, Manorama* Year Book, Kottayam, 2008, p. 381.
7. Rashmi Sharma (2008) cit, Ibid, p. 68. In the 1970s the rate was 85 divorces for every 100 marriages.
8. The recent election based on multi-parties system held in the month of October 2008 and elected the long-timed Political prisoner, Mohamed Nasheed as first democratically elected President. See Indian Express, Nagpur, November 11, 2008, p. 1 also see This is the first multiparty elections have been held freely and fairly. "Gayoom's 30-year reign ends in Maldives", *Hitavada,* Nagpur, 30/10/2008.

9. "Vote's the Message", *Hitavada*, Nagpur, November 3, 2008.
10. See, detail US Department of State Maldives country Report on Human Rights Practices for 1997, released by the Bureau of Democracy. Human Rights and Labour January 30, 1998. (cited in Rashmi Sharma (2008), Maldives and SAARC, p. 109).
11. Rashmi Sharma (2008) *Ibid.* p. 112.
12. *Ibid*. p.112.
13. See, UNDP support to the Human Rights Commission of Maldives Project Document (Male: UNDP 2004, p. 3.
14 www,hrcm.org.mv. dated 4.10,2008.
15. *In 1991, at a United Nations-sponsored meeting in Paris, a retailed set of principles on the status of national human rights institutions was developed. The United Nations Commission on Human Rights and the General Assembly subsequently endorsed the Paris principles. Key criteria include:*
    1. *Independence guaranteed by statue or constitution*
    2. *Autonomy from government*
    3. *Pluralism, including in membership*
    4. *A broad mandate based on universal human rights standards*
    5. *Adequate power of investigation*
    6. *Sufficient resources*
16. On the section of Arbitrary or unlawful File://G: \Maldives_US *Gov.*report_2007 on Human Rights.htm. On 10/11/2008.
17. Country Report on human Rights Practice released by the bureau of Democracy, human rights, and labor March 11, 2008.
    Detailed report See, www.state.gov maintained by the Bureau of Public Affairs. 10/11/2008
18. "Anni heralds new era in Maldives" *Indian Express*, Nagpur, November 12, 2008.
    Nasheed, is also better known as Anni, who defeated Maumoon Abdul Gayoom.
19. V. Gangadhar (2008) "Change At Maldives", *Hitavada*, Nagpur, November 14, 2008.
20. *India Today*, New Delhi, November 24, 2008, p. 21.

9

Recent Developments in Nepal and Indian Foreign Policy Dilemma: A Neo-realist Perspective

Rajneesh Kumar Gupta

Introduction

Nepal, also known as the Himalayan Kingdom, has now established Democratic system. The protests by the people against monarchy forced King Gyanendra to revive the Nepali parliament. The political parties are now gearing up to set up the democratic rule, the first step towards which was appointing Girija Prasad Koirala the Prime Minister of Nepal. Declaration of Nepal as a secular state and formation of a constituent assembly could be seen as second step to establish a liberal democracy. There was reader debate over the fate of age old Monarch than ever before. Even those who are in favour of keeping this institution, believe just for the ceremonial value of Monarchy. So, Nepal has marched on the path of democracy and a government elected by popular vote, having power in true wisdom, is now just a matter of time. There is an obvious question of role of India as a regional power, in this whole transformation. Some scholars have not appreciated Indian foreign policy in this regard; critics have alleged that Indian response was quite inadequate and confusing. This paper attempts to explain internal and external compulsions of India, which play a crucial role in making any policy towards Nepal in general, and particularly in the recent development.

Dilemma of Indian foreign policy in recent development was what to choose and whom to support since there were three major parties involve-The Monarch, Mainstream political parties and Maoist parties. India tried to choose a mid path supporting democratic movement but at the same time sympathetic attitude towards monarch and dialogue with extremist groups like Maoist for peaceful negotiations in the Nepalese democratic process. The paper analyzes Indian response in the recent Nepal crisis within the framework of neo realist approach of international relations. While realism believes that national interests are supreme in foreign policy of any country, they are not unanimous on the question of 'national interests'. Neo realism is an advanced approach of the realism, which was largely, evolved during later half of the twentieth century. There are various dimensions in neo realism, this study has adopted 'security studies' stream of neo realism. For proper understanding of the issue, article began with theoretical definition of neo realism, then discusses a brief history of Monarchy and materialization of democratic movement in the Nepal. In view of an intact approach, the paper examines various security issues, which were prominent determinant factor in making of Indian foreign policy towards Nepal in recent years in general and in the last year's development in particular.

A Brief History of Monarchy and Materialization of Movement for Democracy

Nepal has been known for very traditional political structure. Due to traditional feudal social structure and lack of political modernization, monarchy is not only surviving since last several hundred years but also manifested its extreme form till the recent past. As an institution monarchy in Nepal is a product of historical development. Though, historical evidence give an idea about existence of primitive monarchy in the Kathmandu Valley by the Lichchhabis from Gangetic plains around third century AD, but modern centralized monarchial system was built in late eighteenth century under the leadership of King Prithvi Narayan Shah of Gorkha.

In the colonial era, the British attitude towards Nepal was governed by strategic and commercial interests. For the British Empire, Nepal was a buffer state of vital importance along India's strategic frontiers. It also became a recruiting ground for the Gurkha soldiers who formed an important part of the Indian Army. For obvious reasons they neither had any sentimental attachment towards Nepal nor were they guided by any particular ideology aiming at the conversion of Nepalese society towards liberal western ideals. Hence, the British government tried to maintain its friendly relations with Nepal by allowing the Ranas the widest possible latitude in preserving their family oligarchy and feudal system (Dharamdasani, 2004: 136). And this colonial legacy led to continuation of Monarchial system even after the decolonization of the entire Indian sub-continent.

But, continuation of monarchy is only one facet of the coin, there is another and probably much more important side i.e, movement for a liberal democracy can't be overlooked in this story. The trace for the said movement goes back to early twentieth century. Initially democratic movement in Nepal was considered as an extension of the Indian national movement. By the 1930's, this movement got distinct identity. Some prominent Nepali leader like Girija Prasad Koirala and Tulsi Mihir who were influenced by the democratic philosophy expressed by the Indian leaders, and particularly inspired by Gandhian way of freedom struggle. They formed a group to pressurize the Ranas to have a liberal political system in Nepal. On the other hand, T.P. Acharya who were inspired by the revolutionary movement in India, brought into existence a secret organization known as the *Praja Parished* in the mid 1930's, but the Rana suppressed it in 1940. Later in early 1940's, when Indian leader launched 'Quit India' movement, GP Koirala and others launched a countrywide Satyagrah in Nepal on Indian pattern for their cause (Dharamdasani, 2004: 134-135).

The nascent movement of the Nepalese people against feudal autocracy resulted in the formation of the Rana-King-Nepali Congress coalition government in 1951. The coalition government for the first time promulgated an interim constitution for Nepal, which separated the executive, legislative and judicial functions of the state. The interim government also established a Public Service Commission, Election Commission, High Court, and Office of Attorney General. This represented a substantial modernization in the organization of the government, gradually opening up spaces for participation to increasing sections of Nepalese society.

Since then, under the flag of democracy, different systems of governance have been installed and advocated in Nepal over the past years. The 1951's experiment did not lost long. In 1959, King Mahendra, who had assumed the throne in 1955 after the death of *Tribhuvan*, approved a constitution which provided for a parliamentary system of government based on the Westminster model, following which elections were held for the parliament. However, the king could not reconcile with the parliamentary system of democracy. In less than 18 months of parliamentary constitutional experiment, he exercised his royal prerogative and used military power to overthrow the system in December 1960. The duly elected government was dismissed, parliament dissolved, political parties banned and political leaders detained.

Following a popular mass movement within the country and a strong international wave of democracy around the world, after 30 years of absolute monarchical rule in the garb of the 'party-less *panchayat* regime', democracy was restored for a second time in 1990. King Birendra, who succeeded King Mahendra in 1972, agreed to abide by the principles and norms of democracy and limit his role to that of a 'constitutional monarch'. Accordingly, a new constitution was framed on the basis of multiparty democracy, constitutional monarchy and parliamentary system of government.

After the restoration of democracy in 1990, there have been three general elections for the lower house of Parliament in Nepal. In 1991, 1994 and 1999 general elections were held on the basis of first-past-the-post election system, citizens of the country participated in the democratic exercise esthetically in hope of better governance. But even in this democratic phase elites of the society continued to control national politics and state affairs, with major landowners and comprador bourgeoisie dominating the higher ranks of police, military and bureaucracy and thus as an institution Monarchy remained a vital force in the state, with the support of above said elite class. However, the post-1990 constitutional democratic experiment came to a dead-end following the premature dissolution of the House of Representatives in May 2002. King Gyanendra assumed executive powers on 4 October 2002 dismissing the duly elected government. Elected governments and political parties were blamed for all the miseries – incapacity to govern and visible corruption. Brushing aside the internal situation and international opinion, the king went a step further and assumed total control over state power in February 2005 by declaring emergency and suspending constitution. In fact, it was murder of democracy and cheating with the peoples sentiments. People of the Nepal marched against such brutal act and twisted to a strongest movement in the known Nepalese history. Despite mutual differences, the political parties of Nepal were unanimous on the issue of the restoration of democracy in the state. Eventually, in November 2005, there emerged a twelve-point agreement between the seven party political alliances and the Maoist to launch a unified movement for democracy. After another agreement of the concern parties in March 2006, strategy was formulated for a comprehensive agitation to bring about democracy, with a commitment to a constituent assembly to draft a new constitution. This was followed by a call for a four day strike, begining in the first week of the April 2006. There was a massive participation of the common people in this strike. The state machinery made all possible effort to suppress this movement. Due to Police hostility against peaceful demonstrators, several deaths were reported. This led to further aggression in the movement and extension of strike for indefinite period. Finally, people's movement came to a success on April 24, 2006, when King Gyanendra agreed to reconvene the dismissed parliament. The resumed parliament unanimously passed a motion to curtail the power of the king and declared Nepal a secular state, abolishing its time-honoured official status as a Hindu Kingdom. An election for the Nepalese constituent assembly was held in April 2008 and after months of power-sharing discussions and deliberations, Mr Pushpa Kamal Dahal (Prachanda) was elected as Prime Minister in August 2008. It was expected that the constituent assembly will draft a new constitution within two years. However, resignition of the Prime Minister Mr Dahal in fist week of May 2009 has once again put the question mark on fate of democracy in Nepal.

Dilemma of Indian Foreign Policy

Founding father's of Indian national movement was not only concerned for decolonization of the country and building up a democratic system of governance, but their ultimate goal was to achieve it world wide. Nepal was not exception of that. Pandit Jawaharlal Nehru, the architect of Indian foreign policy said in a speech at Lok Sabha on 6 December 1950:

"In the nature of things, we stood not only for progressive democracy in our own country, but round about also... We talk about it not only in Nepal but also in distant quarters of the world and we are not going to forget it when one of the neighbouring countries; when a country on our door step, was concerned." (Bhasian, 1970: 24).

But at the same time our national interests were also played a fundamental role in making any policy decisions. Architects of our foreign policy were well aware of the fact that sometimes ideals do not match with reality, and our national security should be given first priority. The neo realist approach of international relations which was advanced by American scholars in late 1970's, could be mark out in Indian foreign policy towards Nepal even in Nehru's era; where guiding principle of foreign policy was not to increase power or influence over other country but to safeguards national security and promote strategic interests in the Himalayan kingdom through a stable liberal political system. At this point, it would be appropriate to quote Nehru once again where he said,

> "...And now our interest in the internal conditions of Nepal becomes still more acute and personal, if I may say so, because of the developments across our borders, because of the developments in China and Tibet, to be frank...and regardless of our feelings about Nepal, we were interested in our own country's security" (Bhasian, 1970: 24).

In the post Nehru era, though there was demand for democracy continued but Monarch achieved a very strong position in Nepal. While, to meet national security and strategic interests, India supported 'Two Pillar Theory' in the subsequent years, its Nepal policy was based on constitutional monarchy and multiparty democracy. But recent developments in Nepal posed new challenged to Indian foreign policy. After royal massacre in Nepal, king Gyanendra throne in 2001. Due to his wrong policies, he lost support of Nepali people and after the declaration of emergency, he faced a massive peoples protest. In changed circumstances, India once again confronted a dilemma of choosing between security and democracy. King Gyanendra's coup on 1 February 2005, assuming direct power and unleashing oppression against the political parties, presented this dilemma in a far sharper and acute form than at any time in the past.

India reacted strongly against this step and expressed firm support for the restoration of democracy in Nepal. All the statements issued by India since then, officially and by the External Affairs Ministry and the prime minister, have been clear and categorical. It would be useful to quote a *suo Moto* statement of External Affair Minister Mr. Natwar Singh-

"...the developments in Nepal constitute a serious setback to democracy and bring the monarchy and mainstream political parties in direct confrontation with each other. This can only benefit the forces that not only wish to undermine democracy in Nepal but the institution of monarchy as well. As a result, the task of both India and Nepal to address their shared security concerns has become difficult and complicated. We continue to believe that the principles of multi-party democracy and constitutional monarchy, enshrined in the country's constitution will be adhered to in order to ensure political stability in the country...The Government of India responded promptly and unambiguously to the developments in Nepal. We have in a fraternal spirit called for the early restoration of multiparty democracy, immediate release of political leaders and lifting of restrictions on their constitutional rights and removal of media censorship. We have stressed the need and importance of forging a national consensus between the two constitutional forces, namely political parties and constitutional monarchy, to effectively deal with the political and economic challenges facing the country" (Singh, 4 March 2005).

Going beyond the formal statement, India recalled Indian ambassador from Kathmandu to New Delhi for consultation and all military supplies put were under review.

This was clear cut signal of Indian attitude towards King's undemocratic action. Further, India refused to participate in the Dhaka SAARC summit scheduled for 4 and 5 February, as that could have been exploited by King Gyanendra to seek international and regional legitimacy for his anti-democratic action. India's defense supplies to Nepal were put on hold and two of the king's messengers, his aide Sharad Shah and his Foreign Minister Ramesh Pande, were sent back empty handed. India has also rallied the international community behind its firm position that the king must roll back his action and ensure a meaningful role for the political parties and the democratic system. On the other hand, India made all possible effort to resolve the crisis peacefully by negotiating with all the concern and parties. Indian approach was to fulfill peoples sentiment for democracy and avoid arms conflict in the naighbourhood. As Deb Mukharji, a former Indian Ambassador to Nepal point out at:

> "India also facilitated the agreements between the Maoists and the Seven Party Alliance only to falter with the dispatch of Karan Singh as the Prime Minister's special envoy, followed by the hasty and ill-judged welcome to Gyanendra's meaningless iniotial offer of April 21. Subsequent explanations from Foreign Secretary Shyam Saran and Communist party of India (Marxist) leader Sitaram Yechuri's effort to find a meeting ground between the Maoists and the political parties have put India back on course, giving its undiluted support for the people" (Mukharji, 2006: 18).

The effort made by India in bringing up democracy is not only acknowledged by common citizens and mainstream political parties but also by communist parties in Nepal.

Nepal's communist icon, Mr. Pushpa Kamal Dahal, popularly known as 'Prachanda, in a recent statement lauded India's role in the Nepal peace process, saying New Delhi helped to create the ground for launching a people's movement against the monarchy. "India allowed a 12-point accord between the Seven Party Alliance and the Maoists in Delhi in December last, which created ground to launch the joint people's movement against the autocratic monarchy to establish democracy. Had India not allowed, the accord could not have been signed in Delhi, and it was not possible to do the deal within the country due to the circumstances". Referring to India, he said some foreign powers were helping in the peace process and in building a prosperous Nepal, while others such as the United States were still obstructing the peace process and helping the feudal forces (Dhakal, 2006).

Causes of Dilemma: The Security Issues

Nepal, a landlocked country, located at Himalayan mountain is bordered by two countries—India and China. Three sides of the country i.e., south, east and west are surrounded by India; while in the northern side Nepal is bordered by the Tibetan region of China. India and Nepal shares around 1700 km. long borders, and it is not separated by any natural barriers and, in fact, there is a free movement of people and goods. In present world order, there are very few countries where such system exists. This indicates a very special and cordial relationship between both countries. But, it also poses a security challenges. This is the reason that any internal development and external involvement in Nepal are closely looked by India. There are many security related issues which play a vital role while making Indian foreign policy towards Nepal, only some of them are dealt here.

Fear of Chinese involvement: The geo-strategic significance of Nepal's location between India and China has been emphasized as a prominent variable in defining India's security perceptions towards it. If British India regarded Nepal as a 'buffer' between the Indian and Russian empires, independent India considered it as a `principal barrier to India' defending the northern frontiers. The security concerns of India became alive after the annexure of Tibet by China. To, consolidate its security interests India signed treaties of Peace and Friendship with Nepal in 1950; with distinct clauses that continue to bind the security of Nepal with that of India. In 1949, India and Nepal had also signed an agreement on the recruitment of the Nepali Gorkhas in the Indian Army, which bound the two countries with a military link. India also sent military missions to help Nepal to re-organize its Armed Forces. The need to re-organize the army first appeared in 1952, when a small armed force revolted against King Tribhuvan. In fact, India's security concern was not only to keep China away from Nepal, but also to assist in achieving political and economic stability that could act as a guard against any foreign intervention.

However, fissures in the commonality of the security interests were visible in the late fifties and early sixties. Nepal had signed agreements with China such as the Treaty of Peace and Friendship in 1960, road construction project from Kathmandu to Kodari (1961) and resolving the boundary issue between the two countries (1961) coinciding with strained Sino-India relations. The road had immense strategic and political importance because it was a major breach of Nepal Himalayas from the North from where there was connectivity to India (Thapliyal, 2003).

In later years, China has developed very cordial relations with Nepal. And China also became an important supplier of military equipment to the Royal Nepal Army

(RNA) increasing Chinese influence in Nepal, has always been a point of anxiety to India. Even, this anxiety lauded in Indian parliament, on August 11, 2005. Answering one question related to whether the dominance of China has increased tremendously in Nepal and anti-India atmosphere is building up there after the transfer of power in the hands of royalty, Minister of State in the Ministry of External Affairs (India) Shri E. Ahamed accepted that :

"Government of India is aware of reports suggesting that some military supplies have been sent by China to Nepal or are under consideration. Both countries have been sensitized to our views in this regard. Government is closely monitoring the issue and will take steps as appropriate. India and Nepal share a long tradition of cordial and mutually beneficial relations both at Governmental and people-to-people levels. We remain committed to support all efforts for the restoration of multi-party democracy and political and economic stability in Nepal." (Rajya Sabha Un-starred question, No. 1932: 11 August 2005).

China has granted military aid to the Royal Nepalese Army. In addition, the Indian Express reported in November 2005 that Nepal purchased 4.2 million rounds of bullets, 80,000 grenades and 12000 AK-47 from China (Tompson, 2006). Fear of Chinese involvement was further advanced in Indian circle due to a statement issued by Chief of Royal Nepal Army. He was of the opinion that Nepal's relations with India and China were in the ratio of 60:40. The latest reports shows that China is planning to built a railway network in Nepal border which could pose another security threat to India. Again, this issue was raised in Indian parliament and External Affairs Minister Shri Pranab Mukherjee replied: "Government has seen reports in the

Chinese media suggesting that there are plans to extend the Qinghai-Tibet railway to the border between China and Nepal...Government is constantly vigilant about all developments on India's periphery.' (Lok Sabha Un-starred question No. 47: 22 November 2006).

Maoist Forces in Nepal and Naxal insurgency in India

Nepal is one of the poorest and least developed countries in the world. Agriculture is the mainstay of Nepal's economy. It accounts for more than forty percent of Nepal's gross domestic product. Industry is much smaller, primarily based on processing of agricultural produce and related activities. Urban industrial workers are a tiny minority of the workforce. Poverty in Nepal is grinding. Over forty percent of its more than twentyseven million people live below the poverty line, with the gross national income averaging 240 US Dollar per person, according to the World Bank. The average income can be as low as forty US Dollar for women, people from lower castes, *dalits* or "untouchables," and ethnic and religious minorities. More than eightyfive percent of Nepal's people are peasants in the countryside. They are uniformly poor and suffer malnourishment and exploitation by corrupt officials, landlords and moneylenders. In rural areas, people lack social services, basic sanitation, clean water and solid infrastructure. This low level of human development and feudal social structure, provide a fertile ground for the communist insurgence. Nepal has a long history of communist movement, inspired by the triumph of the Chinese revolution, and this has obtained a strong support over the years. There was a phenomenal growth in the number of communist parties in the decade of 1990's (see table 1). During this period, radical left parties begin their revolutionary activities; they formed revolutionary army and started guerilla warfare in the country against the elite class. The revolutionary army initially numbered a few hundred, but it has since grown to more than 25,000 including local militias. Despite of RNA's all possible effort to curb this guerilla warfare, the Maoist influence in Nepal has increased significantly in past few years. In fact, one of the mouthpiece of these revolutionary groups claimed to have control over eighty per cent of the countries land (Nepal Revolution at Crossroad). In some places, they have set up their own courts and other institutions and virtually heading a parallel government.

Maoist forces have usually tried to exploit the prevailing 'anti-Indian' sentiments prevailing in the country. They define India as a capitalist state, and a major hurdle for Maoist revolution in Nepal. Bretil Lintner in his article "Nepal Struggle to Cope with Diehard Maoist Violence" (1999: 45) has mentioned some of the pamphlets issued by Maoist leaders, spreading hatred against India. In a pamphlet called "Two Momentous Years of Revolutionary Transformation", Comrade Prachanda brands the Nepalese authorities "this government of Indian Stooges", and Bhaurai in his "Politico Economic Rationale of People's war in Nepal", calls his country "India locked" and goes on to state that "the biggest direct manifestation of world imperialist oppression and exploitation in Nepal is Indian expansionist exploitation and oppression" (Pattanaik, 2002: 130).

Maoist forces pose a serious danger to existing Indo-Nepal relations. Indo-Nepal Treaty of 1950 has been abrogated and Mahakali Treaty on rulled. Maoists claim that these treaties give subordinate status to Nepal and detrimental to the country's national interests, though they don't offer any concrete alternative proposal. Besides this, there is a more serious problem of Maoist linkages with Naxal forces in India. It is well known that both have ideological linkages. There were several reports in the last two years indicating possible connections among them. In 2004, CPI (Maoist) was formed by the merger of India's two major Naxal groups. Maoist Communist Centre (MCC) and Peoples War Group (PWG). The some members of Nepali's Maoist groups took active role in this merger. Some experts believe that the idea of establishing a "red-corridor", which includes Nepal and Naxal affected parts of India, has become a prime and combined agenda of these forces. The Annual Report of Ministry of Home Affairs, India (2005-6: 25) exposes the close linkages between Maoist of Nepal and Naxal forces in India. The Report says :

"Available reports indicate continued fraternal and logistic links between Communist Party of Nepal (Maoists) and Indian naxalite groups. Communist Party of Nepal (Maoists) are reported to have come to various parts of the country, especially bordering States such as Bihar and Uttar Pradesh, mainly for medical treatment. In the last four years (2001-2004), over 140 Communist Party of Nepal (Maoists) cadres / sympathisers have been apprehended in Bihar, West Bengal, Uttar Pradesh and other parts of the country. Around 40 activists / supporters of CPN (Maoists) have been arrested in the year 2005."

In fact, any close coordination of the Maoist and Naxal groups functioning in both the countries could create more problems for maintaining law and order situation in some parts of India. So, again there were securities interests involve in dealing with recent crisis in Nepal.

Concern of Indian Diaspora

Due to geographical proximity and close cultural interaction, citizens of India and Nepal have been moving either side since ages. Even after the emergence of the concept of modern states there was no restriction in the movement of people between India and Nepal. In post Independence period this age old binding got boost by Indo-Nepal Friendship Treaty, 1950. The treaty of 1950 had provisions regarding benefits accorded by India and Nepal to each others citizens. Art. 6 of the treaty states that. "Each government undertakes, in token of neighbourly friendship between India and Nepal, to give to the nationals of the other, in its territory, national treatment with regard to participation in industrial and economic development of such territory and to the grant of concessions and contracts relating to such development". According to, Art. 7 of the treaty, "The governments of India and Nepal agree to grant, on a reciprocal basis, to the nationals of one country in the territories of the other, the same privileges in the matter of residence, ownership of property, participation in trade and commerce, movement and other privileges of a similar nature." (Murthy, 2000: 196).

The above provisions of treaty encouraged large scale migration from India to Nepal. Today, Indian citizens or People of Indian Origin are visible in almost each parts of Nepal involve in various professions. The 1961 census of Nepal reported 110,061 foreign citizens in Nepal. Indian citizens constituted 69.3 per cent. In 1971, Indian citizens constituted 94.4 per cent of the total of 136,477 foreign citizens in Nepal. But in 1991, the number of foreign citizens decreased to 90,427 persons. Out of this 75.7 per cent were Indian citizens. In urban areas only there were 32,435 foreign citizens and 81.7 per cent of them were Indian citizens. Foreign citizens living in the urban areas in 1991 constituted 35.9 per cent of the total foreign citizens in the country. In 2001, the number of foreign citizens was 116,571 of which 90 per cent were Indian citizens (Kumar, 2003: 15-

16). According to Kadekar, Indian Diaspora constitutes about 27.12 per cent of the total population of Nepal (2005:1).

Though, Indians are spread in almost every part of Nepal, their major concentration is in the Tarai region of Nepal and they are commonly known as 'Madhesi'. The Indian Diaspora in Nepal has, in the course of time, contributed in the tremendous way to the growth of Nepalese society and economy in general and particularly in the Tarai region. 'It is a fact that it was the Indian community which turned the swamps and forests of Tarai into a rich agricultural belt. At a time when the hill people of Nepal were not prepared to move into Tarai, Indians took pains to settle down in the Tarai region. Needless to state that, today Tarai constitutes the richest agricultural and industrial belt of Nepal and it is considered as the backbone of the Nepalese economy.' (Upreti, 2003: 46).

Acknowledging contribution of Indian Diaspora to the Tarai's development, Kansakar (2001) writes,

"There has been significant contribution of the Indian technical manpower and skilled immigrants to the industrialisation of the Tarai. During the period of Prime Minister Juddha Shumsher, a lot of industries were established in Biratnagar, Birganj and other areas of the Tarai in the process of industrialisation in the Tarai. Industries were established in jute, cotton and textile, matches, plywood and bobbin, pulses, rice, flour, oil, etc. The skilled, semi-skilled and unskilled labour for these industries came from India. Those living in the Tarai who had enough land to till for livelihood were not in need of employment outside agriculture, while people from the hill areas, who lacked technical and industrial skills, were reluctant to move down to the hot, humid and malarial Tarai and were more inclined to migrate to India for employment. Thus employment opportunities generated by industrialisation in the Tarai benefited and attracted the Indian immigrants."

But since last few decades Indian Diaspora has been facing tremendous trouble Denial of citizen status to the *Madhesi* people has been a major complaint of the Indian migrants against the Nepalese government. Complexity in the citizenship laws has practically disabled Indian migrants to acquire Nepalese citizenship. The 1964 Citizenship Act stipulated twelve years of stay in Nepal for migrants as an essential qualification for the acquisition of citizenship. Further, it was extended to fifteen years by an amendment in 1975. It is reported that a large number of people in the Terai region have been awaiting Nepali citizenship (Upreti, 2003: 48). Between 1975 and 1993, eight citizenship teams and three investigative committees were formed to investigate citizenship issue. According to Gurung (2000), the number of Indian citizens has increased only in the western tarai, western inner tarai and Kathmandu Valley. In the eastern Tarai, there was a drastic decrease in Indian citizens, by nearly half. Region wise, the number of Indian citizens declined by eighty-four percent in the mountain, 55.1 percent in hill, 35.6 percent in Tarai and 27.2 percent in the inner tarai. Author reveals that, only nine out of 75 districts had an increase in Indian citizens: Kathmandu, Bhaktapur, Dang, Chit-wan, Kanchanpur, Kailali, Bardiya, Banke and Parsa. In all other districts, their number declined.

Apart from citizenship issue, Indian Diaspora in Nepal has been facing various socio-economic problems. The Land Reforms Act, 1964 prohibits them to purchase of land or other immoveable property. Being foreigner Indian citizens can't own small scale industry and they can't have majority share in medium scale industries. These issues have come and again in the different levels of discussion between India and Nepal. While indigenous people of Nepal have been complaining against Indian communities for minimizing their livelihood and economic opportunities, anti-social elements take advantages of sentiments of locals. There have been various reports of violence against Indian workers, professionals and entrepreneurs in recent past. In April 2004, there was violent attack on Indian cargo vehicles and fuel tankers. There were few reports of harassment and extortion of Indian businessmen and professionals. The Maoist-affiliated All Nepal Hotel and Restaurant Workers Union openly threaten that, only Nepalese should be given jobs in the country's casinos, asking non-Nepalese, including Indians, to leave the country or face consequences (www.indianmuslims.info, 2006). Even sources of Ministry of External Affairs, India accepted that situation is alarming for Indian Diaspora in Nepal. The spokesperson of the ministry, Mr. Navtej Sarna informed that "We have strongly taken up the issue with the Nepal government through our embassy in Kathmandu"(www.indianmuslims.info, 2006). According to news published in Indian Express (1 November 2006), Indian ambassador Mr Shiv Shankar Mukharjee is also believed to have raised the issue of harassment Indian business houses and employeesby Maoist forces, in Nepal during his meeting with Maoist leader Prachanda. Mukharjee had conveyed a similar concern to Prime Minister GP Koirala, which was promptly conveyed to Prachanda.

Economic Interests

India is Nepal's largest trade partner and source of foreign investment. India is also the major transit providing country for Nepal. Today, India accounts for nearly two third of Nepal's foreign trade. Besides formal trade, Nepal also enjoys substantial assistance from India. Presently, there are about 100 projects worth more than 8000 million rupees, which are being implemented or under consideration. These projects are related to infrastructure development, health, education, irrigation and hydro power development etc. They have vital importance for both countries. Further, numbers of private Indian firms are operating in Nepal either independently, or through their Nepalese counterpart. According to Ministry of External Affairs, India:-"Indian firms are the biggest investors in Nepal, accounting for thirtyfive per cent of total approved foreign direct investment of Indian Rupee 14.5 billion (a little over 300 million US Dollar) and also for thirtyfive per cent of 792 operating ventures with foreign investment...Indian ventures in Nepal are found in manufacturing, services (banking and insurance) and tourism industries. Some large Indian investors include Dabur, ITC (for cigarettes), Hindustan Lever, SBI, PNB, LIC, Oriental Insurance, Asian Paints, Colgate-Palmolive, etc. In September 2003, a consortium of VSNL, TCIL and MTNL, together with a Nepali partner, became the first private sector player in the telecommunication sector in Nepal. The Indian partners have 80% share in this venture and offer basic telephony service through WLL technology." (Country Report-Nepal, 2005: 9).

The safeguarding of economic interests could be seen, one of the major objective of the foreign policy of any country, and this is also true in case of India and Nepal relations. One of the major concerns of Indian foreign policy makers was, to keep ongoing projects running and providing security to Indian companies and their employees in the host country. Violent struggle could resultin more suppression and further anger, which could have led to a complete collapse of the system. And this presumed anarchical situation, was neither in the interest of India nor the people of Nepal. Therefore, India was very cautious in dealing with recent developments of Nepal.

Conclusion

On the basis of above analysis it can be concluded that Indian foreign policy towards Nepal has been primarily guided by national security. At the same time India always firmly supported democracy and development of democratic institutions in this Himalayan Kingdom. But, in recent past, with the changing security dynamics in the region and emergence of certain new security threats, Indian foreign policy faced a dilemma of choosing between national security and democracy. This dilemma was in its acute form, after the take over of the democratic government and proclamation of emergency in the country by Monarch and subsequently nationwide strike in Nepal, which led virtually a chaotic situation at least for few days. Task of the Indian foreign policy was, to establish calm in the Nepal and support democratic movement without harming national security interests. Government of India used various channels, to bring all the concerned parties on a negotiation table and to avoid any external powers involvement. At the same time, government appointed special envoy to persuade King, mainstream political parties and Maoist. The biggest success was a smooth transformation towards democracy.

In 2008, country transitioned from a monarchy to a parliamentary republic under the leadership of Pushpa Kamal Dahal (Prachanda). Howevever, dispute over sacking the army chief and consequent resignation of Mr. Dahal, have put the question mark on fate of democracy in Nepal. In May 2009, Nepal plunged into political Crisis with the resignation of Maoist Prime Minister Pushpa Kamal Dahal alias 'Prachanda'. Hopefully new government-in-formation led by Madhav Kumar Nepal, would bring change in foreign policy of Nepal. There is an obvious question of role of India as a regional powers in this whole transformation towards democracy and thereafter developments.

The Maoist government's anti-India posture is no way either a novel thing or a sudden somersault. Since 1950 Indo-Nepal agreement treaty the undercurrent of hostility towards

TABLE- I[1]

Ideologies of the Major Political Parties in Nepal

Parties	*Year of formation*	*Programme / identity*
Nepali Congress (NC)	1947	Social democratic
Communist Party of Nepal (UML)	1991	Moderate left
Rastriya Prajatantra Party (RPP)	1990	Conservative
Communist Party of Nepal (ML)	1998	Radical left
Nepal Sadbhavana Party (NSP)	1990	Regional party (Terai)
Nepal Workers & Peasants Party (NWPP)	1975	Moderate Maoist
Communist Party of Nepal (UPF)	1991	Maoist
Communist Party of Nepal (NPF)	1995	Radical left
Communist Party of Nepal (Maoist)	1993	Ultra-Maoist
Communist Party of Nepal (United)	1993	Moderate left
Communist Party of Nepal (Mashal)	1978	Radical Maoist

1. *Source*: ESP 2001, cited from Lama M.S., "The Working of Democracy" Seminar April 2005.

New Delhi is always there. Reasons may vary from the allegation that New Delhi would like to bring back Monarchy again into Nepal or the alleged interference of Indian Ambassador in internal affair of Nepal. Or Kathmandu's hobnobbing with China to leverage its position vis-a vis India is another tangent in simmering unfriendliness towards Big Brother India. Nepal, after all, suffer from curse of geography and history and that has much to do with present Indo-Nepal equation as it was a recent or distant past.

References

1. "India concerned over harassment of citizens in Nepal" *Indian Muslim Info*, New Delhi, 02 Aug. 2006 [Online :web] Accessed 04 Dec. 2006 URL: http://www.indianmuslims.info

2. Ministry of External Affairs, India (July 2005) *Country Report-Nepal*. [Online: web] Accessed 15 Nov. 2006 URL: http://www.mea.gov.in/

3. Ministry of Home Affairs, India (2006) *Annual Report 2005-06*. New Delhi: Government of India.

4. "Nepal Maoist held in J-K, LeT link suspected," *Indian Express*, New Delhi, 1 November 2006.

5. Ahamed, E. 2005. Rajya Sabha unstarred question, no. 1932: 11 August 2005.

6. Baylis, John Baylis and Steve Smith. 2004. *The Globalization of World Politics*. Oxford: University Press.

7. Bhasian, A.S. 1970. Documents on Nepal's Relations with India and China New Delhi quoted in Dharamdasani, MD. 2004. 'India's attitude towards the democratic movement in Nepal,'

Journal of Contemporary Asia and Europe, Jan.-June 2004 p.135.

8. Dhakal, Ameet. 2006. 'Historic beginning to new Nepal,' *Hindu*, 09 November 2006.

9 Dhar MK. 2006. *Fulcrum of Evil: ISI-CIA-AL Qaeda Nexus.* New Delhi: Manas Publication.

10. Dharamdasani, M.D. 2004. "India's attitude towards the democratic movement in Nepal", *Journal of Contemporary Asia and Europe*, Jan.-June 2004 pp.133-144.

11. Ghimire, Yubaraj. 2007. 'Indian envoy, Prachanda discuss peace glitches,' *Indian Express,* New Delhi. 13 February 2007.

12. Gurung, Harka. August 2000. 'Nepali NationalismNepali Nationalism A Matter of Consolidation,' *Himal South Asian* [Online: web] Accessed 13 Dec. 2006 URL: http://www.himalmag.com/march2001/essay.html

13 Jamwal N.S. 2002. 'Management of Land Borders,' *Strategic Analysis*, Vol. XXVI, no. 3, pp.406-425.

14. Kadekar, L.N. 2005. *Global Indian Diaspora: An Overview.* Hyderabad: University of Hyderabad Research Monograph.

15. Kamath, M.V. 2006. 'Nepal and Pakistan's ISI,' *News Today* [Online: web] Accessed 13 Dec. 2006 URL: www.newstodaynet.com/guest/1505gu1.htm

16. Kansakar, VB Singh. 2003. 'Nepal-India Open Border: Prospects, Problems and Challenges,' *Nepal Democracy* 11 Nov. 2003 [Online :web] Accessed 04 Dec. 2006 URL: *http://www.ncpaldemocracy.org/documents/treaties_agreements/nep_india_open_border.htm* Kumar Bal KC, 2003. *Migration, poverty and development in Nepal.*

17. Bangkok: Economic and Social Commission for Asia and the Pacific ESID/EGM/INF. 10.

18. Lama M.S. 2005. 'The Working of Democracy' *Seminar* April 2005 [Online: web] Accessed 15 Nov. 2006 URL: http://www.indiaseminar.com/semframe.htm

19. Lintner, Bretil. June 1999. 'Nepal Struggle to Cope with Diehard Maoist Violence,' *Jane's Intelligence Review*, [Online :web] Accessed 04 Dec. 2006 URL: http://jir.janes.com/public/jir/index.shtml

20. Mearsheimer, John J. 2002. *Tragedy of Great Power Politics.* New York: W.W. Norton.

21. Mukharji, Deb. 2006. 'A New Equation.' *Frontline* 19 May 2006. pp. 16-18.

22. Mukherjee, Pranab. 2006. Lok Sabha Un-starred question no. 47: 22 November 2006.

23. Muni, S.D. 2005. **'Neighbourly concerns,' *Seminar* April 2005** [Online: web] Accessed 15 Nov. 2006 URL: http://www.india-seminar.com/semframe.htm

24. Murthy, Padmaja. 1999. 'India and Nepal: Security and Economic Dimension.' *Strategic Analysis,* Vol. XXIII, no. 9, pp. 1531-1547.

25. Murthy, Padmaja. 2000. 'Movement of Citizens on Indo-Nepal Border: Some Issues,' *Strategic Analysis* Vol. XXIV, no. 1, pp. 196-199.

26. Singh, Natwar. 2005. Suo Moto Statement by External Affairs Minister Shri Natwar Singh on developments in Nepal 4 March 2005 [Online: web] Accessed 12 Feb. 2007 URL: http://www.satp.org/satporgtp/countries/india/document/papers/india_nepal_natwar05.htm

27. Taliaferro, Jeffrey W. 2000/2001. 'Security-Seeking Under Anarchy: Defensive Realism Reconsidered,' *International Security*, Vol. 25, no. 3, pp. 152-86.

28. Tompson, Ian. 2006. 'People's movement advances against Nepal's monarchy,' *S&L Magazine*, February 2006 [Online: web] Accessed 13 Dec. 2006 URL:http://socialismandliberation.org/mag/index.php?aid=561

29. Thapliyal, Sangeeta. 1999. 'Movement of Population between India and Nepal: Emerging Challenges,' *Strategic Analysis*, Vol. XXIII, no. 5, pp.777-789.

30. Thapliyal, Sangeeta 2003 "Contesting Mutual Security: India-Nepal Relations" [Online: web] Accessed 13 Dec. 2006 URL: http://www.observerindia.com/analysis/A004.htm

31. Upreti, B.C. 2003. 'Indian Community in Nepal,' in Ajay Dubey, ed., *Indian Diaspora: Global Identity*, New Delhi: Kalinga Publication..

32. Waltz, Kenneth. 1979. *Theory of International Politics*. New York: McGraw Hills.

10

Civil Society and Struggle for Human Rights in Nepal

Arjun Karki and *Neeraj N. Joshi*

Civil society in Nepal encompasses all institutions, for example NGOs, media, trade associations, sports clubs, advocacy groups, and special interests that are innately the structures that lie outside the governmental framework. While the debate continues with regard to a precise definition of Civil Society and their functions, this paper argues that civil society in Nepal plays a critical role in protecting and promoting human rights besides influencing the political system by means of advocacy and campaigns for well functioning of the government, be it democratic or otherwise.

This paper first presents a brief description about the emergence of modern civil society in Nepal and its relationship with the State. It then highlights the recent trend of human rights in Nepal, followed by a description on the contribution of CSOs to the Struggle for Human Rights in Nepal and the significance of such a struggle. The paper also presents the challenges, facing Nepali CSOs.

CSO-State Relationship: Confrontation or Synergy

The CSOs in Nepal have emerged from the earliest period of history. However, the modern civil society structures in Nepal have developed only with the establishment of democracy in 1990. Since then, the building of civil society has followed, both the strategies of 'involvement of' and 'confrontation with' the State. Both the strategies flow from the provisions of the 1990 Constitution, which envisions a plural, equal and liberal society, in which all civil society organizations have a crucial role to play and engages both the State and civil society in social, economic and political processes (Karki, 2005).

The CSOs in Nepal represent special interest groups, ranging from the development and social groups, outside the institutional framework of the government, involving themselves in mobilizing masses of citizens to participate in the development projects and those involved in advocating and campaigning political issues and demanding implementation of legislations in favour of the general public. There are other CSOs, which often have come to work as organisation of social, economic and political liberalization, when the state somehow fails to perform or fulfil its promises, such as social and gender inclusion, maintain law and order, human rights obligations, women empowerment, including social and economic service deliveries to the vulnerable communities.

In the area of development too, CSOs play a role in modern Nepal by supplementing the government effort to provide social and economic service to citizens, and by raising awareness in society, about development issues such as health, education, natural resource management, institutional development, employment/income creation etc, which is not less important than just implementing development projects. Despite the important role of the civil society, the State has not been engaging in dialogue with civil society at all. Instead it has assumed the opposition role: arresting and harassing NGO workers, journalists, academicians, lawyers, human right defenders and others, limiting their freedom of movement, and curtaining their basic freedom to work (Karki, 2005).

Though different civil society groups have been engaging in different activities as per their respective interests, agenda and priorities, the recent trend is that, in the course of their work, almost all CSOs engaged themselves against the unaccountability or even hostile approach of bureaucracy. Therefore, it is part of the strength of Nepalese democracy, that the CSOs have by no means been the looser in all these tug-of-wars.

Human Rights Trend in Nepal

With the advent of democracy in 1990, and the ratification of major international human rights treaties in the world, Nepal has been exposed to the international arena of politics and people's rights related issues. The ratification of such international tools opened up Nepal to an extended field of international human rights laws that created opportunities for the country to be more visible with its commitment, to nurture a democratic governance system and promote human rights, at the same time requiring the fulfilment of these obligations. To date, Nepal is a state party to 22 United Nations (UN) and seven International Labour Organisation (ILO) conventions, including the International Covenant on Economic, Social and Cultural Rights (ICESCR) and is entrusted with obligations to provide provisions for these instruments.

Contrary to its commitment to promote human rights related issues, Nepal has sadly failed to record any significant progress in addressing the obligations of respecting and promoting human rights that correspond with national and international human rights related instruments. During the decade long violent political conflict faced by the country, the structured and systematic denial of human rights that manifested in state governance, was the worst political incident experienced, and dealt with by the nation. The period witnessed a serious situation of human rights violations, exacerbated by arbitrary arrests, illegal detentions, disappearances, extra-judicial executions, abductions, and torture in the context of the armed conflict and disrespect for the rule of law.

Nepal's human rights situation deteriorated, since the King assumed direct executive authority as Chairman of the Council of Ministers, and imposed restrictions on the citizens' fundamental rights on 1 February 2005. The King also staged a coup against the civilian government, which he claimed was a necessary step to tackle the nine year old Maoist insurgency. Security forces arrested all leaders of major political parties. Authorities severed all communications links within Nepal and with the outside world. Many civil and political rights, including freedom of movement and freedom of assembly, were suspended.

Despite the King's promise to resolve civil war, the conflict continued with the same brutal intensity till September 2005, when the Maoists declared a unilateral ceasefire. The Government said that it doubted the sincerity of the ceasefire and at the time of writing this report had not reciprocate. In spite of renewed commitments to abide by international standards, both sides continue to engage in serious violations of international humanitarian law. The establishment of a UN human rights office gave rise to some hope that the tide of abuses might be curtailed, through vigorous monitoring and public censure of violations.

Even during the decade long (1996-2006) violent conflict, between the Government and the Communist Party of Nepal (Maoist), the structured and systematic denial of human rights that manifested in state governance, was the worst political incident experienced and dealt with by the nation. The period witnessed a serious situation of human rights violations exacerbated by arbitrary arrests, illegal detentions, disappearances, extra-judicial executions, abductions and torture in the context of the armed conflict and disrespect for the rule of law. The root cause of the conflict, can be attributed to the socio-economic and cultural inequalities that resulted from the state's failure to realize ESCR, including the right to development.

In the months after the royal takeover, the King maintained emergency powers through legislative changes, that solidified control over key institutions, such as the National Human Rights Commission (NHRC), civil services, and media. The Human Rights Commission Act was amended, to allow the King to change the composition of the NHRC appointment committee, undermining its independence and neutrality. Human Rights Watch found, that the Government and the Royal Nepal Army (RNA) have consistently hampered the work of the judiciary and the NHRC, despite cosmetic steps designed to give a contrary impression. Strict media regulations had prohibited the broadcasting of any news critical of the King and the royal family.

The government imposed prohibitions and bans on the citizens' fundamental rights among may others, their right to freedom of expression, right to peaceful assembly, right to freedom of movement, among many others. As the people could not resist the situation of oppression, hundreds of thousands of them spontaneously took to the streets, demanding an absolute end to the feudal monarchy system. The movement continued for 19 consecutive days, leading to a great success on 24 April 2006.

However, contrary to the expectations, the trend of killings, abductions, torture, intimidation and extortion, persisted even after the establishment of the 'democratic interim government'. The failure of the government to make its presence felt as well as to take action against the perpetrators and maintain law and order, rather promoted the state of impunity. The emergence of violence in the country in general, and the *Terai* region of Nepal adjoining the Indian border in particular also resulted in widespread human rights violations. The *Terai* violence started especially after the promulgation of the interim constitution, with demands among others for a federal system of government and proportional representation of the *Terai (Madhesi)* people at the political level. The delayed action by the government to address this demand, led to evolution of more than 20 small groups, of which while some were of political in nature and others criminal in nature.

During the first period of emergency in 2001 and 2002, state security forces killed a total of 992 people. Out of them, 59 were children below 18 years. In 2005, though the emergency period was only for three months, security forces killed at least 333 people; out of this 13 were children. Furthermore, even after the establishment of *Loktantra* a total of 371 persons have been killed and 7,668 people have been abducted by different groups. This certainly depicted the fact, that the government has not been able to protect the people's social, cultural and economic rights (INSEC, 2007).

Even today, NGOs and human right defenders, including journalists who work in a very precarious environment, because of the proliferation of rebel groups, continue to get regularly threatened by the authorities, they accuse, The rebels in the Terai region of Nepal, where the major abuses (kidnappings, assassinations and other forms of violence) are committed by armed groups. Therefore, it is not surprising, that the government are harassed is criticized for ratifying human rights treaties and conventions, but not incorporating the human rights laws into legislation and implementing subsequently.

Contribution of CSOs in the Struggle for Human Rights

The civil society organizations in Nepal are playing a very significant role in the promotion and protection of human rights and peace in the country. The CSOs have been lobbying for the right to ESC rights and right to development, besides other several human rights. In this endeavour, CSOs have become the media's key allies in advocating the issues of injustice and clear violations of rules.

In post 1990 days, the CSOs have played very significant role in Nepalese society, in a number of ways, including successfully arousing consciousness and making advocacy a of human right issue. The CSOs had played significant role in the movement for overthrowing the autocratic non party panchayat polity and pressuring the post 1990 democratically elected governments, to be responsive and accountable to the people.

Even, since the beginning of the armed conflict in Nepal, civil society groups and organizations have been in the forefront advocating for peace, human rights and humanitarian aids for people in need. The past two dialogues between the government and CPN (Maoist) were held in the initiatives of civil society organizations. The CSOs had participated in civic mediation to bridge the gap between the two conflicting parties the governments and the Maoists and creating favorable background for two rounds of talks in 2001 and 2003. Human rights organizations and several civil society groups have also initiated peace movements in different parts of the country. As for the peace dialogue, several road maps for the conflict resolution and conflict transformation were formulated and discussed by the civil society groups (Pradhan, 2008).

The role of civil society in the political process is no less important. In this context, as the civil society experts point out, the concept of CSOs in Nepalese society has emerged as a part of oppositional politics and has, in many respects, contributed to respect for and observance of human rights of the citizens and making the government more accountable and responsible to the people.

Between 2002 and 2006), the CSOs have contributed much for the restoration of 'Multi-party democracy' with in the 19 day mass uprising, which concluded the midnight declaration made by King Gyanendra on April 24, 2006 that restored the House of Representatives, elected in 1999.

As it appears, the CSOs in Nepal have been able to contribute to the country's political harmony, strengthening social foundation of democracy, within the context of the pluralistic society. Therefore, for a country like Nepal, with its multitudinous ethnic, racial, religious, cultural groups and political, the theme of 'solidarity among CSOs' appears to be an ideal approach, which should be aspired, in order to struggle for promoting and protecting human rights and bringing about democratic development and governance in the country.

Continuing the Struggle[1]

In Nepal, the struggle by the CSOs to influence the government, for making more accountable to citizens, is an ongoing process. Even after the major successful political events in the country, the struggle of the CSOs continues. This is because, the current post conflict situation is marked by fragility in all respects, demands urgent and utmost attention of all stakeholders.

Common Nepalese are facing the problems of securing basic needs; the Maoist ex-combatants are still languishing in the cantonments; the rural infrastructures necessary for supporting livelihoods of the returnees are in a devastated state; socio-cultural attitude towards returning women migrants, has been of stereotype stigmatization making their reintegration into the society difficult and the list goes on - despair, dispossession, disappointment and disillusionment. All in all, the brunt made by the conflict is being borne by the already disadvantaged - women, children, youths and senior citizens including widows, single women, orphans and the handicapped. made by the conflict. The country situation spells out a climate of fear, distrust, anarchy and volatility. The very issues of poverty, exclusion, denial, exploitation and lack of opportunities, that partly fuelled the decade long violent conflict, have ironically been further aggravated than mitigated.

The share of the long awaited peace dividend has been confined to the top brass of the political parties, ruling elites and public servants, within Kathmandu and other urban centers, outrightly denying to the common people in general and to remote rural Nepal, in particular. At the grassroots, fear of insecurity, poverty, violence against women and blatant violation of human rights continue, The poor and the marginalized have failed to receive any peace dividend, that they are rightfully entitled to. For the majority of the Nepali citizens, who have been deprived of their basic rights, peace dividend translates into reclaiming and securing the right to food, shelter, livelihoods, employment, education, health and every other socio-political, economical and cultural rights without any fear of discrimination, marginalization and humiliation, in the manner of true spirit and concept of substantive equality. Unfortunately, the priceless peace dividend has remained Kathmandu-centric, in the corridors of power, leaving no room for peace building from below!

Since Nepal is reeling through a delicate transitional phase - with the ongoing peace process and having recently declared Nepal as a federal republic state, it is imperative that the civil society, by adequately representing the voices of the people, plays a significant role towards realizing the establishment of an inclusive new Nepal, where the State fulfil its human rights obligations and the people enjoy such rights.

Challenges Facing Civil Societies in Nepal

The Nepalese CSOs in the current changed national, regional and global context, has to face a number of challenges regarding the functions, due to the rising expectations of the people particularly in post 1990 periods. Due to the high and growing expectations of the people, the CSOs have to involve a number of areas including the empowerment of the state (Dahal, 2007).

In Nepal, the great political events, such as the end of the state of emergency, which had been in force since February 1, 2005 until the restoration of the Nepali Parliament in April 2006, and the signing of the Comprehensive Peace Agreement (CPA) between the Government and the Communist Party of Nepal - Maoist in November 2006, the establishment of a Parliament in January and an interim Government in April 2007. Finally the declaration of Nepal as a federal democratic republic in May 2008 has put an end to large-scale repression and led to a marked improvement in the situation of human rights in the country. However, human rights defenders and people working for CSOs continued to be subjected to various acts of intimidation and repression by both State and non-State actors.

In the changed political context, there is a paramount importance of the role, that NGOs can play. By taking an issue of state restructuring among general public, the NGOs could take opportunities to contribute for social transition, through a massive social mobilization on how to create an environment to participate poor, Dalit, women, ethnic, disabled, and other backward communities. However, the upcoming days are not less challenging for the NGOs. In the changed context, responsibility of the NGOs has been further increased. Along with the transition of the whole society, the transition of the NGOs is also necessary. These comments may not hold true for all the NGOs, it has become an overarching challenge to the NGO sector (Timsina, 2007)

As the evidence depict, the right–to–development as a human right, of the majority of the poor and excluded people, has been totally ignored. The whole "peace" process has now become Kathmandu-centric, top-down and dominated by political elites based in Kathmandu. There have been no sincere efforts till now, to share the peace dividend to people, living in war torn rural and remote Nepal. As a result, there seems to be mass frustrations amongst Dalits, tribes, ethnic minorities, youths and other traditionally marginalised communities in conflict affected Nepal, as there are no signs of improvement, which they desperately aspired for.

It is also a fact that, the current state structure still creates and perpetuates injustice, inequity, exclusion and exploitation. Therefore, restructuring of the whole state including the security, bureaucracy and the politics is a must, for inclusion of the poor and excluded masses, belonging to different classes, castes, gender, ethnicity and region. Without radical restructuring of the state, a lasting democratic peace still remains a wishful dream. Given this situation, the challenge for the CSOs seems even bigger than ever before, especially in terms of ensuring the rights of the people, by exerting pressure on the government for fulfilling the human rights obligations.

Conclusion

Nepal entered a political transitional phase after the successful People's Movement in April 2006. The movement toppled the autocratic regime of the monarch and compelled the followers of violence to shun it for the sake of the people and the country. Amid hopes and efforts for sustainable peace, inclusive and progressive restructure of the State, political activities have been organized to protect the aspirations and mandates of the movement. The change was a big political advance from autocracy to democracy and from armed conflict to peace. More importantly, it delivered a message and created hope that the future course of state governance, will uphold the issues of economic, social and cultural rights (Joshi and Khadka, 2008).

In this context, what is required, is strong and coordinated action by the CSOs, leading to improvement in the human rights situation. Improved human rights situation in terms of protection and monitoring, is the most significant confidence building measure, open to both sides, so that the government and political parties can operate freely and effectively in support of a peace process. This is because, to take the CPA to a logical conclusion is still due.

CSOs need continue to exert pressure on the government, to implement its commitment to prevent the culture of violence, and end practice of impunity. CSOs need to be prepared to face all these challenges in the coming days. Again, it is still worth to say, that the CSOs must continue their struggle, in an effort to render the government more democratic and accountable to the citizens of Nepal.

The resignation of Maoist Prime Minister Pushpa Kamal Dahal, led to political crisis in Nepal. It is not even six month of Panchanda's government, a veteran communist leader Madhav Kumar Nepal staked claim to form new government. Hope this new government-in-formation, would look into the interest of civilians as well as army and maintain peace and stability in Nepal.

Endnote

1. This section draws upon the **Kathmandu Declaration 2008, Respect and Uphold the Right to Participatory Development, brought out by the** representatives of civil

society, including 17 leading federations, alliances and networks from more than 55 districts of Nepal convened on 14-15 February 2008 in the National Civil Society Forum on "Peace, Development and Foreign Aid: Civil Society Concerns" held in Kathmandu.

References

1. Dahal, R.K. (2007). The Civil Societies in Nepal. Excerpts from the paper presented at a seminar, the Institute of Foreign Affairs on March 27, 2007 in Kathmandu.

2. FIDH (2007). Nepal: Observation for the Protection of Human Rights Defenders. In: Steadfast in Protest, Annual Report, International Federation for Human Rights (FIDH), France. http://www.omct.org/pdf/Observatory

3. INSEC (2007). Human Rights Situation in Nepal after *Loktantra.* Kathmandu: Informal Sector Service Centre (INSEC).

4. Joshi, N. and S. Khadka (2008). Human Rights Situation in Nepal: A Politico-economic Perspective. Paper prepared for publication in Social Watch 2008.

5. Karki, A. (2005). Sharing Experiencing of Civil Society Building. In: Confronting the State, Engaging the State Civil Society Building Strategies under Adverse Political Conditions Seminar, May 10, 2005, The Hague, The Netherlands, pp. 2-4.

6. Pradhan, G. (2008). Civil Society in Conflict Transformation – Nepal, http://www.nepaldemocracy.org/conflict_resolution/index.htm

7. Timsina, N. (2007). NGOs in Nepal: Social Responsibility and Governance System, 26 September 2007.

11

Human Rights in Pakistan A Heuristic of Hope and Despair

Sangeeta Mahapatra

The Hobbesian State of Nature, described as "solitary, poor, nasty, brutish and short", presents the existence of a state, devoid of human rights. The principle that every individual has an inherent moral worth and enjoys certain natural rights, forms the rationale of the doctrine of human rights. This acceptance of the moral universalism of human rights, predicates a major breakthrough in man's march towards civilisation from a state of barbarism. These basic ethical guidelines draw attention to the economic, social and political conditions required for all individuals to lead a minimally good life. Thus, they provide the standard by which social, political and legal systems of a country, entrusted with the task of guaranteeing human rights, are judged.[1] Pakistan has a poor track record, when it comes to assuring these fundamental prerequisites of life.

When one is asked to write about human rights in Pakistan, it is commonly felt that one might just spare the ink and send in a blank page. Though this observation reflects a deep sense of dissatisfaction, about the ground situation in the country, it stems more from the common people's inability to do something about it. Their rights are often breached in order to strengthen the iron triangle and strangle hold of the military, feudal lords and religious leaders. Implementing internationally sanctioned ideals of emancipation, would be a direct threat to the despotic regimes as it would lead to a more egalitarian system of governance. It is thus to the advantage of Pakistan's power elite, to maintain the status quo and keep human rights in a state of suspended animation. To reverse this situation is simply a matter of political will and civil society activism.

However, the thorny question about national sovereignty superseding any amorphous conception of human rights rather than finding an answer ,has led to many complex questions. One such query is related to the concept of natural rights, and whether it can exist independently of legal acknowledgment. According to political philosophers like Aristotle in his *Ethica Niomachea*, the Sophists, the Contractualists, and many others, these inalienable rights are not given to man by any higher divine authority; it is by the very fact that he is a human being; that he is entitled to rights, such as that of life and livelihood. Investiture of authority is contingent on the recipient providing for and protecting these basic natural rights of individuals. The twentieth century, a bloody century gave legal form to this notion and the twentyfirst century added a qualitative dimension to it, that is, it is not just life and livelihood that matters, but also human dignity. Thus, any belief, value or action, that contravenes these rights, should be condemned and made punishable, even if these rights have not been made into laws in the country, that is guilty of such violation. Therein lays the value of these rights as an auditing mechanism that prevents the abuse of governmental power and authority.

This idea of overarching rights has a sanctity that few dare to question. But cultural anomalies and differences often intrude upon rationalisations on these rights. For instance, while some countrie,s believe it is enough to guarantee the right to physical security, others jump ahead with the holistic idea of human security. The latter group gives equal weightage to normative and empirical considerations. But it might have the unintended consequence of making its implementation much more difficult as there can be no end to the demands for rights that enhance the quality of one's life. In a society such as that of Pakistan's, which is characterised by linguistic, cultural, religious, and regional and other divergences, the idea of what constitutes human security and dignity may vary. However, given the rootedness of human concerns and recognition of natural rights that allow man the enjoyment of certain basic goods, national sovereignty cannot be an excuse for states to neglect their human rights obligations. Thus, the government of Pakistan is accountable to both the Pakistani people and the international community if it fails to respect human rights irrespective of whether these rights have previous legal and political recognition in that particular country as they are validated by the principle of natural justice. As Aristotle stated, "Of political justice, part is natural, part legal."[2] While, private citizens and civil society organisations play a role in the protection of these rights in what is termed as "privatising rights", the onus is on the government to ensure the institutional delivery of these rights, to create opportunities for the people to lead a stable and secure life, and to co-operate with autonomous, national and international organisations that act as the paladin of human rights.[3]

The purpose of the article is to review the human rights scenario in Pakistan. Divided into three parts, it will first briefly touch upon the concept of human rights that is widely accepted and assess the extent to which Pakistan has legalised these precepts. The second part will deal with those groups of the society that continue to suffer human rights abuse in Pakistan and Pakistan occupied Kashmir (PoK), despite unflagging passion of and efforts by Pakistan's Human Rights Commission and international organisations to put an end to their privations. The article will especially focus on the different religious minorities and women who have been subjected to draconian laws and have no one to turn to but an indifferent establishment. The concluding part will evaluate the political-institutional, religious and societal dimensions of ensuring human rights in the country.

Formalising Human Rights

The philosopher Brian Orend contends that the object of human rights is to secure "minimum levels of decent and respectful treatment".[4] Ronald Dworkin takes this view forward by his concept of "rights as trumps", that is, claims over rights take precedence over other considerations, when a policy is formulated. Thus, a minority's right against discrimination trumps over considerations of benefit of the majority, if the benefit ensues from an act of discrimination.[5] A government loses its moral authority, if it is biased towards the state religion and promotes it at the expense of other religious denominations.

The case for according equal value to all human rights is idealistically sound. In reality, conflicts often arise between claims over different rights. This is more prevalent in developing societies saddled with problems of poverty and limited resources. A triage mentality seeps in when the government tries to prioritise rights and implement those that are absolutely necessary for living, while keeping the rest that provide conditions for a qualitatively better life in hold, till the desired level of growth and progress has been attained. While many might find fault with this approach, it is more practical to understand the constraints faced by the implementing agency. T.M. Scanlon has pointed out in his work '*What We Owe to Each Other*' that an action is wrongful, if they are disallowed by whatever first-order principles has broad consensus among the populace.[6] Conceptual delineation of rights in the twentieth century owes much to W.N. Hohfeld (1919) who classified rights into claim rights, liberty rights, power rights and immunity rights. Peter Jones (1994) divided the substantive categories of rights (rights to life, to freedom, to protection of rule of law, to political life and to fundamental social, economic and cultural goods) into liberty and claim rights. The claim rights can be held '*in personam*' (rights one holds against an authority) and '*in rem*' (rights that apply to all). [7] Thus, Pakistan's human rights record can be evaluated keeping in mind how far it has been able to ensure to its people basic liberties and opportunities to enjoy a decent life.

Cutting across societal experiences, the concept of natural rights was the manifestation of the primordial sense of belonging to a human family and as expounded by Thomas Aquinas, they constitute a natural code, which imprints on man, a directive principle of human actions. However, its implementation first requires the recognition of the procedural status of an individual, the ascription to an individual of bedrock, that is, a fundamental right. The Universal Declaration of Human Rights adopted by the General Assembly of the United Nations (U.N.) on December 10, 1948, which has been translated in about 334 languages, is the benchmark by which, individual states formulate their own human rights policies. As an expression of the "legal conscience of mankind" and based on the principle of equality of all human beings, it covers the three generations of rights:

(a) Rights to freedom: freedom of life, liberty, security; equal protection of law; right to fair hearing by independent and impartial tribunal; freedom from interference in private life; freedom of religion, expression and assembly/association; freedom against arbitrary detention and *ex-post facto l*aws and the right to marry and protect one's family.

(b) Socio-economic rights: Right to education, welfare, social security, right to participate in cultural life, right to work and free choice of employment.

(c) The last generation of rights are associated with the right to self-determination, rights of minorities and right to a secure and clean environment.

One cannot just make a categorical statement that denies the existence of human rights in Pakistan as it would be a negation of society and state: human rights or certain fundamental rights of life exist *hic et unique* and form the basis of community living. The difference in the degree and range of observance and implementation of these rights marks out a state as a shining exemplar or a defaulter. In 1947, in spite of being founded on a common religious identity, Pakistan projected itself to be a secular and liberal democracy with the Preamble to the Constitution of Pakistan stating, "Adequate provisions shall be made to safeguard the legitimate interests of minorities and backward and depressed classes". Expanding on this, the law provided that the linguistic, cultural and religious minorities will be allowed to pass on their heritage to the people of their community. Further, they would not be discriminated against by the state, especially when it came to education and employment opportunities on grounds of their particular identities. The *Quaid-I-Azam*, Mohammad Ali Jinnah, founder of Pakistan, declared that, "You may belong to any religion, caste or creed- that has nothing to do with the business of the state. In due course of time, Hindus will cease to be Hindus and Muslims will cease to be Muslims, not in the religious sense, because that is the personal faith of each individual, but in the political sense as citizens of the state...We are starting with this fundamental principle that we are all citizens and equal citizens of the state."[8]

However, in pursuit of power and dominance over acknowledgment of equal rights has firmly entrenched the former in human psyche and when a country is still in a state of flux, the desire for more power motivates the practice of states. The *Ulema* and privileged members of Pakistan's society, who belonged to particular religious sects and linguistic groups, were determined to forestall any measures that would reduce their control over the resources of the country. Falling back on Great Britain's tried and tested formula of asserting racial superiority as a justification for their continued rule, a leading member of the Constituent Assembly who also belonged to the *Ulema*, claimed that the non-Muslims "cannot be entrusted with the responsibility of framing the general policy of the state or dealing with matters vital to its safety and integrity."[9]

Though the tenures of the military presidents, General Ayub Khan (1958-69) and General Yahya Khan (1969-71) and of the civilian ruler Zulfikar Ali Bhutto (1972-77) were often marked by unrest, the discriminatory attitude of the state to the non-Muslims (*dhimmi*) was not as intolerable as it became after Zia ul Haq wrested power in a military coup in 1977. The following decade witnessed a massive campaign to rid Pakistan of what was perceived to be the corrupting influence of "*Magribi Adab*" (Western influence) and enforce an eleven-point agenda for restitution of Islamic principles of governance and rulings that covered every aspect of one's life.[10] His goal was establishment of Nizam-i-Mustafa in the country. Important positions in political, executive and judicial branches of the government as well as in the military were earmarked for the Muslim citizens and non-Muslims were reduced to being *de facto* non-citizens. The religious institutions were given a lot of power to spread their doctrinaire interpretation of Islam and maintain their hold over the populace. The basic canon of democracy that guarantees its citizens not just their physical but also their cultural plane of existence, was flouted as state intervened in its citizens' personal sphere by illegalising anything that was deemed as un-Islamic. For instance, the Hudood Ordinance allows Christians to call for divorce only on grounds of adultery and if it is proved, the guilty party has to face a severe penalty. This makes it almost impossible for them to divorce as the price they are made to pay, is too high.

The Revised Constitution Order of 1985, set the seal on government's discretionary power and the minorities and non-Sunni Muslims found themselves at the receiving end of unfair laws like paying taxes for practising a different faith, being forced to conform to *Shariat* Bill and witnessing the steady erosion of their culture. Their properties could be taken away by the state and its favoured faction for the furtherance of their own interests. Women, who had always been second class citizens, had to endure injunctions that further restricted their choice and made them increasingly vulnerable to the high-handed writ of a male dominated society.

Though the organisational arrangement to ensure equality of citizenry was laid, during the inception of Pakistan, the will to back it up was not strong enough, to contend with the might of the reactionaries who transposed the purpose of the government institutions to suit their interests and further their dominion.

The Marginalisation of the Minorities

Under Zia's rule, an exclusive brand of Islam spread into Pakistani society, like a prolific weed that fed on the insecurities of two largest minorities, the Christians and Hindus, and the fear of other smaller denominations, like the *Ahmadiyas, Parsis, Buddhists,* and *Sikhs.* The institutionalisation of their minority status, by means of separate electorate, ensured their continued marginalisation.[11] The Hindus, viewed as a fifth columnist, have always had to bear the brunt of Muslim ire, when there has been a communal conflagration in India. After the demolition of the Babri Masjid in 1992, their properties in Lahore, Peshawar, Quetta, Charsadda, Dera Murad and Jamali, were raided and more than sixteen temples were burned down. Their life was made unbearable as Muslim shopkeepers and hoteliers refused to sell and serve them. The Hindus and the Kohli community of Sindh were harassed, and their complaints went unheeded. They were forced to migrate to India *en masse.* A report pegged the number of migrants in one month alone, to be five hundred.[12] Many human rights organisations have given detailed accounts of systematic state sponsored discrimination against Hindus, and how many were coerced into becoming "bonded labourers". The Hindus who accounted for 23 percent of Pakistan's population in 1947 have now declined to only 2 percent.[13]

The Christians form the bulk of the labouring class like brick-kiln worker, sweepers etc, and find the law unfavourable to them. Their land is seized without prior notice and often churches and graveyards are given away to power tribal lords. For example, a Christian settlement in Bhindor in Faruqbad, was demolished by local Chowdhuris as was their cemetery, in Chak Peero in Sialkot. The kidnapping of Christian girls and their re-appearance as Muslim brides and the ransacking of missionary schools, are common occurrences. They are often slapped with charges of blasphemy. Under the blasphemy law, a person is convicted on the same day on which he is accused of the offence, and often this law is used to settle personal scores or to seize property. In one such case, against Ayub Masih of Pak Pattan, fourteen Christian families were deracinated and made unregistered refugees on canal bank.[14] On May 6, 1998, Bishop John Joseph fired a bullet into his head in a court to protest the death sentence of a Catholic under the blasphemy law on April 19 of the same year.[15] On September 25, 2002, unidentified gunmen shot dead seven people at a Christian charity in Karachi's central business district. Pakistani Christians have claimed that they have been increasingly victimised following the United State's "war on terror."[16]

The most besieged lot are the *Ahmadiyas*. Denounced as heretics, they are often persecuted under the blasphemy law. In 1984, a law that was passed, led to their ex-communication. They have been denied basic freedoms, on ground of their interpretation of Islam. Apart from being denied employment, they are frequently arrested and not been given a fair hearing in the courts. There are countless cases of human rights violations of *Ahmadiyas*. In 1989, the Deputy Commissioner of Hazara ordered the Director of Tarbela Dam Project without giving any reason to summarily remove all *Ahmadi* families from their places of residence . The official *Ahmadi* mouthpiece, *Al-Fazal*, and other publications have been banned. A Mustaq Ahmad of Khushab, was sentenced to a year of rigorous imprisonment for reciting the *Azan*. The Muslim orthodoxy led by Anjuman Thaffuz Khatm-e-Mabuwwat and other fanatical organisations, indulged in acts of terrorism against *Ahmadiyas*, they likened their heinous mission to a holy war, to purge the society of "apostates" of Islam.[17] Just to live without constant fear, the *Ahmadiyas* were asked by the Majlis-e-Ahrar to either declare themselves to be non-Muslims, or seek Minority status or convert to Islam as defined by the Majlis or be prepared for punishment for being religious deviants.

According to a trend analysis done by Aleyha Ahmed, a Human Rights Commission of Pakistan's (HRCP) intern, there has been a rise in kidnappings of religious minorities for forced conversions from Christianity and Hinduism to Islam. In 2006, there was 145 percent increase in suicides and attempted suicides among minorities. Most common causes were "domestic troubles, unemployment and admonishment." [18]

The ideal of humanity becomes a falsehood in a country, whose government turns a blind eye to the ill treatment of minorities and in some cases, is a party to it.

Women: Forced to Pay the Price of their Gender

In a conservative society like Pakistan, women have been fighting to empower themselves and stand at par with their male counterparts in different spheres of life. The obduracy of religious leaders, feudal rural elite and tribal warlords forecloses any possibility to degenderise the society. Even if a proposal for the emancipation of women finds favour with the government, the latter simply caves in when pressurised by conservatives to reject such a bid for gender equality. For instance, the proposed Women's Commission to examine discriminatory laws and practices against women was stillborn despite the Pakistani Senate's unanimous approval for its institution.

There is no equality of and before the law when it comes to women as the law, especially the Hudood ordinance is biased against them. According to an HRCP report, 75 to 80 percent of women languishing in prisons, were convicted on Hudood offences. During the release of the HRCP's 1997 annual report on March 10, 1998, Asma Jahangir, the Chairperson of the Commission, claimed that violence against women in personal and public life, continued unabated and that, forced marriages were often followed by marital abuse. Trafficking of women in North West Frontier Province (NWFP), is taken to be an established fact. In Karachi, around 100 to 150 women are trafficked every day.[19] The *Shirkat Gah*, a famous Lahore-based women's group, which promotes women's rights relating to child-marriage, discriminatory marriage laws, polygamy, divorce, property rights and so on, has continuously been targeted by hard-line Muslim clerics and their supporters. The group along with the WLUML network, produced the 'Great Ancestors Project', which challenges myths about the place of Muslim women in society by sharing the narratives of women from the 8th to the 20th centuries.

The Asian Human Rights Commission in an article, *"Ten Years of Human Rights Violations in Pakistan: 1997-2008"* stated that there has been a substantial increase in human rights violations especially since 2005. Though many do not make it to the press, one horrifying case that did, was that of the abduction and rape of a seventeen year old girl by police officials, who kept her in custody for sixteen days and forced her to confess to the murder of her fiancée. As a pressure tactic, her elder sister was also kept nude in jail for three days.[20]

According to Aleyha Ahmed, in 2006 honour killings, *Karo Kari* (killing due to suspicion of adultery) and murder committed against women, increased by 29 percent over the 2005 statistics. The same year witnessed a 129 percent increase, in gang rape and rape of minors and married women, while kidnappings almost doubled from 633 in 2005 to 1113 in 2006. According to Pakistan's Interior Ministry, there have been more than 4,100 "honour killings" since 2001.[21] There were 78 cases of reported domestic violence, while incidents involving women being burnt or acid being thrown on them have increased. The most alarming finding was that, the accused were relatives, neighbours or prominent members of the society.[22]

In most of these cases, one finds individuals in the society, committing human rights violations against others. Usually, they belong to the influential and/or majority groups of the society. There is state's culpability in its inaction against the violators, its abetment of such crimes and participation in these acts.

The Heavy Hand of the State

With the formation of the society and state, individual code of violence gave way to the legitimisation of state violence, that was needed to maintain law and order. But this violence was not to be arbitrary and definitely not directed at the citizenry. Observance of human rights, that is not favoured towards the powerful factions of the country but is pervasive, is a feature of states having democratic ethos. Pakistan has not had a continued experience of democracy, as its military has an iron grip over the country. Being a part of the international community, Pakistan's military dictators often resorted to the formation of what is called a 'bonsai democracy' or an appearance of democracy by engineering sure win elections. These elections appeased the conscience of their supporters in the West as well as gave the Pakistani people superficial assurance that the intention of the military was not, to establish an absolutist state. Pakistan's political parties are deeply divided by regional origins, ideologies, and opportunism. The brief interludes of democracy experienced by the country, was characterised by maladministration and graft. It was not a difficult task to discredit such a set up and look good in comparison. The military excelled at this.

What the military could not grasp was that while the political representatives might be weak, the people they represent are not: they cannot be subdued for long or be mollified by short-term prophylactic measures. In 1999, General Pervez Musharraf, the then chief of staff, staged a coup and exiled his major political rivals. At first, the people of Pakistan accepted him as he promised a slew of progressive measures. His cosmopolitan image won favour with Pakistan's middle class. However, Musharraf's subsequent alignment with the United States in its "war on terror" proved disastrous for him. By neglecting to factor in the clout of the clerics and the rising Talibanisation of Pakistan's tribal belts, he incurred the wrath of many Pakistani followers of extremist philosophy, in both urban and rural areas. His response was what makes the difference between an autocracy and a democracy evident. The strongarm methods used by Musharraf to quell all opposition, marks one of the darkest phase in Pakistan's history. The government used the National Accountability Bureau (NAB) and a host of anti-corruption and sedition laws to jail political opponents or blackmail them into changing their political stance and desist from criticising the military authorities.

On November 3, 2007, Musharraf suspended Pakistan's constitution, fired two-thirds of the country's senior judiciary and arrested thousands of opponents, many of whom were eventually released because of international pressure. He then sacked the Chief Justice of the Supreme Court, Iftikhar Mohammad Chaudhry, for questioning the whereabouts of about six hundred (unofficial figures record more than a thousand) Pakistanis who had been arrested for their alleged terrorist links. Most of the lawyers, who took to the streets demanding the Chief Justice's reinstatement were put behind bars. He imposed Martial law and passed an executive order that took away the power of judicial review, which is the key legal instrument to safeguard against human rights violation. The media was censored and riot police attacked the Islamabad offices of the Jang Group, which housed the newspapers Jang and The News, and Geo TV. The Muttahida Quami Movement (MQM), a major coalition partner of Musharrafs government, issued a statement naming twelve eminent Pakistani journalists as "enemies" and continued with their targeted killings of dissenters with impunity.[23] The assassination of the Balochi leader Nawab Akbar Ali Bugti showed that, there was no difference in the trial and judgment procedures of the Islamabad government and kangaroo courts.

According to the Human Rights Watch (HRW) Report of 2005, sectarian violence increased significantly in Pakistan in 2004. It was estimated that at least 4,000 people, largely from the minority Shiite Muslim sect, died as a result of sectarian violence since 1980, with the preceding five years, witnessing a steep rise in incidents of sectarian violence. Sunni extremist organisations in concert with the militant Sipah-e-Sahabah targeted Shiite professionals, like doctors, and murdered many Ahmadis. Even Pakistan's ally in the West, the United States labelled it as a "Country of Particular Concern", following the recommendation of the US Commission on International Religious Freedom (USCIRF) because of its continued human rights violations. The US State Department report stated that "Under emergency provisions, Pakistani authorities also arrested approximately 6,000 opposition political party workers, human rights advocates, lawyers, and judges".[24] The paramilitary forces acting in conjunction with the army, also killed and tortured farmers, who refused to cede their land rights to the army. The HRW Report relates a particularly gruesome incident of such land grab in the Okara district of Punjab.

All this paints a Stygian picture of human rights in Pakistan. Is the country mortgaged to the military fiat and the religious orthodoxy? In 2007, the protest of the legal community, turned into a groundswell of public outrage that subsided only when Musharraf agreed to hold elections that took place in February 2008 bringing the Pakistan People's Party (PPP), led by slain Benazir Bhutto's husband Asif Zardari and Pakistan Muslim League (N) led by Nawaz Sharif back to power. The jailed lawyers and human rights activists were released and curbs on the media were lifted. Following the start of impeachment proceedings against him, the self declared president of Pakistan, preempted his downfall by tending in his resignation in August 2008. What is noteworthy, keeping in mind the history and political culture of Pakistan, is that the agent of political change, was not some discredited political parties or the military, but the people of Pakistan. This is a clear repudiation of the cynics' contention that it was not a grass root movement but mere astroturfing, which was limited to the educated, urban youth of Lahore, Islamabad and Karachi. The determining force was not external pressure but the ructions within that shook the mighty military enough for it to make such concessions. Taking stock of public opinion, the newly appointed military chief of staff, General Ashfaq Kiyani, clearly stated that the military would not interfere in politics. Whether the military actually toes the line is dubitable, but the very fact that such a statement was made demonstrates the impact of the public protests of 2007-08.

Before reviewing the institutional and societal dimensions of human rights implementation, it is necessary to briefly dwell on the situation in Pakistan occupied Kashmir (PoK). Often the plight of the people residing in PoK is skirted over, due to the fact that it is a disputed region and any opinion of either a Pakistani or an Indian on this, might be open to criticisms of bias or worse, treated as treason. Many militant organisations operate in PoK, and it is an open secret that they receive training and logistical support from Pakistan's Directorate of Inter-Services-Intelligence (ISI) and the Jammat- e-Islami party.[25] The militants have murdered hundreds of civilians, both Hindus and Muslims, for their suspected support to the Indian government. Incidents of kidnapping, assaults and extortion are viewed as a part of life there. Rape has been used as weapon of coercion and degradation. More than militants, it is the state sponsored militias, who have enchained society in poverty and uncertainty. Land meant for growing food crops, are instead used for cultivating plants from which narcotics are made, which is far more lucrative. Drug trafficking would not flourish without the tacit approval of the government. Crime and poverty plague the region and terrorists find a safe haven here.

The Judiciary's Role as a Custodian of Rights

On the occasion of the Golden Jubilee of Pakistan's Supreme Court (S.C.) on August 11, 2006, the Asian Human Rights Commission (AHRC) remarked that, there was no cause for celebration as its fifty-year performance belied the event's theme of "justice for all". Institutionalised corruption, lack of judicial independence and the culture of impunity of the privileged has made justice a class based phenomenon. At that time, the cases pending before the SC were around 15,000 and roughly 3,500 in other courts across the country. The local body system was so devolved that feudal lords, big land owners, tribal chieftains and unscrupulous police used their influence to subvert law and carry on human rights violations like honour killings, extra-judicial killings, rapes, torture. They forced disappearance without fear of reprisals. For instance, in May, 2006, more than 1,250 cases of police torture were reported as having been committed, in the past sixteen months, despite the setting up of public safety commissions at district level, judiciary could do nothing about it. The media reported that an Inspector General of Prisons in Sindh, who was allegedly responsible for the torture and death of five high profile prisoners in Karachi in 2005 and 2006, did not even face judicial probe. The military's detention facilities are off-limits to the judiciary.[26]

The military has time after time gained indemnity, by subverting the rule of law. On November 21, 2007, an executive order to amend the constitution, withdrew the power of judicial review. The military also appropriated the powers of the judiciary by amending the 1952 Army Act, that gave it the power to try civilians in special military courts, on a wide range of offences. The government could also disbar lawyers if they felt that the lawyers were involved in anti-government activities by an amendment to the 1973 Legal Practitioners and Bar Councils Act.[27]

In this context, the whole Iftikar Chaudhary episode becomes significant. The Chief Justice and his colleagues, who took a principled stand not to sign the order of suspension of the constitution, and preferred detention to submission, actuated the legal community to take up the cudgel and fight for justice. Supported by many civilians, the protest march signalled the end of Musharraf's authoritarian rule and the movement for democracy gained steam. Hassan Abbas, a research fellow at Harvard's John F. Kennedy School of Government said that, "This is unprecedented in Pakistan's history". Through his *suo moto* action, Chaudhry demanded greater accountability from the government and even from the intelligence agencies, something that had never been done before.[28]

The Conscious Civil Society and Media: The Cerberus of Human Rights

What the events of 2007 clearly demonstrate is that there are many in Pakistan's civil society (community based organisations, think tanks, trade unions, informal associations) who have internalised human rights concerns and prioritised it over class and cultural affiliations. The rising influence of an extremist variant of Islam, in many rural and tribal areas, and in some parts of Pakistan's major cities, notwithstanding, young Pakistani students and middle class are on the *qui vive* for any breach of human rights and use the media, especially the internet, to put pressure on the government to get its act together. This was evident during the Martial Law, in what is popularly described as a revolution of the bloggers, who sidestepped censorships placed on print and audio-visual media and brought to world attention the atrocities committed by the government.

In 2001, Civicus, an international alliance of civil society groups, described Pakistan's civil society as a "collection of incoherent voices, conflicting worldviews and opposing interests" characterised by "unresolved struggle between the practices and values of pre-capitalist society and new modes of social life, between authoritarian legacies, and democratic aspirations". It stated that the country had around 12,000 active and registered non-governmental organisations (59 percent of which were in Punjab, followed by Sindh and NWFP), 60,000 unregistered NGOs and some 8000 trade unions.[29] According to Hassan Abbas, they are slowly gaining ground and are challenging arbitrary acts of the government, especially the military.

Pakistan's Human Rights Commission, comprising of notables like Hina Jilani, the United Nations Secretary-General's first Special Representative of Human Rights Defenders in 2000, Asma Jehangir, Special Rapporteur of the UN Human Rights Commission, and IA Rehman, Director of the Human Rights Commission of Pakistan; has been the voice of Pakistan's human rights movement for a long time.

In recent times, Pakistan's vibrant media has been spearheading the campaign against governmental excesses.

While newspapers like *The Dawn*, *The News, Frontier Post, Daily Times, Jung*, *The Friday Times* and *Daily Khabrain* reache out to the 47 percent literate Pakistanis, television channels like Geo TV, Aaj TV and ARY-TV have mobilised the masses across the literacy divide. A journalist, Shahan Mufti, told *On the Media, a weekly national radio programme,* that before Musharraf opened up the media, "Pakistanis were used to being told things through the state media". Private news channels now "allowed all sorts of voices of all political persuasions to appear on TV". [30] In 2007, Musharraf felt so threatened by their growing reach and influence, that he pulled the plug on several private channels, jailed many journalists and imposed restrictions on live coverage of political events. However, he had to soon relax these restrictions and restore freedom of press, under pressure from Pakistani people and the international community. Pakistan's military and power elite, are slowly waking up to the fact that civil society groups and the media form the backbone of the irreversible process of democratisation. One also has to factor in the contribution of international media in highlighting the human rights violations. To take just one random example will suffice. Nicholas Kristoff, a *New York Times* columnist wrote articles on Mukhtarin Mai/ Bibi, a victim of serial rape as per norm of tribal justice and whopping $ 165,000 dollars were raised for her cause. She opened educational institutions in her village and travelled to USA despite President Pervez Musharraf's conspicuous displeasure.

Islam and Human Rights

A major constituent of political Islam is the concept of "*khilafa*", which means representation. A human being is the representative of Allah on earth. Every individual in an Islamic society enjoys the rights and powers of the caliphate of Allah and in this respect all individuals are equal and nobody can deprive any person of his rights and powers. Thus, Islam is inherently democratic. While democracy in the West rests on popular sovereignty, in Islam, it is based on the sovereignty of Allah. Here people are Allah's caliphs and follow His law. In Islam, a Muslim *ipso facto* becomes the citizen of an Islamic state as soon as he sets foot on its territory with the intention of living there and thus enjoys equal rights, along with those who acquire its citizenship by birth. Islam decrees that the life, property and honour of non-Muslims are to be respected and protected in exactly the same way as that of a Muslim citizen and no difference is to be made between a Muslim and a non-Muslim citizen in respect of civil or criminal law. All this can be gleaned from the Cairo Declaration on Human Rights in Islam that was adopted by the members of the Organisation of Islamic Conference (OIC) at the nineteenth conference of Foreign Ministers held on August 5, 1990. Thus, the religious extremists' view of democracy and human rights being some sort of post colonial interventionism is merely a smokescreen to hide their true intentions of maintaining their sway over a pluralist society like, that of Pakistan's and preventing it from becoming a healthy and cohesive political entity.

Pakistan proclaims itself to be an Islamic republic. However, it contravenes the principles of political Islam by its discriminatory attitude towards non-Muslims, Shiites, Ahmadiyas and women. The Muttahida Majlis-e-Amal, a coalition of religious parties, such as Jamaat-e-Islami (JI), Jamiat Ulema-e-Islam (JUI) and Jamiat Ulema-e-Pakistan, runs the government in North West Frontier Province and is part of a coalition in Balochistan with PML (Q). It is reported to have strong ties with the Taliban. There are more than two dozen religious militant groups, most of which have been officially banned, yet continue to operate under new names and in new places. They often target religious and linguistic minorities and foment sectarian violence and dissension. In typical Jekyll and Hyde stance, the ruling establishment at times is not averse to use them for creating mayhem and violence across the line of control against India and across Durand Line against Afghanistan. Some of the religious militant outfits have clandestine linkage with ISI. However, progressive Islamic intellectuals and professionals are slowly asserting themselves and making their voices heard above the din of bigotry.

Conclusion

The eminent Indian jurist, Nagendra Singh, one time judge of International Court of Justice, Hague, Netherlands, has outlined four aspects of human rights that exist beyond its cultural and temporal relativity. The first is the national aspect of human rights, that is, the existence of human rights is a matter of its enforcement by the various branches of the government. The second is the international aspect, where inter-governmental organisations and NGOs must recognise their obligations to protect human rights. The third and fourth aspects cover the observance of human rights in conditions of peace and war or conflict. [31] The purview of rights is thus all encompassing.

While we tend to focus more on setting up institutional mechanisms that guarantee such rights, what is equally, if not more important, should be the focus on the actualisation of human rights. In the introductory part of the article, it was felt that internal constraints play a major role in determining the government's policies when it comes to realising internationally sanctioned tenets of human rights. While liberties function in controlled environments, the extent of restriction must not be such as to undervalue the right of liberty itself. In Pakistan, the traditionally privileged feudal classes, have been politically mobilised and there is intense inter-group rivalry for control over resources. The military wields the iron rod as do the tribal overlords in the western frontiers of the state. None of them are willing to relinquish their power. The political parties divided along language, religion and regional lines, are constantly bickering amongst themselves and often fail to come together as a countervailing force against the organised and highly committed military, whose thumb rule of success is that restriction equals to domination.

The civil society has been characterised as an inchoate mass of conflicting opinions; one, that continuous struggle between authoritarian legacies and democratic aspirations. There is also a heady cocktail of Western democratic practices and Islamic *Shariat*. However, as Pakistan is opening up uneasily to the world, due to forced of globalization, there are many bright and perspicuous Pakistanis, who have realised that the only way to enjoy their rights is, to fight for these, rather than repose their faith in a government, that changes its tune according to the wishes of their principal backers. In this, the role of Western educated and influenced intellectuals cannot be underestimated.

Reformist religious movements often spring from social causes and are not declamations about alien morality but are an appeal to ethical notions of right and wrong. There is nothing contextual about human rights and on what should be done and not done in the exercise of one's rights. This reasoning will help to separate the *soi-disant* social movements that are led by zealots and those guided by genuine societal concerns. The former is regressive and conservative, while the latter is progressive. The, apologists of Islam, who tend to blame discrimination and atrocities committed against women on a patriarchal society, must first understand why certain practices take root in such a society; why a particular religion is interpreted in a manner, that is biased against women and views them in terms of the role, they perform rather than as individuals. Cultural practices and religion often dictates one's life to such an extent that restrictions inconsistent with universal principles of human rights are accepted as indicators of identity and tolerated even by those who are at the receiving end of unfair treatment like for instance, women's submission to various restrictions right, from their dress code to how they interact with outsiders. In Pakistan, discrimination is legalised and this makes it all the more difficult to counter, especially if proceedings against violations take place in a Pakistani version of Star Chambers of medieval England, characterised by closed hearings and arbitrary rulings.

Human rights violations committed against political workers, media, human rights activists, lawyers, judges, women and religious minorities can tear asunder the social fabric of the society. The explanation to human rights' continued pretermission, can be found in Pakistan's hierarchical power structure, the might of its military, the pervasive influence of religious extremists, and the weakness of the legislative, political and judicial branches of the government. Without belabouring the point, it is sufficient to point out that the situation, till the imposition of the Martial law on November 8, 2007 was grim enough, for many to dismiss Pakistan as a "failed or failing state". This was presumptuous as events that followed the dismissal of Justice Chaudhry proved that there was still hope for Pakistan to redeem itself and exorcise the ghosts of its past.

Following the elections in February 2008, a new government has been formed in Pakistan. People are hopeful that the current dispensation, having learnt from the mistakes of the previous regime, would be more mindful of the needs and concerns of the people. Some important steps that must be taken if human rights are to be observed in practice are as follows:

- Restrictions on the freedom of expression, like the PEMRA code of conduct imposed on the media, must be removed and media as well as NGOs must not be harassed for their views

- Minorities and non-Muslims must be treated as citizens and there must be procedural guarantees for their security. Laws that deny the expression and practice of their cultural and religious identities must be repealed. The practice of different religions and cultures must not be termed as treason

- Women must be accorded equal status before the law and the provisions of the *Qisas* and *Diyat* law, which allow the next of kin to "forgive" the murderer in a so-called "honour killing" should be scrapped

- All detainees and under-trials must be allowed legal representation and their families must be given visitation rights

- All cases filed under the Anti-Terrorism Act and sedition law for acts that are already protected under international human rights laws and which are not cognizable criminal offences, must be withdrawn

- Arbitrary laws and amendments to the constitution that have been in effect since November 3, 2007 must be revoked

In fine, the government must be made accountable for its actions and no branch of the government must exceed its jurisdiction so as to make the state virtually a hostage to the whims of its power elite. While assuring human rights to all citizens is the *raison d'être* of the state, special care must be taken to ensure that minorities and the traditionally disenfranchised lot, are empowered and treated with fairness. National sovereignty is the privilege of a state that looks after its people. It cannot be a pretext for disallowing international scrutiny and avoiding worldwide condemnation as human rights is not territorially bounded. The present coalition government under PPP-PML (N), is in the process of drafting lustrous laws to deal with past human rights abuses and injustices and implement policies to restore those rights, that had been suspended during the Martial law. Pakistan is a signatory to many international human rights conventions and is a member of the UN Human Rights Commission. As such, it is responsible for its actions to both its citizens and to the international community. Its inability to observe these rights or indisposition to do so, would be a defeasance, which would invalidate the moral authority of the government.

The idea that human beings enjoy rights *qua,* human beings is the crux of the discourse on human rights. The people on the streets of Pakistan are no longer mired, in the existential slough of despond. They have hope as they have realised, that they have a say in determining the fate of their country. There are some political commentators, like Krishnan Srinivasan, a former Foreign Secretary of India, who question the motivations behind the February elections, that is, whether it was a campaign against Musharraf or a support for a strategy of reforms. [32] Unless the federal model, skilfully combines regional identities with national one and the mainstream political parties connect with the needs and aspirations of the people, Pakistan will sink into chaos and become vulnerable to extremist forces. This will once again allow the military to displace the democratically elected government, as it will be viewed as the only institution strong enough to ensure security and stability. For Pakistan to be a progressive and more tolerant state, human rights having legal force, political will and popular acceptance is the *desideratum*. Human rights thrive in a democratic setting. The government should strengthen democracy and not undermine it by resorting to vindictive politics. Pakistan can aspire to be democratic only, when its leaders have electoral sanction; when there are institutional checks and balances; when it promotes a culture of individual autonomy, and when there is harmonious civil military relations.[33]

The next phase is crucial: If Pakistan's government stays the course by upholding human rights of its people, it will keep the hope and optimism of the people alive. Only a sustained pursuance of these moral imperatives, will lead to the country's overall development. Yet one caveat is well in order. Victim of today, at times become oppressor and violator of human rights tomorrow.

Endnotes

1. Nickel, James, Making Sense of Human Rights: Philosophical Reflections on the Universal Declaration of Human Rights, Berkeley, University of California Press: 1987, pp. 561-2.

2. Singhvi, L.M, A Pioneering Role-Forty years of the United Nations, Edited by Bajpai, U.S.A, Lower International, New Delhi: 1987, p.159.

3. Pogge, Thomas, referred to in the chapter on Scope of Human Duties, Available in The Internet Encyclopedia of Philosophy at www.iep.utm.edu/h/hum-rts.htm , Accessed on May 12, 2008.

4. Orend, Brian, *Ibid.*

5. Dworkin, Ronald, Taking Rights Seriously, Duckworth, London: 1978, p.153.

6. Mack, Eric, 'Scanlon as Natural Rights Theorist', The Journal of 'Politics, Philosophy and Economics', Published by the Murphy Institute of Philosophy, London: 2001, p.46.

7. Jones, Peter, Rights, referred to in the chapter on Claim Rights and Liberty Rights, Available in The Internet Encyclopedia of Philosophy at www.iep.utm.edu/h/hum-rts.htm, Accessed on May 12, 2008.

8. Pakistan Constitution Assembly Debates, Volume 1, Number 2, pp.19-20.

9. Constitution Assembly of Pakistan Debates, Official Report, Government of Pakistan Press, Karachi: 1947, Volume 5, Number 3, p.5.

10. Singh, Indu and Saksena, Ajay, Human Rights in India and Pakistan, Deep & Deep Publications Pvt. Ltd., New Delhi: 2004, pp.64-67.

11. *Ibid.* p.71.

12. State of Human Rights in Pakistan, Islamabad: 1990, p.79.

13. Available on Internet Encyclopedia, Wikipedia: http://en.wikipedia.org/wiki/Human_rights_in_Pakistan, Accessed on May 17, 2008.

14. *Ibid.* p. 82.

15. Available in Asian Human Rights Commission website: http://www.ahrchk.net/statements/mainfile.php/2006statements/683/, Accessed on June 5, 2008.

16. http://en.wikipedia.org/wiki/Human_ rights_ in_Pakistan, Accessed on May 19, 2008.

17. Singh, Indu and Saksena, Ajay, Human Rights in India and Pakistan, Deep &Deep Publications Pvt. Ltd., New Delhi: 2004, pp.74-75.

18. Pakistan Human Rights Commission website: www.hrcp-web.org/hrcpDetail_2. cfm?catld=166 &catName= Reports, Accessed on June 7, 2008.

19. Reference 16, pp. 83-84.

20. Available in Asian Human Rights Commission website: http://www.ahrchk.net/statements/mainfile. php/2006statements/683/, Accessed on June 5, 2008.

21. Universal Periodic Review of Pakistan, Human Rights Watch's Submission to the Human Rights Council, May 5, 2008, http://hrw.org/english/docs/2008/04/11/global 18516_txt.htm, Accessed on May 28, 2008.

22. Pakistan Human Rights Commission website: www.hrcp-web.org/hrcpDetail_2.cfm?

catId=166&catName=Reports, Accessed on June 7, 2008.

23. Universal Periodic Review of Pakistan, Human Rights Watch's Submission to the Human Rights Council, May 5, 2008, http://hrw.org/english/docs/2008/04/11/global18516_txt.htm, Accessed on May 28, 2008.

24. The International News, Washington, Wednesday, March 12, 2008, http://www.thenews.com.pk/top_story_detail.asp?Id=13523, Accessed on May 18, 2008.

25. Singh, Indu and Saksena, Ajay, Human Rights in India and Pakistan, Deep &Deep Publications Pvt. Ltd., New Delhi: 2004, p.113.

26. Available in Asian Human Rights Commission website: http://www.ahrchk.net/statements/mainfile.php/2006statements/683/, Accessed on June 5, 2008.

27. Universal Periodic Review of Pakistan, Human Rights Watch's Submission to the Human Rights Council, May 5, 2008, http://hrw.org/english/docs/2008/04/11/global18516_txt.htm, Accessed on May 28, 2008.

28. Bajoria, Jayshree, "Pakistan's Institution and Civil Society", Council for Foreign Relations, December 27, 2007, http://www.cfr.org/publication/14731/, Accessed on June 7, 2008.

29. A Preliminary Report on the Civicus Index on Civil Society Project in Pakistan, Occasional Paper Series, Volume 1, Issue 11, p.6.

30. Bajoria, Jayshree, "Pakistan's Institution and Civil Society", Council for Foreign Relations, December 27,

2007, http://www.cfr.org/publication/14731/, Accessed on June 7, 2008.

31. Singh, Nagendra, Human Rights and the Future of Mankind, Vanity Books, Delhi: 1981, pp.7-8.

32. Srinivasan, Krishnan, "After Musharraf", The Telegraph, Tuesday, August 19, 2008, Volume XXVII, Number 43, p.10.

33. Mahapatra, Sangeeta, "Pakistan: A Democracy as Scripted by the Military", The International Gazette, Published by the IJS, Kolkata: February, 2008, Volume 1, Number 1, p.5.

References

1. Nickel, James, *Making Sense of Human Rights: Philosophical Reflections on the Universal Declaration of Human Rights*, Berkeley, University of California Press: 1987.

2 Singhvi, L.M. *A Pioneering Role-Forty years of the United Nations*, Edited by Bajpai,U.S., Lower International, New Delhi:1987.

3. Dworkin, Ronald, *Taking Rights Seriously*, Duckworth, London: 1978.

4. Mack, Eric, *'Scanlon as Natural Rights Theorist'*, The Journal of 'Politics, Philosophy and Economics', Published by the Murphy Institute of Philosophy, London: 2001.

5. Pakistan Constitution Assembly Debates, Volume 1, Number 2, pp.19-20.

6. Constitution Assembly of Pakistan Debates, Official Report, Government of Pakistan Press, Karachi: 1947, Volume 5, Number 3.

7. Singh, Indu and Saksena, Ajay, *Human Rights in India and Pakistan*, Deep & Deep Publications Pvt. Ltd., New Delhi: 2004.

8. Singh, Indu and Saksena, Ajay, *Human Rights in India and Pakistan*, Deep & Deep Publications Pvt. Ltd., New Delhi: 2004.

9. The International News, Washington, Wednesday, March 12, 2008.

10. A Preliminary Report on the Civicus Index on Civil Society Project in Pakistan, Occasional Paper Series, Volume 1, Issue 11.

11. Singh, Nagendra, *Human Rights and the Future of Mankind*, Vanity Books, Delhi: 1981.

12. Srinivasan, Krishnan, *"After Musharraf"*, The Telegraph, Tuesday, August 19, 2008, Volume XXVII, Number 43.

13. Mahapatra, Sangeeta, *"Pakistan: A Democracy as Scripted by the Military"*, The International Gazette, Published by the IJS, Kolkata: February, 2008, Volume 1, Number.

12

Self-Determination, Sovereignty and Democracy: The Reality Behind the Rhetoric in Sri Lanka

Rohini Hensman

Introduction

Journalistic accounts of the crisis in Sri Lanka refer to it as an 'ethnic conflict' between the Sinhalese majority and Tamil minority, and there is an element of truth in this perception: the war that broke out in 1983 and has continued ever since, despite periods of ceasefire, is primarily between the armed forces of a state dominated by a Sinhala nationalist agenda and the Liberation Tigers of Tamil Eelam (LTTE) fighting for a separate Tamil state. Yet this description is inadequate to capture the complexity of the situation in Sri Lanka. It simply cannot account for episodes like the following:

Norms of civilisation and humanity today seem assailed from all quarters, leaving one sickened, bewildered and despairing as never before. The actors in this grim scenario include the forces of the state, violent forces opposed to the state, shadowy vigilante groups...The gruesome tally of deaths mounts daily.

Chief News Editor of Rupavahini, Kulasiri Ameratunga, was shot in his home by unidentified gunmen; the Ven. Soragune Pannatissa Thera, taken out of his temple in Haputale and shot; young lawyer Kanchana Abhayapala shot at his home by an unidentified gunman; seventy five year old Wellatota Pannadassi Nayake Thera shot, when returning to his home in Kamburupitiya, and burnt; SLFP organiser in Kurunegala, H.P.Wijesekera, shot in Dompe; Rubber Research Board Chairman and former Deputy Minister Merril Kariyawasam shot in his office at Ratmalana; seventy five year old Kahawe Wimalasiri Thera shot by an unidentified gang in his temple at Kala Oya, Anuradhapura; Moratuwa University Vice-Chancellor Prof. C. Patuwathavithana and Chief Security Officer P.A.K. Ranaweera, slain on the campus premises at Katubedde; State Pharmaceuticals Corporation Chairman Dr. Gladys Jayawardene, shot in her car at Slave Island on her way home from office.

These are some of the names that had made the newspaper headlines. The fact and manner of these deaths is at least known. In addition there are the eyewitness accounts of unidentified corpses, of headless bodies floating down waterways, of

> numerous bodies – sometimes singly, sometimes in heaps, often hideously mutilated – burning on the roadsides. (Civil Rights Movement 1989)

This is an account of what was happening in the rest of Sri Lanka when the Indian Peace Keeping Force (IPKF) occupied the North and East, after the Indo-Lanka Accord of 1987. While the total death toll has never been established, it amounted to tens of thousands – some estimates say 60,000, including disappearances – so the carnage was on a scale comparable to the loss of life in the war between the government and the LTTE. But this was not an ethnic conflict; it was a conflict between the Janatha Vimukthi Peramuna (JVP or People's Liberation Front) and the government, with both sides killing others who did not belong to either side, like the 32 schoolchildren of Embilipitiya killed by the state. It was a case of Sinhalese, including Buddhist monks, being killed by Sinhalese. Both sides used shadowy death squads: several squads in the case of the state, with names like the 'Black Cats,' 'Yellow Cats,' 'Eagles of the Central Hills' and 'Scorpions,' while the JVP used the Deshapremi Janatha Viyaparaya (DJV or Patriotic People's Movement).[1]

In the case of Tamils, the killing spree started earlier, continued into 2008, and included the internationally recognised war crime of conscripting children and sending them to the battle front:

> The LTTE took on the TELO at the end of that month [April 1986]...The manner in which the TELO members were killed, shocked Tamil people everywhere. Many died without knowing what hit them. Twelve were killed near Manipay while they were asleep. Several were caught unawares, shot

and burnt at junctions at Tirunelveli, Mallakam and Tellipallai. Eight persons were killed at the camp behind St John's principal's bungalow...The people were so terrified that few had the courage to give shelter to the fugitives...Some went home saying things such as: "We have produced our own Hitlers". (Hoole et al. 1990, pp. 81-82).

In the early 1990s, very young children from poor families taken by the LTTE in Jaffna were corralled in camps...In July 1991, most of the thousand or so killed in the LTTE's desperate bid to overrun Elephant Pass, were women and children...A woman in the Vanni regularly met young members of the LTTE fighting cadre, who told her about their gruelling life...They told her, *"Once you come into this organisation, there is no alternative. You must make up your mind to die. When volunteers are called for a dangerous job, we all raise our hands".* (Hoole 2001: 404, 415, 416)

These aspects of the LTTE's politics have aptly been described as 'the political culture of auto-genocide,' (Hoole 2001: 403), and this epithet could apply equally to the politics of the state and JVP in the late 1980s. A characterisation of the crisis in Sri Lanka must account for these phenomena, as well as the fighting between the state and the LTTE.

Identity and Politics

Ethnic identities in Sri Lanka are neither as clear-cut nor as rigid as they are often assumed to be. As an important entrepot in ancient times, Sri Lanka (previously known as Ceylon, and even earlier as Serendip and Taprobane) attracted traders and settlers, mostly from India but also from West and East Asia, who mingled with the indigenous

Väddas – rather than exterminating or subordinating them (Obeyesekere 2002) – and with one another. Most of the major religions of the world were represented among these settlers, including Christianity, which was present in Sri Lanka long before it became a European colony. From the early 16th century onwards, with successive conquests by the Portuguese, Dutch and British, settlers from Europe as well as European colonies in Africa and elsewhere added to the mixture. Both intermarriage and non-marital unions were common at all levels of society, producing large numbers of children of mixed ethnicity (Jayawardena 2007). Most Sri Lankans with European ancestry, eventually came to be called 'Burghers'.

Initially, there were Tamil speaking as well as Sinhala speaking Buddhists, and close links between Buddhists in Sri Lanka and Tamil Buddhists in South India (Bandaranayake 1984: A.xvii). The kinship system among both Sinhalese and Tamils resembles that of South India, with parallel cousins (a father's brother's children or mother's sister's children) regarded as brothers and sisters, and therefore marriage with them being forbidden; whereas cross cousins (a father's sister's children or mother's brother's children) are encouraged to marry. This contrasts with the Indo-European kinship system, which prohibits marriage between cross cousins as well as parallel cousins. Along with other anthropological and textual evidence, this suggests that both Sinhalese and Tamils come from the same stock (Guneratne 2002). Furthermore, immigrants often adopted the language of the area where they settled, so that identities based on language could and did change.

'[A]t the 1891 Census, the total population was 3,007,800. Of this,

2,044,762 (67.3 per cent) were Sinhalese
488,644 (16 per cent) were Sri Lanka or 'homeborn' Tamils
197,381 (6.5 per cent) were Moors [Muslims]
21,289 (0.7 per cent) were Burghers
10,120 (0.3 per cent) were Malays [Muslims of South-East Asian origin]
235,109 (9 per cent) were 'Indian Tamil' immigrants
6,356 (0.2 per cent) were Europeans

Colombo's population then was 127,836. Colombo then was already a truly multi-communal, multi-religious city. By 1946 its population had 'naturally' grown to 362,074, of which 38.5 per cent were Buddhists, 18.1 Hindus, 20.5 Muslims and 22.7 Christians...Of those in it, who were 3 years and over, 38 per cent could speak both Sinhala and Tamil, 28 per cent could speak English, and 14.4 per cent could speak all three languages. 47 per cent could speak Tamil, but that was partly because 40 per cent of its population had Tamil as their first language (Piyadasa 1988: 21).

Prior to Independence therefore, Sri Lanka could have been described as a 'melting pot' or 'hybrid island' (Silva 2002), a fitting illustration of the Buddha's vision of universal human identity:

Behold the grasses and the trees;
They do possess the mark of birth
And species each from other distinct.
Then behold the beetles, moths and ants...
And four-footed creatures, big and small;
The reptiles, snakes and long-backed animals,
The fishes and creatures of the water,
And birds that cross the sky on wings.

Consider them, they possess the mark of birth
And species each from other distinct.
As in these kinds of creatures there is
The distinction based on birth,
So there is not, among human beings
The distinction based on birth...

(Speech to Vasettha, quoted in Palihawadana 1989: 4-6)

If on the one hand, linguistic communities had boundaries that were blurred and fluid, on the other, they were divided internally – in some cases so deeply – by caste, class, religion and region. Distinctions between Sinhalese Goyigama and lower castes, Tamil Vellala and lower castes, employers and workers, Sinhala speaking Buddhists and Christians, Tamil speaking Hindus and Muslims, Kandyan and Low Country Sinhalese, or Jaffna and Eastern or Hill Country ('Indian'). Tamils were often more important markers of identity than language (Daniel 15-19). Conversely, there were instances in the labour movement, when class solidarity trumped other elements of identity, bringing workers together across linguistic, religious and caste boundaries in common struggle (Jayawardena 2003: 18-19).

This was not a promising scenario for communal politics, which could take off only by constructing monolithic and mutually exclusive ethnic identities.[2] Two of the stories central to the construction of a Sinhala Buddhist identity are those of Vijaya and Dutugemunu. According to the first, Vijaya – the grandson of a lion (*sinha*) – is exiled from the kingdom of his father in India for bad conduct, arrives in Sri Lanka, which is inhabited by *yakkhas*. He marries a *yakkhini*, Kuveni, and establishes a kingdom there. But he needs a

This led directly to the first large-scale post Independence outbreak of communal violence. Faced with the threat of a satyagraha organised by the Federal Party (FP) led by S.J.V.Chelvanayakam, which advocated a federal form of government, with equal status for Tamil as a national language, Bandaranaike signed the Bandaranaike-Chelvanayakam (B-C) Pact in 1957, recognising Tamil as the language of a national minority and of administration in the Northern and Eastern Provinces, where regional councils with limited powers over administration – including education and the allotment of land for settlement schemes – would be established. A year later, in response to a militant agitation by Buddhist monks, Bandaranaike tore up the Pact. Tamils protested in Jaffna by blacking out the Sinhala letter 'sri' which had been substituted for the English letters on vehicle number plates, and this was followed by an orgy of arson and murder against Tamils by Sinhalese hoodlums in other parts of the country, including Colombo. Banadaranaike at first refused to intervene; then, when the violence appeared to getting out of control, he handed over authority to the Governor-General, who declared an Emergency (Vittachi 1958). It has been suggested that stopping the riots would inevitably involve shooting at Sinhalese gangs, and Bandaranaike wanted to avoid the unpopularity which would follow (Vittachi 1958: 77). If so, he failed. In 1959, an organisation of Buddhist monks, the Eksath Bhikku Peramuna (EBP), hatched a plot to eliminate him, and One of its members assassinated him (Samarasinghe 2007).

By 1964, the LSSP and CP were allied with the SLFP (now led by Sirimavo Bandaranaike), and abandoned their support for the rights of Hill country Tamils and parity for Sinhala and Tamil. Just as earlier, the UNP had opposed the B-C Pact, all these parties now opposed a similar pact between UNP leader Senanayake and Chelvanayakam. Breakaway groups from the LSSP and CP, stood by their earlier positions, yet the fact that the only major non-minority parties, which had supported minority rights, now abandoned that cause which, exacerbated the communal polarisation. In 1968, the SLFP, LSSP and CP formed a United Front (UF), which was elected to power in 1970.

In 1970, the UF government introduced a measure which made a significant contribution to the growth of a militant movement of Tamil youth. This was the 'standardisation' system, whereby the minimum university entrance marks for a Tamil medium student, were higher than those for a Sinhala medium student. This formula and subsequent modifications of it, were rationalised as an attempt to improve opportunities for educationally underprivileged sections of the population, but these sections would hardly have been affected, since less than 1 per cent of all students entering Grade 1, went on to enter university. The overwhelming majority of the latter, would have been from middle and upper class strata (Bastian 1984). The new system put Tamil students at a disadvantage, by comparison with Sinhalese students from the same social strata, creating a group of frustrated and embittered Tamil youth, especially among Jaffna Tamils, whose university entrance results had traditionally been very good (Hyndman 1988: 171).

Given all these attacks on equality, aimed at giving Sinhalese privileges at the expense of Tamils, it is paradoxical that the first large-scale violence of Sinhalese against Sinhalese was during the JVP insurrection of 1971 in which, an estimated 5-10,000 people were killed (Wickramasinghe 2006: 237). The JVP drew its membership and supporters precisely from the strata that were supposed to benefit from the Sinhala Only policies; the depth of dissatisfaction among these sections, should have alerted the UF government to the fact that, discrimination against Tamils did not benefit the majority of Sinhalese. That and other policies to address issues of poverty and unemployment were needed. Instead, it simply went further along the same trajectory. In the name of nationalising the plantations – which might have been a progressive measure, had it been carried out differently – plantation land was distributed to Sinhalese supporters under the Land Reform Law No.1 of 1972 and the amendment to it in 1975. Tamil plantation workers and their families were physically assaulted and driven out, their dwellings looted and burned, some were killed and others were left to starve (Vije 1987: 60-63).

The 1972 Republican Constitution presided over ironically, by Minister of Constitutional Affairs Colvin R. de Silva, who had earlier predicted that Sinhala Only could lead to the creation of 'two torn little bleeding states' not only gave constitutional status to Sinhala as the sole official language, but also provided a special place to Buddhism, omitted the protection of minority rights in Section 29, declared Sri Lanka to be a unitary state; effectively making it a Sinhala-Buddhist state (Hyndman 1988: 72). It also omitted the second chamber, the independent Public Service Commission (intended to guarantee impartiality in public service appointments), the Judicial Service Commission (intended to guarantee the independence and integrity of the judicary) and prohibited judicial review of legislation (Jayawickrama 2008). Thus, in addition to further depriving minorities of their rights, it centralised power in a manner that could be used against the majority. The 1978 Constitution enacted under J.R. Jayawardene, leader of the UNP, which had came to power in 1977, further centralised power in the hands of one person – the Executive President – and omitted the fundamental right to life.

Thereafter, attacks on democracy followed thick and fast. SLFP politicians had used lumpen gangs, but these had no institutionalised status. After 1977, Jayawardene set up the Jatika Sevaka Sangamaya (JSS), which carried out similar functions, but on a larger scale as an organised and centralised force: 'After the massive election victory of the UNP, several political leaders emerged, who had access to and control, over the slums and anomic areas of the city…Jobs in the working class sector were increasingly given to members of this lumpen proletariat, who swelled the ranks of the JSS. Soon members of other unions were intimidated into joining it…They were now organised and effectively controlled government offices and wielded enough power to transfer and intimidate even high officials…MPs have created in small market towns through the JSS and other local groups a complex, powerful network of organisations that can be put to political use. (Obeyesekere 1984: 160-62)

These gangs were used to intimidate voters in the October 1982 presidential elections, from which Jayawardene's main rival, Mrs Bandaranaike, was barred. despite this, he got only 52.91 of the votes cast. He enacted the Sixth Amendment of the Constitution in December, evicting TULF MPs from their seats in Parliament and simultaneously used massive violence in a referendum in which the citizens of Sri Lanka supposedly voted to deprive themselves of the right to vote in the general elections due in 1983 (Perera 1989)! The JSS was used to intimidate and kill opposition supporters and judges, who gave verdicts against violent offences by UNP supporters (Senewiratne 1986: 30, 83). It was used repeatedly against workers and trade unions, breaking strikes, assaulting and killing trade unionists, getting members of existing unions dismissed and even abusing and assaulting management personnel who attempted to discipline them. That, its members had protection from the very top, was made obvious from the fact that, the police never acted against them; while around 80,000 public employees, who opposed them and went on strike, lost their jobs (Civil Rights Movement 1981; Nadesan 1981). It has been suggested that 'the totalitarian power of this extremist group can be compared with the stormtroopers in Hitler's Germany' (Senewiratne 1986: 84), and it certainly appears that in its mode of operation vis-à-vis the labour movement and opposition parties as well as its relationship to the ruling party and police, the JSS resembled an amalgam of the fascist storm-troopers and 'unions' of Hitler and Mussolini (see Guerin 1973: 104-05; 132-34; 179; 185-86).

The parallel with fascist storm-trooppers is, perhaps most striking in the way the JSS was used to assault and kill Tamils, loot and burn their shops and homes and drive them out of the areas, where they had been living. The anti-Tamil pogroms of 1977 started, just a month after the UNP took office: 'Violence spread through the entire country. Plantation areas were widely affected, including estates, towns and villages. Tamils were massacred in their hundreds and their property was looted, burnt or otherwise destroyed. It was estimated that between 5000 and 7000 families, besides being subject to bodily injury and in some cases rape and murder, lost all or nearly all the goods they possessed' (Vije 1987: 64).

In May 1981, violence broke out in Jaffna, on the eve of the District Development Council elections: 'On 24 May, a UNP candidate was assassinated, and the army went on a rampage of looting and torture. And then, on 31 May, an unidentified gunman fired some shots at an election meeting. The tense atmosphere exploded into state sponsored mayhem. With several high-ranking Sinhalese security officers and two Cabinet Ministers...present in the town, uniformed security men and plainsclothes thugs carried out some well organised acts of destruction. They burned to the ground, certain chosen targets, including the Jaffna Public Library, with its 95,000 volumes and priceless manuscripts, a Hindu temple, the office and machinery of the independent Tamil newspaper Eelanadu, the house of the MP for Jaffna, the headquarters of the TULF and more than 100 shops and markets' (Murray 1984). This was followed by island wide violence: 'It is clear that subsequent violence in July and August, which was directed against Sri Lankan Tamils in the east and south of the country, and Indian tea estate workers in the central region, was not random. It was stimulated, and in some cases organised by members of the ruling UNP among them, intimates of the President. In all, 25 people died, scores of women were raped and thousands were made homeless, losing all their meagre belongings' (Eads 1981).

However, all these exploits of the JSS were overshadowed by their role in the pogroms of 1983, which gathered strength from March 1981 onwards. Then on 25 July,

Organised action against Tamils in the streets and in buildings and against Tamil establishments was being taken by squads which had taken up their positions and armed themselves with hit-lists and weapons ...The General Secretary of the government 'union', the Jathika Sevaka Sangamaya (JSS), was identified as the leader of the gangs which wrought destruction and death all over Colombo...One of the most remarkable exploits of the 'heroes' was the massacre, that day, in Welikade Prison (Sri Lanka's most important) of 35 people,..most either on remand or arbitrarily detained by the military. All were Sri Lanka Tamils. We are convinced that this massacre could not have been carried out without government and National Security Council authorisation...

The pogrom continued less intensely in Greater Colombo, for three more days in spite of the curfew. On Tuesday, 26 July, some of the action squad were transported to Kandy, some 70 miles away and that afternoon, there was a similar sharp and quick action there...It then moved further up-country, past towns like Matale (devastated) and Nawalapitiya towards Badulla and Nuwara Eliya. Hindu temples had been added to the hit list. Army action had resulted in over 60 per cent of Badulla city being reduced to rubble. On the 27 July, incredibly, the second massacre of Tamil political detainees and remand prisoners was successfully carried out. This time, 18 were killed...By the end of the week, the majority of the some 600,000 Sri Lanka Tamil children, men and women, in the predominantly Sinhala-speaking areas and in Colombo, and many of the 800,000 'Indian Tamils' had been driven out or fled from their homes and places of work... (Piyadasa 1988: 89-91)

Many of these refugees were displaced again and again. For example, Hill country Tamils who had fled the plantations in 1977 and 1981 were settled on Kent and Dollar farms near Vavuniya, in the Northern Province, which had been donated by a wealthy Tamil landowner. In 1984, 'On the plea that these had become "terrorist infested" areas, government troops launched search-and-destroy missions and literally chased these hapless plantation Tamils from the areas, making them refugees on the run again' (*Saturday Review* 1987). The government then took over the farms and settled Sinhalese ex-convicts and their families on them. (The aftermath of this 'experiment' will be described in the next section.) An account of the attempt to settle 45,000 Sinhalese villagers in Batticaloa District in the Eastern Province, showed very clearly that this was not spontaneous migration by the villagers, but an attempt by Sinhalese politicians and Buddhist monks, to bribe them with the offer of free land (Gunaratna 1988). Along with the pogroms and other means, by which Tamils were driven out, these 'colonisation' schemes, which continued into the 21st century, constituted government programmes of population transfer, defined in international law as a crime against humanity.

By 1983, the character of the state security forces had changed too. With the introduction of the Prevention of Terrorism Act, in 1979, and invocation of provisions of the Public Security Act, to allow the security forces to dispose of dead bodies without inquest, torture, disappearances and extrajudicial executions became routine. Amnesty International documented the grim record of sadism and murder, including rape and other forms of sexual torture, in the North and East. The Special Task Force (STF), created in 1984 by the president's son Ravi Jayawardene, was responsible for even more atrocities than the regular armed forces. Armed Home Guard units were created, supposedly for self-defence, yet, 'during the entire history of the homeguard units, they have hardly been of any use in preventing massacres. Their claim to fame, rests on their use in reprisal killings under cover, provided by the army' (UTHR-J 1990: 5).

This was the background against which, the Indo-Lanka Accord was signed by Rajiv Gandhi and JR Jayawardene in July 1987. While recognising the unity, sovereignty and territorial integrity of Sri Lanka, it also affirmed the country's multi-ethnic, multi-lingual and multi-religious character; the Northern and Eastern Provinces were termed 'areas of historical habitation of Sri Lankan Tamil-speaking peoples' and were merged, subject to a referendum on or before 31 December 1988, when the people of the Eastern Province could decide by a simple majority, whether to remain merged or to de-merge. The Thirteenth Constitutional Amendment made Tamil an official language and provided for limited devolution of power to Provincial Councils. In an Annexure to the agreement, provision was made for the President to invite an Indian Peace Keeping Contingent to guarantee and enforce the cessation of hostilities. According to JN Dixit, who was India's High Commissioner in Sri Lanka at the time, Jayawardene requested that the Indian army be deployed in the North and East so that Sri Lankan troops could be redeployed to maintain law and order in the South (Rediff.com 2000).

Powerful sections within the government opposed the Accord, including Prime Minister R. Premadasa. He succeeded Jayawardene after the presidential elections of December 1988 in which, fraud and violence exceeded anything Sri Lanka had seen before (Perera 1989). His opposition to the Accord explains Premadasa's support to the LTTE, which had started fighting the IPKF in October 1987 (UTHR-J 1990: 1; Jayaweera 1990: 11, 24). The Accord was also opposed by the JVP, which had re-emerged as a political force, and started killing opponents in 1986. Daya Pathirana, leader of the Independent Students' Union which supported the rights of Tamils, was one victim (Hoole 2001: 220-21);

there is also a great deal of evidence that, in February 1988 the JVP assassinated Vijaya Kumaratunga, a rising political star, who was popular among Sinhalese and supported the Accord, although he opposed the presence of Indian troops (Hoole 2001: 294-305).

The ideology of the JVP was a mixture of socialist and Sinhala Buddhist nationalism. Its leader Wijeweera chose the pseudonym 'Rohana' to evoke the province (Ruhuna) from which Dutugemunu waged his campaigns. Prior to the formation of the JVP, he had been in the Ceylon Communist Party (Peking Wing) led by N Shanmugathasan. In 1966 was disciplined by the party for his participation in demonstrations against the Senanayake-Chelvanayakam pact, that provided for the reasonable use of Tamil and regional devolution of power. Later, one of the five lectures by means of which, the JVP propagated its ideology took the position, that the plantation workers were an arm of Indian expansionism and all should be repatriated to India. The putchist conception of revolution and authoritarian structure of the party were also notable. After the 1971 insurrection was defeated, many survivors engaged in a critique of the authoritarian and chauvinist elements in the JVP's ideology left the party (Ismail 1983).

In 1986, those who remained in the JVP, still led by Wijeweera, were the hardliners. The response of the leadership, to those who opposed them inside or outside the organisation was simple: kill them. The state, controlled by the UNP, was equally ruthless and far more powerful. This is what resulted in the gruesome atrocities and massive death toll during the second JVP insurgency, which ended with the execution of Wijeweera in November 1989.

Tamil Nationalism: A Parallel Trajectory

The course of Tamil nationalist politics was set by the murder of Alfred Duraiappah in July 1975. Soon after the 1972 constitution was enacted, various Tamil parties, including the FP (led by S.J.V.Chelvanayakam and A.Amirthalingam), Ceylon Workers' Congress (CWC, representing Hill country Tamils) and Tamil Congress, came together in the Tamil United Front (TUF). The TUF became the Tamil United Liberation Front (TULF) in May 1976, after adopting a resolution, calling for a separate state at its Vaddukottai Conference. However, Alfred Duraiappah, independent MP 1960-65, several times mayor of Jaffna and a popular figure, aligned himself with the SLFP. 'He had a vote bank in the significant business, Muslim and Sinhalese communities and the urban poor. This popularity of Duraiappah irked the nationalists...From 1972, the TUF (FP) launched vicious attacks on Duraiappah, calling him a traitor worthy of death...On 27 July 1975, Duraiappah was shot dead, when he arrived by car in the Ponnalai Varadaraja Perumal Temple with two companions was his custom on Friday evenings. Prabhakaran was among the group of assassins who formed the incipient Tiger Movement...We may say that the TULF pointed a pistol at Duraiappah and looked the other side, knowing that someone would pull the trigger' (Hoole 2001: 17-19).

According to a former Government Agent of Jaffna, Duraiappah told him of an earlier attempt on his life, which failed, adding, 'The extremists hate and fear me as a politician, who believes in unity between Tamils and Sinhalese people...Did you see that statue of a tough looking youth with a hand to his mouth?..That's the villain who boobytrapped my car. When he was to be captured by the Police, he swallowed cyanide. These shameless MPs call him a hero and put up a statue. Is it to this hero worship of murderers, that our MPs want to lead the poor Tamil people? My vision is different' (Devendra 2008).

This incident encapsulates many of the themes that come up again and again in the history of Tamil nationalism. One is the worship of violence, which was extolled even by the supposedly non-violent leadership of the TULF. Making a fetish of violence could only end in self-destruction. The murder of TULF leaders Amirthalingam and Yogeswaran by the LTTE in Colombo in 1989, was strongly reminiscent of the murder of Bandaranaike by the EBP. Like Bandaranaike, the TULF leaders created a Frankenstein's monster, which eventually destroyed them. It also destroyed many others, supposedly fighting for the same goal of Tamil Eelam. 'Able members of other groups, were marked by the LTTE and "switched off" when opportunity arose...It was in May 1986, that the LTTE revealed its intentions openly, by attacking the TELO when there was a split in its leadership and likewise the EPRLF in December 1986. The PLOTE had already destroyed itself by its internal killings' (Hoole 2001: 423). The Indian government made no small contribution to this violence by its policy of arming and training Tamil militants after July 1983: 'Several militant leaders and expatriate Tamils have been frank about the links the Indian government and its intelligence agency RAW had with the militant groups' (Hoole et al. 1990: 199-200). The murder of Rajiv Gandhi by the LTTE in 1991, was a classic case of 'blowback' resulting from this sponsorship of militancy. Yet the policy was justified by the Jain Commission enquiry into the assassination (Koshy 1997).

The cult of violence also found expression in attacks on Sinhalese and Muslim civilians. One of the earliest was the massacre of ex-convicts and their families settled in the Kent and Dollar farms in 1984. Among other major attacks were, the massacre of Buddhist pilgrims at Anuradhapura in 1985, the Kattankudi mosque massacre in 1990, the massacre of Muslims in Eravur in 1990, the Central Bank bombing in 1996, the bombing of a commuter train in Dehiwela in 1996, and the Kebithigollewa massacre in 2006. These are only the worst of hundreds of attacks on civilians. An obvious purpose of the attacks in the North and East, was to drive out Sinhalese and Muslims i.e., transfer of population.

Given that in almost every case, the state and Home Guards reacted by inflicting even greater violence on Tamil civilians, it has been suggested that another purpose of these massacres, was to 'keep the Tamils in a state of insecurity, subjecting them to contrived reprisals – a state in which the LTTE appears as their champion' (Hoole 2001: 346). A similar strategy was adopted with the IPKF. Thus in October 1987, the LTTE fired at the Indian army from Jaffna hospital, as a consequence of which, the IPKF stormed the hospital and seventy civilians were killed. Then it fired at the IPKF from Kokkuvil Hindu College, which was being used as a refugee camp. The IPKF retaliated by killing over 30 civilians (Ibid 420). While the brutality of the Sri Lankan state and IPKF cannot be excused, it is also significant, that the LTTE deliberately provoked such reprisals, knowing that Tamil civilians would suffer. Its only strategy for retaining the support of the people it claimed to represent, was to maximise the overall level of violence.

A second theme is the assassination of Tamil civilians, who dissent from the LTTE, especially those who reject the goal of a separate Tamil state. The list of those who shared

Duraiappah's fate, is far too long to enumerate, but the LTTE's murders include those of Rajani Thiranagama (1989), Sarojini Yogeswaran (1998), Neelan Thiruchelvam (1999), T.Subathiran (2003), Lakshman Kadirgamar (2005) and Kethesh Loganathan (2006). This theme is linked to another: complete subjection to the totalitarian rule of the leader, V Prabakaran and stamping out of thedissent or competition of any kind. Anyone who disagrees with the leader, is branded a traitor worthy of death and killed sometimes incarcerated and tortured. This treatment was meted out even to LTTE members. 'Dissidents in the North-East...place the total number of Tamils killed by the LTTE at 20,000...including Prabhakaran, nearly all those from the 1987 leadership, are dead. Thirteen of them, including Thileepan, committed suicide on orders from the Leader. Several top leaders were killed or suffered an unknown fate like Mahattaya...Every leader feared the "Uzi Group" – an internal spy group, whose members were known only to Prabhakaran' (Hoole 2001: 424, 428).

However, Prabakaran overreached himself, when he tried to liquidate Karuna Amman, his Eastern commander, who expressed dissatisfaction with LTTE policies in 2004. Despite a confrontation in which hundreds of Karuna supporters were killed, he failed to destroy Karuna, who then formed the Tamil Makkal Viduthalai Pulikal (TMVP) and teamed up with the government of Sri Lanka to defeat Prabakaran's forces in the East. In fact, 'Karuna's challenge to Prabhakaran's authority was more than a personal matter. It was driven by more deeply rooted historical, cultural and regional differences and political-economic inequities between Tamils of the north and the east' (Bandarage 2008).

The LTTE split illustrates another feature of Tamil nationalism: its marginalisation and exclusion of large sections of Tamil speaking people. The CWC, representing Tamils from the central hills of Sri Lanka, left the TUF when the TULF was formed, since it had no interest in a separate state in the North-East. Although Chelvanayakam did support the demand for citizenship and franchise of the Hill-country Tamils, this demand was dropped in the B-C Pact of 1957. In 1964, Mrs Bandaranaike came to an agreement with Indian Prime Minister Lal Bahadur Shastri that 525,000 of the Hill-country Tamils would be accepted as Indian citizens within fifteen years. In 1974, the Sirimavo-Indira Pact was agreed upon, by which 75,000 more were to be deported to India. However, by mid-1984, only 445,000 persons in all were repatriated to India - most of them against their will' (Daniel 1996: 115). The Tamil nationalists ignored the persistent demand of Hill country Tamils for citizenship of Sri Lanka and the rights associated with this status, because it did not fit in with their demand for a separate state in the North-East.

A partially overlapping exclusion was that of Tamil Dalits. The Sri Lankan Dalit Development Front was set up in 2006, to fight for their rights. It held its second meeting in London in 2008. Its Dalit Declaration chronicled the untouchability, caste discrimination and violence, inflicted on Dalits by uppercaste Tamils, as well as struggles by Dalits for access to temples, teashops, water, franchise (opposed by Tamil politician Ponnambalam Ramanathan), education and political representation. It stated that 'Political power, if any, earned in the name of Tamil nationalism would in no way serve the interests of the Dalits, who are denied their due social respect and basic human rights.'[44]

Another section excluded by Tamil nationalism were the Muslims of Sri Lanka. At first, the attempt was to deny their specificity, by including them in the category of 'Tamil-speaking people,' but this was rejected by Muslims (Ismail 2005: 123). The LTTE's response to this refusal was brutal in the extreme: massacres of Muslims in the East and the wholesale expulsion of Muslims from the North - a clear case of ethnic cleansing. 'In October 1990, all over the Northern Province, close to 75,000 Muslims were compelled to vacate their homes at gun point, hand over their belongings, and leave...These people lost their homes, possessions, livelihoods, communities and personal histories in one day...Today they live in overcrowded settlements in the impoverished district of Puttalam' (Haniffa 2007: 16).

It appears that Tamil nationalism is as exclusive and totalitarian as Sinhala Buddhist nationalism. The only adequate embodiment of either, would be a fascist state.

Human Rights and Democracy as the Alternative to Ethno-Nationalism

When the government of Sri Lanka is accused of violating human rights, the usual reply is that it is fighting terrorism and defending its sovereignty against a separatist threat. The LTTE, on the other hand, claims that everything it has done, is in pursuance of the goal of self-determination for the Tamil people of Sri Lanka. Since the UN Charter supports both 'self-determination of peoples' and 'the sovereign equality of all its Members,' both these apparently contradictory goals, seem to have validity. How can this dilemma be resolved?

The dilemma arises only because of the way, in which 'sovereignty' and 'self-determination' have been defined by the two protagonists. The notion of sovereignty originally referred to the power of the ruler in an absolute monarchy.

It has been adapted to modern democracy by stipulating that in a democracy, sovereignty resides in the people, yet this definition immediately runs into difficulties. If the 'people' are divided on the basis of age, sex, class, caste, language, religion etc., how can they constitute a single ruler? It appears that 'this mandate of political thought that only the one can rule, undermines and negates the concept of democracy' (Hardt and Negri 2004: 328). Indeed, state sovereignty is compatible with the denial of democratic rights to all the people and the rule of a totalitarian state or single individual.

The 'right of nations to self-determination' has also been contested. In the early 20th century, Lenin supported the right of neighbouring nations, which had been annexed by Russia to form separate states, but Luxemburg asked, who determines the will of the nation? It was a valid question. Self-determination of an individual is easy to understand, but who defines the 'self' of a nation divided by age, sex, class, caste, language, religion etc ? Again, this formula is compatible with totalitarian rule by a group or individual who is seen as embodying the nation. So long as the clash is between a Sinhala Buddhist totalitarian state, fighting for sovereignty over the whole of Sri Lanka and the self-determination of an equally totalitarian Tamil nation, fighting to control a large part of Sri Lanka, there is no solution to the crisis in Sri Lanka.

Clearly, the UN was defending neither of these definitions. The Charter itself, as well as the Universal Declaration of Human Rights which followed in 1948, made it very clear that both sovereignty and self-determination were defined, in terms of fundamental human and democratic rights. If we define sovereignty, as genuinely residing in all the people of a nation, they must have all the human rights and democratic freedoms that enable them to control their own lives, including the right to life, freedom from cruel, inhuman and degrading treatment or arbitrary detention, the right to information and peaceful assembly, freedom of expression, freedom of association, equality of treatment and opportunity and the right to self-government either directly or through the election of representatives in free and fair elections. And if we define self-determination as self-determination of the *people,* it must mean that they too have all the rights and freedoms enumerated above. Redefined in this way, there is absolutely no contradiction between the sovereignty of all the people of Sri Lanka and self-determination for the Tamil people of Sri Lanka.

In other words, the only solution to the crisis in Sri Lanka is democracy, and to their credit, many people in Sri Lanka have been working towards this end. Unfortunately, they are confronted by two ruthless totalitarian entities, and this accounts for the fact that every two steps forward seem to be followed by at least one step back.

After Premadasa was killed by an LTTE suicide bomber in 1993, the parliamentary and presidential elections of 1994 brought Chandrika Kumaratunga and her People's Alliance (PA) to power with a landslide victory on a peace platform. She reintroduced democratic rights in the South, acknowledged long-standing Tamil grievances, and made a genuine attempt to protect human rights in the North and East, although there were still lapses. She initiated a ceasefire and talks with the LTTE, but the LTTE soon broke the ceasefire, and fighting resumed. Assisted by Neelan Thiruchelvam, her government drafted a new constitution entailing substantial devolution of power to the North and East and citizenship for the remaining Hill country Tamils, who had resisted deportation to India. She continued these efforts after getting re-elected in 1999, having surviving an LTTE bombing with the loss of an eye. But when a watered-down draft was presented to parliament in 2000, it faced opposition not only from Sinhala and Tamil nationalists, but also from the UNP. Realising that it would not get the two-thirds majority needed to make a constitutional amendment, the PA withdrew it.

Kumaratunga faced formidable obstacles to her agenda. By forcing a resumption of the war, the LTTE made her dependent on military personnel, who ought to have been punished for massacres and disappearances. Human rights violations continued, albeit on a much smaller scale. These, along with the failure of constitutional reform, disappointed Tamil supporters, while the continuation of the war disappointed Sinhalese supporters and encouraged Sinhala nationalists. Yet, it could still be argued that she could have done more, both to clamp down on human rights violations and to counter Sinhala nationalism (Hoole 2001: 454-63).

The PA was the largest party in the 2000 parliamentary elections, but lacked an absolute majorit. It had to rely on minority parties to form a government. When one of these withdrew support, the PA government first turned to the JVP for support, and then fell, leading to the election of a coalition led, by the UNP at the end of 2001, with Ranil Wickremasinghe as Prime Minister. This was the context in which the ceasefire agreement (CFA) of 2002 was signed between the government and LTTE with Norwegian mediation. A Nordic Sri Lanka Monitoring Mission (SLMM) moved in to monitor it. The high point of this peace process was the agreement by both sides, in Oslo in December 2002, to explore a federal solution within a united Sri Lanka, but

Prabakaran swiftly contradicted his negotiator and pulled out of the talks in April 2003.

The fatal flaw in the CFA was its lack of human rights guarantees, which right from the beginning allowed the LTTE to murder critics, even in government controlled areas, and conscript children with impunity. 'The SLMM and UNP remained silent as abductions and killings of persons opposed to the LTTE accelerated...Amidst murder and the abduction of children for use as combatants, the Government and Norway got the rest of the world to praise the peace process. When confronted with violations by the LTTE, they simply said that there was no evidence - evidence for which they never looked...To the Norwegians, those insisting on building and preserving democratic norms were a nuisance' (UTHR-J 2003). The breakdown of such a ceasefire was inevitable. Although it was formally in place, until the government abrogated it in January 2008, the murder of Foreign Minister Lakshman Kadirgamar (representing one party to the ceasefire) by the LTTE (representing the other party to it) in August 2005 could be considered to be the first shot in the new war.

After parliamentary elections in 2004, the PA formed a government with support from the JVP and an extremist Buddhist monk party, the Jathika Hela Urumaya (JHU). These parties were also instrumental in getting Mahinda Rajapaksa of the SLFP elected President in November 2005. Thus, the new government was much more explicitly tilted towards Sinhala nationalism. Nonetheless, it made some initial moves which stirred up hope, including the formation of the All-Party Representative Committee (APRC) in mid-2006 to deliberate on constitutional reform. The Majority Report of the panel of experts in December, authored by six

Sinhalese, four Tamils and one Muslim, went a long way towards satisfying the aspirations of minority communities, and could have formed the basis of a political solution. However, the ruling SLFP and President Rajapaksa proceeded to sabotage the APRC process, finally relegating it to the dustbin, when the President proclaimed in his Independence Day speech in 2008 that a solution to Sri Lanka's problems would have to be found, within the framework of the existing constitution. Meanwhile, the war raged on, with ugly human rights abuses being committed by both sides with impunity.

Conclusion

What emerges from this account is that the conflict in Sri Lanka is primarily between fascism and democracy and only secondarily, between Sinhala and Tamil fascism. The solution, therefore, is the restoration of democracy and human rights. One reason for hoping that this will occur is that there are strong traditions of non-violence, compassion and humanitarianism in Sri Lanka. The people have displayed these qualities in their relationships with people of other communities, even in the most ghastly situations. Thus Tamil survivors of the 1983 pogrom and other massacres spoke movingly of Sinhalese friends, neighbours and even total strangers, who saved and sheltered them, while Muslim refugees from Jaffna spoke with affection of their Tamil neighbours, who were like brothers and sisters, and wept while pleading with the LTTE not to evict them (Hensman 1993). The vast majority of people in Sri Lanka have nothing to gain and a great deal to lose from a continuation of the war, which has brought death, injury and bereavement to many, and falling living standards to all but a small elite. The desire for peace with justice and democracy is strong, and at some point will surely prevail over the totalitarianism of the war-mongers. Now LTTE leader Velupillai Prabhakaran has been killed. In India the DMK (Tamil Nadu) has urged Government of India to put pressure on Sri Lankan Government to protect the rights of Tamils.

Endnotes

1. Rather than clutter up the text with too many references, I would like to refer readers to human rights reports covering the period from the late 1980s to the present by Amnesty International, University Teachers for Human Rights – Jaffna (UTHR-J) and Human Rights Watch, all of which are available on the internet.

2. The classificatory zeal of the colonisers, especially the British, played a part in making communities fixed where they had been fluid before. However, the numerous identities they recognised were neither clear-cut nor mutually exclusive but vague and overlapping. Of these, only two were selected and further elaborated by the Sinhala and Tamil nationalists, who therefore have the main responsibility for constructing these identities. (See Wickramasinghe 2006: 44-50).

3. For many years these people were called 'Indian Tamils', then 'Tamils of Indian Origin' or 'Tamils of Recent Indian Origin'. However, the name by which they refer to themselves (*Malaiyaha Tamirar)* can be translated as 'Hill-country Tamils' (see Daniel 1996: 23).

4 http://www.thuuuu.net/dalite.htm

References

1. Bandarage, Asoka, 2008, 'The Sri Lankan Conflict: A Multipolar Approach,' *Asian Tribune*, 2 July.

2. Bandaranayake, Senake, 1984, 'The Peopling of Sri Lanka: the National Question and Some Problems of History and Ethnicity,' in Social Scientists' Association (ed) 1984, pp. A.i-ixx.

3 Bastian, Sunil, 1984, 'University Admissions and the National Question,' in Social Scientists' Association (ed.) 1984, pp.166-78.

4. Civil Rights Movement, 1981, *CRM Catalogues Complaints of Thuggery,* CRM, Colombo, 5 October.

5. Civil Rights Movement, 1989, *Civilisation and Humanity in Peril,* CRM, Colombo, 2 September.

6. Coomaraswamy, Radhika, 1987, 'Myths Without Conscience: Tamil and Sinhalese Nationalist Writings of the 1980s,' in Charles Abeysekera and Newton Gunasinghe (ed), *Facets of Ethnicity in Sri Lanka,* Social Scientists' Association, Colombo.

7. Daniel, E.Valentine, 1996, *Charred Lullabies: Chapters in an Anthroplogy of Violence,* Princeton University Press, Princeton.

8. Devendra, Tissa, 2008, 'Assassination of Alfred D.', *The Island,* 2 August Eads, Brian, 1981, 'The Cover-Up that Failed: The Prohibited Report from Colombo,' *The Observer* (UK), 20 September.

9. Guerin, Daniel, 1973, *Fascism and Big Business,* Monad Press, USA.

10. Gunaratna, Malinga H., 1988, *For a Sovereign State,* Sarvodaya Vishva Lekha, Sri Lanka.

11. Gunawardena, R.A.L.H., 'The People of the Lion: Sinhala Consciousness in History and Historiography,' in Social Scientists' Association (ed) 1984, pp.1-53.

12. Guneratne, Arjun, 2002, 'What's in a Name? Aryans and Dravidians in the Making of Sri Lankan Identities,' in Neluka Silva (ed.) 2002, pp. 20-40.

13. Haniffa, Farzana, 2007, 'Muslims in Sri Lanka's Ethnic Conflict,' *Polity,* Vol.4 No.2, May-June, pp.16-18.

14. Hardt, Michael and Antonio Negri, 2004, *Multitude: War and Democracy in the Age of Empire,* Hamish Hamilton, London.

15. Hensman, Rohini, 1993, *Journey Without a Destination: Is There a Solution for Sri Lankan Refugees?'* The Refugee Council, London.

16. Hoole, Rajan, Daya Somasunderam, K.Sritharan and Rajani Thiranagama, 1990, *The Broken Palmyra,* Sri Lanka Studies Institute, Claremont CA.

17. Hoole, Rajan, 2001, *Sri Lanka: The Arrogance of Power – Myths, Decadence and Murder,* UTHR-J, Colombo.

18. Hyndman, Patricia, 1988, *Sri Lanka: Serendipity under Siege,* Spokesman, UK.

19. Ismail, Qadri, 1983, 'Inside the JVP,' *The Island,* 17 August.

20. Ismail, Qadri, 2005, *Abiding by Sri Lanka: On Peace, Place, and Postcoloniality,* University of Minnesota Press, Minneapolis.

21. Jayawardena, Kumari, 1984, 'Some Aspects of Class and Ethnic Consciousness in Sri Lanka in the late 19th and early 20th Centuries,' in Social Scientists' Association (ed.) 1984, pp.74-92.

22. Jayawardena, Kumari, 2003, *Ethnic and Class Conflict in Sri Lanka,* Sanjiva Books, Colombo.

23. Jayawardena, Kumari, 2007, *Erasure of the Euro-Asian: Rediscovering Early Radicalism and Feminism in South Asia*, Social Scientists' Association, Colombo.

24. Jayaweera, Neville, 1990, *Sri Lanka: A Multi-ethnic Democratic Society*, PRIO, Norway.

25. Jayawickrama, Nihal, 2008, 'The Philosophy and Legitimacy of Sri Lanka's Republican Constitution,' *The Island*, 2 March.

26. Koshy, Ninan, 1997, 'India and the Struggle for Tamil Eelam: A Consistently Unsound Policy,' *Indian Express*, 30 December.

27. Murray, Nancy, 1984, *The State Against the Tamils. Sri Lanka: Racism and the Authoritarian State*, Institute of Race Relations, London.

28. Nadesan, S., 1981, *The Strike and its Aftermath*, CRM, 1 October.

29. Obeyesekere, Gananath, 1984, 'The Origins and Institutionalisation of Political Violence,' in James Manor (ed.), *Sri Lanka in Change and Crisis*, Croom Helm, London and Sydney.

30. Obeyesekere, Gananath, 2002, 'Where Have all the Väddas Gone? Buddhism and Aboriginality in Sri Lanka,' in Neluka Silva (ed) 2002, pp.1-19.

31. Palihawadana, Mahinda, 1989, 'Identity and Divisiveness,' (Paper presented at a seminar at Marga Institute, Colombo, 6-8 December).

32. Perera, Janaki, 1989, *The Subversion of the Electoral Process in Sri Lanka* (no publisher or place).

33. Piyadasa, L., 1988, *Sri Lanka: The Unfinished Quest for Peace*, Marram Books, London.

34. Rediff.com, 2000, 'India's Vietnam: The IPKF in Sri Lanka: 10 Years On,' March, http://www.rediff.com/news/2000/mar/24lanka.htm

35. Samarasinghe, Stanley, 2007, 'The Bandaranaike Assassination,' *The Nation,* 30 September.

36. *Saturday Review,* 1987, '10 Years of JR's Rule,' 22 August.

37. Senewiratne, Brian, 1983, *The July 1983 Massacre: Unanswered Questions,* Brian Senewiratne, Australia.

38. Silva, Neluka, (ed), 2002, *The Hybrid Island: Cultural Crossings and the Invention of Identity in Sri Lanka,* Social Scientists' Association, Colombo.

39. Sivathamby, K., 1984, 'Some Aspects of the Social Composition of the Tamils of Sri Lanka,' in Social Scientists' Association (ed.) 1984, pp.121-145.

40. Social Scientists' Association (ed), 1984, *Ethnicity and Social Change in Sri Lanka,* Colombo.

41. UTHR-J, 1990a, *Special Report No.1,* August.

42. UTHR-J, 1990b, *Report No. 5,* September.

43. UTHR-J, 2003, 'The Murder of T. Subathiran: Sri Lanka's End Game,' 15 June.

44. Uyangoda, Jayadeva, 1988, "Authoritarianism in Sinhala Buddhist Tradition," *The Island,* 24 July.

45. Vittachi, Tarzie, 1958, *Emergency '58: The Story of the Ceylon Race Riots,* Andre Deutsch, London.

46. Wickramasinghe, Nira, 2006, *Sri Lanka in the Modern Age: A History of Contested Identities,* University of Hawaii Press, Honolulu.

Index

J

Q

R

S

Y

Z